THE MANAGEMENT
OF EDUCATIONAL CHANGE

This is the fourth volume of a series entitled

Monitoring Change in Education

The Management of Educational Change

A case-study approach

edited by

Paul Oliver

Published by
Arena
Ashgate Publishing Limited
Gower House
Croft Road
Aldershot
Hants GU11 3HR
England

Ashgate Publishing Company
Old Post Road
Brookfield
Vermont 05036
USA

British Library Cataloguing in Publication Data

The management of educational change:
   a case-study approach – (Monitoring change in
   education)
   1. Educational change 2. Educational planning
   I. Oliver, Paul
   370.6'8

Library of Congress Catalog Card Number: 96-86409

ISBN 1 85742 379 8

Printed and bound in Great Britain by
Hartnolls Limited, Bodmin, Cornwall

Contents

Notes on contributors

Paul Oliver is a principal lecturer in the School of Education at the University of Huddersfield. He has published articles on multicultural education and most recently has written on the subject of credit accumulation and transfer systems in higher education.

Wendy Bradford is a senior teacher at King James's School within Kirklees LEA. She has completed an MEd with the University of Huddersfield and is now working towards a PhD. She is working in collaboration with officers and a number of secondary schools within the LEA.

Lynn Free has worked in primary schools for nine years as a remedial teacher and in a comprehensive school (as Head of Special Needs for nineteen years, and Head of Lower School for thirteen years). In 1995 she gained an MEd from the University of Huddersfield.

Stephen Billett lectures in the School of Vocational, Community and Technology Education at Griffith University, Australia. He has worked as a TAFE teacher, educational administrator, teacher educator, professional development practitioner and policy developer. His research interests include the social and cultural construction of vocational knowledge.

Ros Carnwell is a senior lecturer at the University of Wolverhampton. She is currently conducting post-graduate research into the experience of distance learning of community nurses.

Helen Trayers is a chartered biologist and taught science in schools and colleges for many years before moving into teacher training. She has recently obtained her MEd and is currently a course tutor for the franchised University of Huddersfield CertEd and BEd programmes at a college of further education.

Pauline James has worked as a teacher educator at the Hawthorn Institute, Melbourne for almost twenty years, after a career as a Chemistry and General Science teacher in Sheffield, UK; Atlanta, USA and Brisbane, Australia. She obtained a university award for her recently completed PhD project which is the subject of her chapter.

Jennifer A. Earnshaw is Deputy Director (Curriculum and Development) in the Business Studies Department of Carlisle College. She lectures in law, on a wide variety of HE, FE and short courses, and undertakes consultancy work in the areas of law and quality assurance. She is also actively involved in overseas marketing and recruitment, particularly in the Far East.

Geoffrey Elliott is Director of Access at Worcester College of Higher Education. He has published on vocational education and training, management and access issues, and he is joint editor of the journal *Research in Post Compulsory Education*.

Geoff Hayton currently is Senior Research Fellow at the Research Centre for Vocational Education and Training at the University of Technology, Sydney. Formerly, he was the Research Centre's foundation director. In 1995 he was leader of a research team undertaking a large project on enterprise training practices in Australia. His research interests include workplace reform and workplace learning.

Kathy Bland is a middle manager in a further education college. She started lecturing in 1988, after spending ten years in industry and commerce. Her management roles have included continuing education and new business development. She is currently responsible for systems development with a focus on quality assurance. She holds an MEd and is currently studying for an MBA.

Paul Hager is Associate Professor in the School of Adult Vocational Education at the University of Technology, Sydney. He has published and researched on philosophy of adult education and vocational education and training, on critical thinking and on professional competence.

John Sheehan is Principal Lecturer in the School of Education at the University of Huddersfield. He is involved mainly in post-graduate work including the supervision of research degrees and working on funded research projects. The investigation of change is one of his current interests.

Preface

It can sometimes seem as if the only prediction which we can make about education is that there is going to be change. Teachers and lecturers in all sectors of education are having to respond to new economic and organisational systems. These changes are providing challenges not only for managers but also for those delivering the curriculum. What is more, change does not seem to be localised, but to be an international phenomenon, with the characteristics of change identifiable across national borders.

This book is about the 'management' of such situations, but not about management as a precise discipline or concept. Management is expressed in this book as the more general notion of the way educationalists organise and administer their professional lives in the context of the challenges they meet and the changes they encounter.

The papers for this book have been written by practitioners drawn from very different parts of the educational system. Represented in this volume are contributions from higher education; secondary education; nurse education; and from further and vocational education. In addition, there are contributions from both the United Kingdom and from Australia. This book is not only a reflection of the work carried out by the present contributors, but a reminder of educationalists throughout the world who are responding to a context of innovation and change.

In conclusion, I would like to express my gratitude to those people who have helped with this book. My thanks to the contributors who have worked very hard to meet deadlines, and to the Editorial Board of the University of Huddersfield, School of Education for invaluable advice. Finally, and very importantly, I would like to thank Jackie Hepworth of the University Academic Typing Services for her painstaking work in preparing the manuscript.

Paul Oliver
The University of Huddersfield
1996

1 The concept of change management

Paul Oliver

Abstract

This paper provides both an introduction to the book and a means of linking together the different contributions. It is argued that change is an integral function of organisational life and of education in particular. Rather than viewing 'equilibrium' as the norm, it is suggested that change and transition are more typical of contemporary life. Learning to live with change has become almost a prerequisite for participating in the education system. Case studies will be viewed not so much as exemplars of stability, but rather as points on a continuum of evolution and change.

Introduction

In many ways it would be very reassuring to be part of an educational system which did not need to change. Such a system would not require changing because in all major facets it would meet the hopes and aspirations of those involved, both teachers, students, parents and employers. There would be an agreed system of values with a consensus view about such issues as equal opportunities or education for the disadvantaged. A general agreement on curricular matters would have been reached, with a clear consensus about curriculum content at different ages and for different purposes such as academic or vocational education. Similarly, there would be agreement about styles of curriculum delivery and of assessment. A compromise would have been reached about different teaching and learning approaches, and although diversity no doubt would exist, there would be a general, common approach within the system. Once all of this agreement had taken place, perhaps the most contentious area would be that of funding the system, but at least there would be consensus on the main points of principle. Both teachers and students would know quite clearly what was expected of them.

This kind of scenario might sound very attractive to some. Teachers would just have to get on with a clearly-defined job year after year, and students would have an agreed curriculum for years to come. For some, however, this might sound a rather dull kind of existence. However, personal views are of little consequence here, since this kind of development is highly improbable. 'Change' seems a much more likely characteristic of education, than 'stability'. Handy and Aitken (1990, p.102) sum this up:

> People will push for change because they are dissatisfied; events will push those who want to hold on to what they've got because they are satisfied. The only certainty about the future is its uncertainty, that there will be changes.

A changing education system is inevitable. Within a country, there is a constantly evolving public perception of what an education system should have as its priorities. To some extent this public perception changes with changes in the economic situation and employment market. When jobs are plentiful there may be a wider tolerance for innovation and experiment within the system. At times of contraction, the public demand may be largely for vocational skills and for a concentration upon the basic skills of numeracy and literacy. Governmental imperatives change as well. All governments are to some extent interested in the capacity of an education system to deliver young people who are able to contribute effectively to the economic wealth of the country. As the needs of the economy vary, so generally will governments' views about the nature of the education system.

Moreover, teachers are not a uniform body. They represent very different subjects and disciplines with different ways of viewing the world. They have been trained as teachers in different times and in different locations. Inevitably, to some extent, they embrace different value systems and ideologies of education. Teachers cannot be expected to respond uniformly to the contentious issues of the time. In addition, as human beings, their attitudes vary with time. An individual teacher may take one view on an educational issue at one point in his or her career, and an entirely different view, at another stage. This is perfectly natural, but is another dimension of the inconstancy which one might reasonably expect in an educational system. Research, too, has an impact upon educational change. It defines problems in new ways and suggests different methods for the resolution of issues. Moreover, research has a significant effect upon policy development at both local and national level, and so is frequently a factor in initiating change.

It is difficult then, to conceive of an educational system which is not changing. In fact, it can be argued that change is a much more 'natural' situation than one of equilibrium or stability. At an organic level, living things go through cyclical processes of growth and decline. At a psychological level, the individual finds that ideas arise, stay for a while, and then disappear. Mental activity appears to follow a similar process of arising and falling away. Even at a cosmic level, it is clear that large aggregations of matter operate within cyclical patterns. If change is 'natural' for the organic, psychological and physical worlds, then there is no reason to suppose that it should not be the 'natural' state for society, for organisations and for human systems. West-Burnham (1990, p.93) argues that:

> Change is axiomatic to organisational life, and an organisation that ceases to respond effectively is balanced on the fine line between stability and stagnation. Neither state is appropriate to an educational institution.

The 'naturalness' of change is not always an easy concept for individuals to accept. There is something very attractive and reassuring about stability and continuity. As individuals we often feel very attracted to the idea of working within the same administrative systems, of working with the same people, and of teaching the same course. Regularity may at times be rather tedious, but it has a very appealing side. Many people, when faced with the prospect of change, particularly if it involves a major readjustment, will try to cling on to the familiar and the predictable.

This view of 'change' sees a transition as a major event which must be 'coped with' rather than a natural consequence of the way things are in the world. If change is viewed as a series of isolated events which upset the pleasant stability of things, then it will be perceived as something to fear, and something to avoid wherever possible. On the other hand, change can be viewed as simply a continuous process of evolution, whereby transition is part of the normal sequence of events. There may well be times of greater change and of lesser change, but generally an organisation or educational system is perceived as being in a state of natural flux. Such a view requires a radical shift in perspective for many people, from a position of distrust about change, to one of beginning to feel adjusted to operating within the process of transition. Within this framework, individuals will develop new approaches to change:

> .... change is not just about the creation of new policies and procedures to implement external mandates. It is also about the development of personal strategies by individuals to respond to, and seek to influence the impact of, structural and cultural change: personal change as much as organisational change. (Bennett et al, 1992, p.2)

Just as one might reasonably make an appeal to individual teachers and lecturers to try to adapt to changing circumstances, and to seek to develop a different view of change, it also is important for those cast in the role of management to attempt to understand the stresses placed upon individuals. Education is an area of work which demands a high level of personal commitment. It is difficult in many ways, to imagine someone working in education without giving an enormous amount of 'themselves' to the job. This level of commitment tends to result in a considerable degree of attachment to various aspects of the work. For example, when someone is a course tutor, we often refer to that course as 'Person X's course'. This is a reflection of a common assumption about the extent of the personal involvement which one has in administering and recruiting for a particular course. When a department goes through a period of intense change, courses are reorganised, and roles reallocated, it is not surprising that this can cause considerable psychological upheaval for individuals.

The process of change and of role reallocation can easily result in a degree of alienation, and the individual is not necessarily in a positive frame of mind to contribute effectively to the change process. An effectively managed transition can not only help to reduce or eliminate this sense of alienation, but can in the process help individuals to become part of the transition. Heichberger (1976, p.113) argues for more of a sense of empathy for those participating in change.

> The process of change will be more humane if the stimulators for change realise that feelings and emotions are of primary importance. These prime movers must realise that the individuals they are asking to change are, first of all, human; they have deep underlying feelings, wishes, defence and fears ....

We are here firmly within the province of what might be termed 'the ethics of change management'. As with many ethical issues, there is a component which is concerned with a value system for ways of treating other people; but in addition, an aspect which involves creating organisational structures which enable people to live their lives in positive and constructive ways.

The functional structures by which change is created are certainly very important in developing an environment in which people can flourish and feel part of the change process. Appropriate discussion forums can help people to participate in the transition, and make a positive contribution. It certainly helps the change process if managers try to project forwards to imagine the possible effects of the developments which they initiate. Newsam (1992, p.253) recounts that in ancient Athens people with proposals for change were rewarded if the ideas were accepted, but executed if they were considered inappropriate.

> At least that ensured that people did not try and institute major changes, as seems to be the fashion these days, without thinking hard about the practical consequences.

Participation is an essential requirement if individual teachers and lecturers are to feel that they are part of the change and not being asked merely to implement changes developed by others. The question of policy development is crucial here. If teachers learn about change through the medium of memoranda and circular, then they will not gain that sense of ownership which is crucial if the change is to be truly successful. It is important that teachers are actually involved in the policy development, and have the opportunity to bring all of their grass roots experience to bear upon resolution of problems. Managers can sometimes be sufficiently removed from the day to day consequences of planning decisions, as to make their solutions to issues sometimes impractical. A climate of participative policy formulation can help to create an atmosphere of stability and security which is essential for effective change.

> Incompatibility between long-term developmental objectives and short-term fashionable objectives is often at the root of much of the current confusion in the post-sixteen world. Responsiveness and change are necessary consequences of a market in further education, but colleges need security and support if they are to develop their contribution. (McGinty and Fish, 1993, p.7)

The involvement of educationalists from all strata of the organisation is very important when change is contemplated, because of the diffuse nature of the change process within human systems. In the natural sciences it is conceivable that a single variable can be altered and that this will result in a change in another specified variable. The possibility of excluding the effects of extraneous variables is one of the characteristics of investigations in the natural as opposed to the social sciences. During organisational change however, it is extremely difficult to identify a feature which is to be altered and to develop a single strategy which will change that feature, and that feature alone. Normally when a variable in a human system is altered, then a network of potential and actual changes is initiated throughout the system. As Hargreaves and Hopkins (1991, p.8) suggest:

> In reality both a weakness and a change designed to cure it interact with all the other factors that contribute to a school's character - strengths and weaknesses included.

When such a change network is established, it is important for the viability of the transition, that change agents are involved who are familiar with the different facets of the organisation and the implications of the proposed change. This is where participative planning and development are important.

It is crucial that those responsible for the initiation and management of change, appreciate the organic nature of the change process, and that sometimes it is difficult to predict all of the consequences of a particular localised transition. There is also an underlying ethical principle here, that within organisations everyone is dependent to a greater or lesser extent upon everyone else. Organisations are inevitably co-operative ventures. Peeke (1994, p.26) emphasises this aspect of organisations:

> Systems Theory conceptualises an organisation as analogous to a biological organism ... A specific characteristic of the systems view is its emphasis on the interrelatedness of the various parts of the system. Change in one part of the system necessitates change in all the other parts also.

It is being increasingly recognised that change is an inevitable aspect of life in organisations and within education in particular. Education planning must involve the establishment of new targets and strategies, and when this happens it is very likely that former goals will lose something of the sense of priority. As education exists primarily in a changing social context, it is almost certain that it will be accompanied by continual transition.

> Competing goals force us to accept that moving towards one may take us away from another. Hence we must be willing to accept a certain amount of instability. (Leigh, 1994, p.12)

Just as the organic world is in a state of adaptation and evolution, so is the world of educational organisations. Arguably, it is not change itself which is undesirable. The challenge is to identify the correct changes to make, and then, importantly, to implement them in a humanistic and sensitive manner.

This volume is less concerned with management theory and perspectives, but rather more with the everyday strategies employed by practitioners to ensure the smooth progress of change and transition. It reflects the notion that all teachers and educationalists are essentially 'managers' in one sense or another. They must 'manage' the classroom learning process and the educational experiences of pupils; they must manage their own allocated resources; they must manage their own time; and they must manage their involvement in the numerous curriculum initiatives which are part and parcel of everyday educational life. Moreover, all educational change inevitably takes place in a corporate or participative environment. Teachers have to work together with each other and with their students in order to make change work. The notion that a single person can act in isolation to 'manage' an educational situation, seems increasingly problematic. A manager must function as part of a collaborative enterprise in order to ensure the success of change in a contemporary educational environment. The papers in this volume have been selected to illustrate the increasingly complex nature of educational change and the sophisticated strategies needed to organise that change.

The chapter by Wendy Bradford reports on recent research on the underperformance of boys in secondary education. There is growing evidence that schools will increasingly have to address this issue. In recent years employers have made various calls for an improvement in the literacy and numeracy skills of the young people who apply for jobs. Lynn Free explores practical strategies for improving literacy skills of secondary school pupils with relatively low literacy levels.

Changes in vocational education and training and the associated transitions in the needs of industry, have resulted in new challenges for vocational teachers. The chapter by Stephen Billett examines a case study involving teachers acting as industry consultants. Increasingly, the educational system is having to develop a range of non-traditional approaches to curriculum delivery. Ros Carnwell's chapter explores the issue of distance education, particularly in relation to community nurses. Related to this is the development of learning systems in which students take much more responsibility for the organisation of their own learning. Helen Trayers describes the development of a Resource-based Learning Centre and the way in which it can be used to manage curriculum delivery.

An important aspect of change is the evolution of the learning experience involving tutor and students. Pauline James proposes an application of collaborative research with students, in order to help manage the nature of student learning. 'Quality' is becoming one of the key considerations behind any new development in education. Jennifer Earnshaw's chapter analyses the Total Quality Management approach and its relevance to a college.

Changes in the funding mechanisms of education have placed greater pressures upon institutions to be cost-effective and efficient. One of the most complex management situations is the merger of two institutions, and Geoffrey Elliott explores a case study which illustrates this; while Geoff Hayton focuses upon education and learning in workplace situations. Kathy Bland examines one aspect of the response of colleges to the need to generate more income. She analyses attempts to develop and extend a commercial unit in a further education college. Such developments are likely to become more significant in the future of technical colleges.

Paul Hager's chapter examines an interesting case study in the exploration of the key competencies which link education and vocational situations. The current examination of new ways of delivering vocational training may create an increasing need to manage tuition in core skills.

The training and preparation of technical teachers is an area which is continually making new demands, as the needs of industry and commerce fluctuate. John Sheehan considers the case of one of the four main technical teacher training institutions in England, and the ways in which change has been managed over a period of fifty years.

References

Bennett, N. et al (1992) Managing Educational Change: the Centrality of Values and Meanings. **In** Bennett, N. et al (eds.) *Managing Change in Education.* London: Paul Chapman.

Handy, C. and Aitken, R. (1990) *Understanding Schools as Organisations.* London: Penguin.

Hargreaves, D.H. and Hopkins, D. (1991) *The Empowered School.* London: Cassell.

Heichberger, R.L. (1976) Toward a Strategy for Humanising the Change Process in Schools. **In** Eiden, R. and Milliren, A. (eds.) *Educational Change: A Humanistic Approach*. La Jolla, California: University Associates.

Leigh, A. (1994) Change in Leadership. **In** Bennett, N. et al (eds.) *Improving Educational Management through Research and Consultancy*. London: Open University and Paul Chapman.

McGinty, J. and Fish, J. (1993) *Further Education in the Market Place*. London: Routledge.

Newsam, P. (1992) Educational Reform: The Past has Lessons to Teach the Future. **In** Simkins, T. et al (eds.) *Implementing Educational Reform: The Early Lessons*. Harlow: Longman.

Peeke, G. (1994) *Mission and Change*. Buckingham; The Society for Research into Higher Education and Open University Press.

West-Burnham, J. (1990) The Management of Change. **In** Davies, B. et al, *Education Management for the 1990s*. London: Longman.

2 The progress of boys in secondary school

Wendy Bradford

Abstract

This study was undertaken to assess differences between the attitudes of boys and girls in Key Stage 4 towards key aspects of their school experience, and differences in performance at GCSE.

In the first phase of work, a survey by questionnaire of 1,049 students in one LEA was carried out within five comprehensive schools - all schools in which girls outperformed boys at GCSE.

From the survey data, a number of interesting differences between the attitudes of boys and girls towards school were noted. In particular, boys' responses showed much higher levels of academic self-confidence. Their seemingly false optimism meant that they significantly over-estimated their likely chances of success in their forthcoming GCSE examinations.

In the second phase of work, the author worked with a large number of schools in one LEA to develop strategies for enhancing the performance of boys at GCSE.

Introduction

The present study was shaped from the author's work, over a period of several years, as Head of Year 10 in an 11-16 mixed comprehensive school. The case study involved collaborative work with officers and schools within Kirklees LEA, and academic support from the University of Huddersfield. At the time of writing, eleven secondary schools are working in the second phase of a project to develop strategies to enhance the performance of boys at GCSE.

In this sense, the case study could be interpreted in one of two ways. Either as a study of a single case - that of the LEA - or as a 'collective case study' (Denzin and Lincoln, 1994) of several cases - a number of individual schools within the LEA, chosen so that an understanding of these schools might offer insights leading to a better understanding of a still larger collection of schools, both within the LEA and beyond.

A number of different methods of data collection were employed within the case study framework over the two separate phases of work - questionnaire, semi-structured interview, observation, analysis of statistical data from the schools. Robson (1993, p.290) offers a justification for such an eclectic approach:

> One important benefit of multiple methods is in the reduction of inappropriate certainty. Using a single method and finding a pretty clear-cut result may delude investigators into believing that they have found the 'right' answer. Using other, additional, methods may point to differing answers which remove specious certainty.

The schools involved in the case study represented different levels of performance at GCSE, but one common factor between the schools was that girls outperformed boys at GCSE. It was the aim of the case study to initiate change in the performance of boys at GCSE in the LEA's schools, in ways which were seen to be appropriate to the particular needs of each school.

Responding to the need for change

It was felt to be particularly important that any change which was introduced would be sustainable over a period of years, and would not, therefore, be seen as an 'initiative'. In terms of managing change within individual schools, this was felt to be an important prerequisite for producing positive outcomes. It was also felt that teachers, subject to years of seemingly transient initiatives, imposed largely from external sources, would respond more favourably to changes which represented modifications to existing ways of working; changes which, it was hoped, would become embedded in a new understanding of 'good practice'. It had to be acknowledged, however, that even with small-scale alterations to customary practice, change could be professionally uncomfortable. As Hutchinson and Whitehouse (1986, p.91) note:

> Only when teachers realise that their views of professional competence are prejudices which have to be tested, rather than uncritically accepted, can they begin to build a constructive critique of their social practice.

Somekh (1995) offers a rather more accommodating model where, rather than seeking to brusquely uproot and supplant teachers' taken-for-granted assumptions, research adds to the available store of understanding and practice. In this way, school-based research (Somekh, 1995, p.343):

> constitutes a powerful means of professional development. The process of change is integrated with the development of new understandings of the implications of personal action, in particular of the unintended consequences of habitual or routinised behaviour ... The routines of professional practice are enriched by the intellectual challenge of research.

How successful the project was in achieving this aim, would be, perhaps, only partially determined by the quality of the final written outcome.

As Alkin (1987, p.319) notes:

> Who is so naive among us not to recognise that who we are as evaluators, our past reputation, our organisational affiliation, and - oh yes - our personality traits have a great impact upon the extent to which someone 'needs', 'cares', or utilises the evaluation report that we produce.

Hutchinson and Whitehouse (1986, p.85) have a pessimistic view of what the outcome of such school-based research projects might be. They see that through the hierarchical relationships of power and responsibility, the project can be:

> emasculated, neutralised and cut down to size by and within the institution.

Elliott, (1991, p. 56) however, views the enterprise in rather a different way, arguing that, through research activity and reflection, the 'insiders' in the educational practice - the teachers - are empowered. Such empowerment helps to initiate a creative resistance in handling change:

13

It involves the transformation of the professional culture into one which supports collaborative reflection about practice and takes the experiences and perceptions of clients (pupils, parents, employers) into account in the process ... Teachers ... develop the courage to critique the curriculum structures which shape their practices, and the power to negotiate change within the system which changes them.

Boys in secondary school

The issue of differential educational achievement according to gender has been a persistent theme in educational research, underpinning investigations into educational performance for many years. Statistics, at both a national and local level, show girls to be increasingly successful at GCSE (DFE, 1995; Kirklees LEA, 1995) and to be maintaining - even extending - their advantage over boys (see Table 1).

In spite of this persistent 'gap' between the performance of boys and girls at GCSE, less research consideration has been given to the attitudes, schooling experiences and academic performance of boys. This may be because, ultimately, boys are seen as being the 'winners' in the educational system - in terms of A level successes and entry to the 'high status' branches of higher education. As Connell (1989, p. 301) states:

A 'compensatory' logic will not work for the privileged sex.

Table 1   Five or more grades A*-C for boys and girls - nationally and Kirklees LEA

	1991	1992	1993	1994	1995
Boys National	30.8	31.1	33.7	36.2	39
Girls National	38.4	40.1	43.1	45.2	48.1
% by which girls out-perform boys, nationally	**7.6**	**9**	**9.4**	**9**	**9.1**
Boys Kirklees	24.9	26.3	27.8	31.9	29.8
Girls Kirklees	33.3	34.7	40.4	39.9	42.6
% by which girls out-perform boys, Kirklees	**8.4**	**8.4**	**12.6**	**8**	**12.8**

14

The fact that there has been little published research on 'the boys' issue' may be one factor encouraging schools to initiate and implement changes in this area themselves. After years of externally-imposed educational change it has, perhaps, been refreshing for schools and LEA's to work together in locating an area of concern where both the identification of the 'problem' and the devising of strategies to produce change has come from the 'inside'. In the case of the present study, higher education has facilitated and supported school-based research to initiate change, rather than suggesting the direction of change itself.

It is, perhaps, anecdotal but, nonetheless, interesting to note that many teaching colleagues were keen to participate in the work relating to the 'boys' issue' because it was 'about things which mattered'. It was closely related to improved teaching and learning opportunities and , therefore, seen as central to their interests and responsibilities. This would seem to suggest some justification for Elliott's emphasis (1991, p.53) that the practitioner-researcher should have 'a felt need' for the subject under study.

This strategy of analysing and modifying practice within one's own area of experience relates to Robson's concept of 'real world enquiry' (Robson, 1993, p.11). He characterises real world research, as opposed to 'artificial' research, as being concerned with solving problems, predicting effects and concerned with factors where change is possible. Such research has strict time and cost constraints, is carried out by 'generalist' researchers working for organisations such as schools and is (Robson, 1993, p.12):

...currently viewed as dubious by many academics.

Fortunately, those academics supporting this project were converts rather than doubters, perhaps sharing Stenhouse's view (1987, p. 74) that:

Educational research has as its overriding aim the support of educational acts - it is not 'pure' but 'applied'.

It is clear from the above that this case study involved 'co-operative inquiry' (Reason 1994, Ch.20). This involves working with groups as both co-researchers - making a contribution to the shaping, management and evaluation of the project - and as co-subjects - participating in the activity being researched.

Differential responses to the process of schooling

There are, however, reasons beyond the 'gap' in performance at GCSE which should lead researchers to look more closely at the educational experiences of boys. A major stimulus for the present research arose from evidence emerging from the school's internal processes of reviewing and recording progress which suggested that boys were being judged by their teachers as making a less positive response to their school work than were girls of the same year group.

The school in which the author is a teacher, attached great weight to the processes of reviewing progress which had been developed over a number of years. A central element of this process was the Progress Review, where teachers awarded effort grades to cover work over the previous two months. A five point scale was used, with 1 suggesting high levels of effort, and 5 suggesting unsatisfactory effort. A single, illustrative example may be useful at this point. In the Autumn of 1994, effort grades were awarded to 160 Year 10 students in school 1. The results of 40 students were seen to be particularly commendable - 31 were girls, 9 were boys. Of the 24 students whose poor effort was seen to be a cause for concern, 3 were girls and 21 were boys. In the same school, in the Autumn of 1995, a summary of referrals from subject teachers to Year Heads for bad behaviour showed a comparable situation.

Table 2   Referrals for 'bad behaviour' from subject teachers to Head of Year from one school for September to October 1995

Year Group	7	8	9	10	11
Girls	3	10	8	4	11
Boys	22	15	12	9	20

A similar 'feel' was evident in all the schools who wished to get involved in the current project. 'Boys take up so much of the time, and it's all to do with troubleshooting rather than planning ahead' was one comment.

There is also evidence on a national level to suggest that boys are presenting themselves as more of a 'problem'. As Hymas and Cohen (1994, p.14) note:

Boys now outnumber girls by two to one in Britain's schools for children with learning difficulties. In special units for pupils with behavioural or discipline problems, there are as many as six boys for every girl.

From a longitudinal study, covering three years, in an LEA of 47,000 students, Imich (1994, p.7) noted:

As in most research on disruptive behaviour there was an overwhelming leaning towards males, who accounted for 80% of all exclusions.

In examining the procedure of statementing children with special educational needs in Sheffield over one year, Hill noted that 67.6% were boys. In examining the underlying processes which shape the decision to statement students, Hill (1994, p.351) notes:

... gender descriptions generated as part of statementing procedure see boys as generally more disruptive, less co-operative, less positive in attitude toward school, but also as more academically able than girls. Girls, however, are seen as less disruptive, more passive, more happy with school life, but less academic than boys.

And after school ......?

An additional reason for focusing on the experience of boys at school arose from looking at destinations of students when they left school at age 16. Whereas academically-successful boys and girls were equally likely to move to sixth form education, there was a difference in the routes chosen by those defined by the school as being of 'middle' ability. Definition of academic potential was often made on the basis of a Cognitive Abilities Test, most usually administered at the age of 11. 'Middle ability' girls were passing sufficient GCSEs at grade C or above to allow them access to further academic or vocational courses, whereas 'middle ability' boys were often gaining more grade Ds and were dropping out of full-time education at that point. The local employment market, having a small and shrinking number of unskilled and semi-skilled vacancies, would not be able to employ these students. Nationally, it is difficult to imagine how dramatic has been the collapse of the youth market for work. For example, in 1976, 53% of 16 year olds entered employment. In just ten years, by 1986, this figure had fallen to 15%. As Furlong (1994, p.126) notes in the Scottish context, 'failure' at school, along with fewer employment opportunities has had a particular effect on the opportunities of boys. Whereas girls leaving school with grades D or E at GCSE are twice as likely as those with five or more grade C and above passes to suffer long-term unemployment, boys with grades D and E were three times more likely to suffer long-term unemployment than their more successful peers.

Furthermore, some sixth form colleges and technical colleges were becoming more selective about their intakes and, therefore, the range of educational opportunities for these boys to re-sit or improve their low level of examination results was also narrowing. From the above it is clear that the eventual destination of many of these boys must be a matter of some concern. As Barber (1994, p.8) points out:

> If there is a growing underclass, poorly educated young men are its vanguard... It is certain that one of the critical equal opportunities issues for the next decade is the motivation and achievement of young men.

The place of boys in school effectiveness research

A final, and broader, rationale for focusing on the progress of boys in secondary school surrounds the notion of school effectiveness. Is it appropriate to examine the effectiveness of a school by treating its students as a single population, or would more useful insights be gained by looking at the effectiveness of the school for particular populations - in this case, girls and boys? Nuttall et al. (1989, p.776) conclude, in response to this question:

> Our research indicates with three years' data in 140 schools ... that it is more meaningful to describe differences between schools for different sub-groups: the concept of overall effectiveness is not useful.

In summary, there were, perhaps, four main reasons for raising a concern about the performance of boys in school. First, boys are less successful than girls at GCSE - in some schools and some areas of the curriculum quite markedly so. Secondly, there is evidence that teachers see boys to be making a less beneficial response to the process of schooling than girls. Thirdly, inferior performance of boys at GCSE raises concerns about their future in education and training and their eventual place in the employment market. Finally, a concern for boys helps to illuminate the concept of differential effectiveness within schools for certain sub-groups of the student population.

Shaping the project

As the author is a teacher is an LEA school, and one of the five schools which was to be included in the first phase of the study, the question of access was significantly eased. Adopting the role of 'practitioner-researcher' (Robson, 1993) provides the advantage of being an 'insider' and allows familiar access to an invaluable base of knowledge, experience and contacts. It could also be suggested that one might be more sensitive to the 'internal politics' of institutions.

Work was divided into two main phases of activity. First, came a diagnostic stage in which the area under concern could be investigated and hypotheses generated which, it was hoped, would lead to the generation of practical strategies. Whilst the literature concerning action research usually emphasises the aim of improving practice, it was important within this study to begin with an enhanced understanding of the current attitudes and aspirations of boys. Second came a phase of implementation and evaluation where strategies could be adopted within the school situation, whilst close attention would be paid to their efficacy in improving the performance of boys. In practice, there was an on-going inter-play between the two phases as developing understanding influenced choice of strategy, and work to implement practical strategies provided a further contribution to the base of understanding. McNiff (1988, p.42) describes this dialectical process in appealing terms as 'a dance of communication'.

The first phase of change - investigating attitudes

It was decided to focus on the performance and attitudes towards schooling of boys within one LEA. Using GCSE data at the level of five or more A to C passes for 1993, it was found that girls outperformed boys in each of the LEA's secondary schools. Through agreement with officers within the LEA and the schools concerned, five schools were selected to form the substance of the first phase of the LEA case study. The five schools represented different measures of social disadvantage, different ethnic mixes of students, and different levels of performance at GCSE. The LEA had already identified 'the boys' issue' as a topic of concern and was keen to support work in this area, as a report indicated (Kirklees, 1992, p.7):

The gender differences in terms of levels of achievement across all subjects are clearly issues for individual schools to identify and consider strategies to address.

The first phase of work involved a questionnaire which was completed by 1,049 of the LEA's students in the five selected schools during the period February to April 1994. All students in the sample were involved in the final two years of schooling, with 62% of the sample in Year 10 and 38% in Year 11. 57% of the respondents were boys and 43% girls.

Results from the first phase of work

The questionnaire included five main sections:

1   Feelings towards school

The general feeling which emerges from this section is one of boys exhibiting less attachment to school than girls, with boys having contacts other than through school as the source of friendship and fun. For girls, however, friendships were mainly school-based. Girls expressed greater commitment to the rules and activities of school-life than did boys. This finding links with other research (Harris et al., 1993) which suggests that boys' social networks are broader and more extensive than those of girls. This apparently greater attachment of girls to school may suggest that they have more 'invested' in success in this context.

There was something of a sense, in a substantial minority of responses, that school was tolerated - endured rather than enjoyed. In response to the statement 'I look forward to coming to school' only 28.1% agreed, or strongly agreed, with the statement, whilst 42.8% disagreed, or strongly disagreed. Boys were significantly more likely than girls to show antipathy towards coming to school. A similar feeling of disenchantment, with deterioration through the years of secondary schooling is noted by Keys and Fernandes (1993, p.1-64)

A fairly substantial minority of students said they found their school work boring ... students' attitudes towards school and learning tend to deteriorate to some extent as they progress from Year 7 to Year 9 in their secondary schools.

20

A similar pattern is noted by Downes (1994, p.8) in the context of Cambridgeshire:

> We develop a picture of the average and below average boy attending school without showing much interest for schoolwork, finding little pleasure in academic achievement ... rarely reading for pleasure and with little long-term motivation to be a high achiever.

2 How do you like to work in lessons?

This section aimed to elicit attitudes towards passive and active teaching/learning strategies. 'I enjoy copying notes from a book or from the board', 'I learn more by doing, rather than just listening'.

In response to items in this section, boys were more appreciative of lessons which involved discussion work, and disliked passive activities such as copying work from a book or the board ($p < 0.001$). 'Class discussion' may be defined by students as oral activity which is primarily student-led, with the emphasis on large group interaction. Other research (Swann and Graddol, 1988; Bousted, 1989) has suggested that boys tend to dominate such 'free' discussions and this may help to explain their liking for such activities.

3 How important are your school subjects to you?

This section looked at subjective importance ratings given to the core subjects of English, Mathematics and Science.

Clear gender-related differences could be noted here. Girls' rating of the importance of English to them was much higher than that given by boys. However, boys rated Mathematics and Science as being of more importance to them than did girls (see Table 3).

It is interesting to speculate about factors which have led boys and girls to see three of their core subjects in this way. The lower ratings given to Science could suggest its failure to attract young people, but it could be due to the relative 'newness' of current Science courses as part of the core curriculum. Looking at patterns of importance attached to English and Mathematics, one could argue that these results reflect past patterns of success for previous cohorts of girls and boys, but this is not, in fact, true. In English, in the schools concerned, girls outperform boys by a much greater degree than the importance ratings would seem to suggest. In Mathematics and Science, boys are only slightly more successful than girls.

21

An alternative explanation may be that students, looking ahead to possible future training, education and career choices, are assessing which subjects will be of the greatest use in that context - a context where, traditionally, girls have been more likely to pursue work involving English, and boys are more likely to utilise Mathematics and Science.

Table 3   How important are your school subjects for you? A response from students in five schools

Subject	'Very important to me' Nos & (%)	'Quite important' Nos & (%)	'Neutral' Nos & (%)	'Not very important to me' Nos & (%)	'Not at all important to me' Nos & (%)
English - boys	437 (73.0)	116 (19.4)	15 (2.5)	4 (0.7)	8 (1.3)
English - girls	363 (80.7)	66 (14.7)	11 (2.4)	3 (0.7)	0 (0.0)
Maths - boys	481 (80.3)	77 (12.9)	3 (0.5)	2 (0.3)	7 (1.2)
Maths - girls	331 (73.6)	86 (19.0)	8 (1.8)	8 (1.8)	0 (0.0)
Science - boy	361 (60.1)	161 (26.9)	36 (6.0)	6 (1.0)	12 (2.0)
Science - girls	221 (49.1)	126 (28.0)	59 (13.1)	22 (4.9)	12 (2.7)

4   How do you spend your time?

This section asked students to list all the activities of the previous evening, giving time allocations for each. A measure was made of how much time, if any, each student allocated to homework.

There was no statistically significant difference between the homework habits of boys and girls, although girls were slightly more likely than boys to spend more than one hour on homework tasks.

5   How do you see yourself?

This section aimed to measure students' feelings of academic self-esteem. It should be remembered when considering responses to this section of items, that, for a significant length of time, girls have outperformed, and increasingly outperformed boys at the age of 16. One would, therefore, perhaps, expect girls to have higher expectations of their current academic standing within their peer group, also to have higher aspirations for their GCSE results and subsequent academic career.

The results gained from the sample of boys and girls studied suggests that this is not the case. Measured in several ways girls seem reluctant to describe themselves as other than 'average', whereas boys seem more confident of their academic standing within their peer group. For example, in response to one item, (see Table 4), 23 boys (3.8%) described themselves as '*The* best' in their year group. Not a single girl described herself in this way. ($p<0.001$).

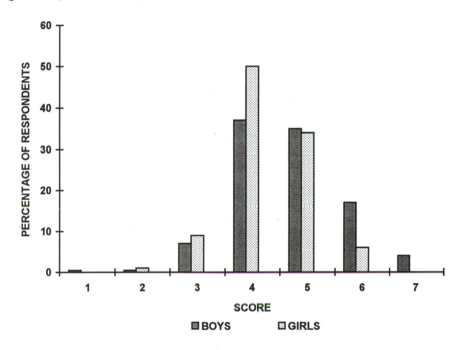

Figure 1 Answers in response to the question, 'Think of all the other classes in your year at school. Where would you place yourself in terms of your school ability?'

In response to the item where students were asked to judge their future level of achievement at GCSE, (see Table 5) there was not a statistically significant difference between the expectations of boys and girls. This lack of difference, is, in itself, interesting, when it is noted that, in line with past years, this cohort of girls probably will gain better results at GCSE than their boy peers, with an LEA average of approximately a 10% difference between girls and boys securing five or more A to C passes.

A slightly higher percentage of girls than boys expected to get grade C or above - 76.4% of boys and 79% of girls. Once again, however, boys were much more likely than girls to see themselves getting the top grades. For example, 10.2% of boys saw themselves as getting mainly grade A, whereas only 3.8% of girls predicted this outcome for themselves.

It is interesting to note the degree to which boys and girls feel they will be successful at GCSE. Guided by results from their schools over the last few years, both groups over-estimate their chances of securing grades C or better. Typically, approximately 75% of students felt they would gain five or more grade A to C passes, whereas, in practice, only 35-50% would gain this level of success. This inaccuracy in prediction, on the part of girls, and more significantly, boys, was particularly noteworthy as 38% of the sample were but a few months away from their final GCSE examinations. The over-estimation of likely outcome at GCSE was particularly marked in the case of boys. Boys consistently rate their academic performance more highly than girls. Girls consistently seem reluctant to describe themselves as anything more than 'average'.

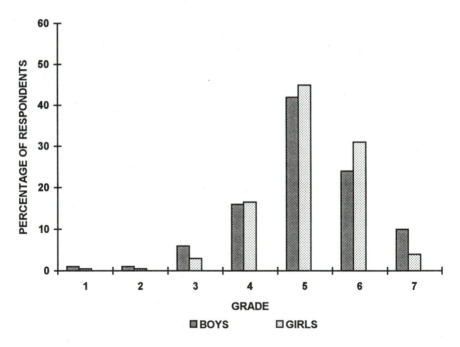

Figure 2   Answers in response to the question, 'What kinds of grades do you think you are capable of getting at GCSE?'

Licht and Dweck (1983, p.75) help to illuminate this issue through their examination of children's perceptions about their academic performance. They note a difference in final academic outcome between those children who attribute failure, or academic difficulties, to controllable factors, such as inadequate effort, and those who attribute difficulties to factors beyond their control, such as lack of ability. For this second group, attitudes are seen to lower expectations for future success. The authors note gender-related differences in this respect.

> Girls are more likely than boys to attribute their failures to ability, while boys are more likely to view their difficulties as stemming from insufficient effort ... While this attribution may result in lower expectations and efforts ... it still allows a boy to maintain confidence in his intellectual abilities ....

It could be suggested that these findings present schools with a double task if they wish to develop the effectiveness of their work for boys and girls. Boys need to be assisted to have a realistic view of their current levels of performance, and to be encouraged to fulfil their high expectations. Girls need assistance in developing a stronger sense of their academic worth and potential.

As will be noted later, these findings may well have implications for the procedures of monitoring and assessment of student performance which a school adopts. An emphasis on regular reviewing, individual feed-back to students on their current progress, and clear target-setting would seem to be essential.

The second phase of change - implementing strategies for improvement

As the LEA and participating schools noted the results from the survey by questionnaire in the early months of 1995, interest moved from an awareness of 'Where are we now?' to a concern with 'How can we change?'.

The LEA was able to provide a small amount of funding, which was matched by the local TEC, in order to allow the case study to be developed, through encouraging work to take place in schools to formulate practical strategies for addressing issues connected with the attitudes and academic attainment of boys at GCSE. The funding allowed the author to be seconded for one day a week for a full academic year. At this point a Steering Group was also created to monitor the project. This consisted of officers from the

LEA, a key representative from the TEC, a representative from the University of Huddersfield - who was also the author's academic tutor - the author, and the author's Headteacher.

Contacts were made with LEA's and schools around the country where there was interest in similar issues. As with schools in Kirklees, many schools around the country had identified the performance of boys as an area of concern. Some schools had undertaken sophisticated statistical work in order to identify their current position for all boys, boys of different ability groupings, and boys in different curriculum areas. Many were, however, only tentatively beginning to move forward in developing initiatives to address 'the issues' they had uncovered.

The response of teachers, mainly Headteachers, was interesting in that, even when they had conceived practical strategies and were in the process of implementing and evaluating ideas, they were noticeably apologetic about their ideas. 'It doesn't look much on paper', 'It's just a common-sense thing we're trying' were comments made in introducing and explaining ideas. It may be that the climate of externally-imposed educational change which has dominated for a number of years has adversely affected the confidence of teachers' in implementing strategies of institutional self-evaluation and self-improvement. It is hoped that as this project moves forward, and teaching colleagues are involved in offering, implementing and evaluating strategies for improvement, that the processes will be found to be of use in addressing other issues within school. The importance of such internally-managed processes of change is emphasised by Everard (1987, p.5):

> ... to help people to become originators rather than pawns, to make a difference to their world by getting things to happen - a problem solved, a decision implemented, an objective attained.

Once again, schools had to be made aware of the new phase of the project. The author spoke to a meeting of Kirklees Headteachers in September 1995 and invited interested schools to participate. One third of Headteachers representing the LEA's secondary schools responded within a fortnight and individual meetings were arranged. Some schools had been aware of the issue for a number of years, seeing a pattern of boys' underachievement spreading back over a prolonged period. Some schools had highlighted the issue in their School Development Plan and were now looking to move forward with practical strategies. Other schools had had the issue raised by OFSTED and others, with OFSTED imminent, felt that the issue would be raised. All were keen to move from their existing position of identifying the need for change, to implementing strategies to produce improvement.

As a starting point for discussion, the author presented Headteachers with a three page document which listed many practical strategies designed to improve both the process and outcome of schooling for boys. It was anticipated that schools would modify and adapt suggested strategies in the light of their own circumstances and priorities.

It was also agreed that participating schools would take part in a further survey by questionnaire, probing issues of academic self-esteem which had produced such interesting results in the questionnaire employed in the first phase of research. It was also suggested that the author would interview small groups of boys in participating schools about their attitudes to school, their academic work, progress and targets set for the future. It was hoped that this would enable a view to be taken about whether, following a range of practical interventions by schools, students now had positive, but more realistic, targets about their progress and aspirations for their GCSE results, than had been suggested by results from the first phase of work. Obviously, the interviews themselves would make a contribution to the school's plans for 'awareness-raising' amongst boys, and would also make a positive contribution to the school's plans for reviewing and monitoring student performance.

Progress in phase two

By the end of December 1995, meetings had taken place with Headteachers and other colleagues in eleven participating schools, and schools were now beginning to give shape to the strategies they wished to pursue. It was, obviously, important that, in selecting strategies to pursue, schools should be clear about the exact nature of the intervention which was being made and, at the same time, be mindful of how the success, or otherwise, of such strategies would be measured. As Fitz-Gibbon (1978, p.8) notes:

> Plans should be laid at this time for evaluation of the program - but they rarely are.

It was agreed that the ability 'to prove improvement' should be built into projects from the outset. As Fitz-Gibbon (1978, pp.13-14), once again, notes:

27

The critical characteristic of any one evaluation study is that it provide the best possible information that could have been collected under the circumstances and that this information meet the credibility requirements of its evaluation audience.

It was certainly felt that each individual strategy within the overall project would need to be subject to formative evaluation in order to assess and, if necessary, re-think underlying assumptions and activities. A key requirement here was that the author would work closely with the teachers who were carrying strategies forward within the participating schools. Additionally, each strategy, and the overall project, would need to be subject to rigorous summative evaluation in order to measure its total impact.

Through a meeting of the project's Steering Group it was also agreed to arrange a joint meeting for representatives of all participating schools, to allow a more comprehensive sharing of strategies to take place. A central, one day conference, with a nationally-recognised speaker was also planned for a further few months ahead. It was hoped that, through these regular meetings, the issue would maintain the sense of interest and commitment it had originally stirred.

From initial meetings, the following strategies attracted significant interest. The need to raise the awareness of issues surrounding the performance of boys with colleagues in schools, boys themselves and their parents had to be addressed. Whilst most schools were confident that this could be achieved through a variety of means - an article in a newsletter, a special letter to parents, inviting parents into school for a Parents' Seminar - one or two schools felt themselves to be in a sensitive position. It was thought that to advertise that a section of the school's population was, in effect, failing to some degree could have an adverse effect on recruitment to the school. It was, therefore, decided to develop authority-wide strategies for raising awareness, in addition to the work carried out in this area by individual schools.

As all schools participating in this project used NFER tests with their students, either at age 11 or at 13, there was keen interest in using information gained from these tests to make early identification of potential underachievers, and to map the progress of boys through the school. There was particular interest in matching NFER data against the current position of students in areas where setting was the means of organising teaching groups. Some schools had already begun to look at this issue, and found that a number of boys were in much lower sets than their NFER scores might have suggested would be the case. It was considered that discussions around these issues would be particularly powerful in helping to change the basis on which setting decisions were taken.

Some schools were keen to evaluate experiments in new ways of grouping students within the classroom. For example, in the author's school, classes in Art and Design would sit two boys and two girls together, as far as was practicable, throughout Key Stage 3. Indeed, after one term of this plan, the Art and Design Team was so positive about the impact of this move on teaching and learning opportunities, that the scheme was also extended to students in KS4.

There was an interest in devoting some attention to boys who were performing well in the school. It was hoped that lessons could be learned from their successes, and it was hoped that their impact upon their year group could be enhanced. This emphasis reflected a desire to counter the ethos which was felt to exist amongst the boys in some schools that it was not appropriate to work well, or, more particularly, to be seen to be working well. Indeed, one school saw the diminution of an 'anti-boffin' culture as a necessary prerequisite for the improvement of the academic performance of boys at GCSE.

A number of schools asked colleagues in each curriculum area, as part of their regular process of reviewing results, to reflect on the 'gap' between the performance of boys and girls and to offer one practical strategy which could be implemented in their curriculum area. This approach had the advantage of developing commitment for the project. If teaching colleagues had recognised an issue, and been encouraged to offer a way of improving matters, surely they would have a greater desire to develop, monitor and evaluate work in this area.

There was a strong desire to improve existing processes for the monitoring and reviewing of progress in order to produce a clearer focus and more regular interactions with students.

Some schools were keen to review their system of rewards for older students. Some felt that a regular private word of praise would be more warmly received by students than a certificate presented in a public, and, possibly, embarrassing manner. There was also a feeling that, whilst schools had worked hard to create a climate in which the emphasis fell on praise rather than criticism, in some areas, particularly during interactions in the classroom, praise was still somewhat of a scarce commodity.

One school was keen to investigate, in greater depth, the characters of the different communities served by the school. It was hoped, in this way, to have an improved understanding of the interests and aspirations of particular groups of boys in the school.

Three schools had secured enhanced funding in order to give a colleague a responsibility point for taking charge of work on boys' underachievement. It was hoped this would make, at least, a partial contribution to raising the profile of the issue within school.

In one particular school, enhanced funding had been used to identify fifteen boys, on the basis of NFER and SATs data, as underachievers. The boys had been made aware of this and the fact that they were to be seen as a 'special' group in school for the two years of their GCSE courses. Their parents were contacted by letter and were invited to come to school to discuss ways of supporting work to improve the performance of their sons at GCSE. This project was, however, very much an exception to the general thrust of work within the case study schools. The ideas receiving most support from schools were not 'initiatives', about which it was felt both teachers and students may well have had their fill, but were policies which would represent a long-term modification of existing practices.

A final emphasis moved away from some of the 'macro'-level considerations above to focus on 'micro'-level processes of classroom and behaviour management - the dynamic aspects of curriculum management - seen as the foundation of effective teaching and learning. One particular initiative, which found favour in a number of participating schools, was to develop schemes for paired learning, based on peer-tutoring. Initially, schemes would involve students working in a pair - one as tutor as one as tutee - to learn a specific skill or piece of knowledge. Over time, roles would be changed so that each student had experience of the role of tutor. It was also anticipated that whilst, initially, pairings would be of the same sex, and of similar age and ability, at a later date pairings would be of mixed gender, mixed ability and would possibly involve cross-age tutoring. Such projects were based on teachers' feelings that students, particularly boys, would respond well to teaching and learning activities which involved a strong emphasis on oral work. Note was also taken of research (Sanderson et al., 1992; Fitz-Gibbon, 1978, 1995) which suggested that, through peer-tutoring projects, the tutee could be expected to make greater learning gains than in a conventional teaching and learning situation, with the tutor making even more substantial learning gains, presumably as s/he had more thoroughly embedded an understanding of the relevant skill or knowledge as a prerequisite to passing this understanding to another person.

Many schools were interested in looking at a combination of short-term strategies, designed to boost GCSE results of those already in Key Stage 4, and longer-term work beginning at age 11 or 13, depending on the structure of the school. 13-18 schools were also interested in using their cross-pyramid links to discuss issues of boys' attitudes and attainment. It is interesting to note that, in a preliminary meeting of representatives from some of the Authority's schools covering KS1 and KS2, there was a keen enthusiasm to work with their partner secondary schools to address 'the boys' issue'. Indeed, many of the concerns which were apparently evident within fifteen year old boys, were also seen to be causing concern at a much earlier age - with first school teachers wishing to address issues such as 'anti-learning peer pressure' amongst five and six year old boys!

A framework for change

At the time of writing, at the end of December 1995, the eleven participating schools had been moving towards a series of interventions which, whilst individually-tailored to meet the specific needs of a particular school, shared the same tripartite approach.

- The need to begin work with a phase of awareness-raising. This should 'touch' all colleagues within school, all students within school - and in the feeder schools within the pyramid - and should involve the community of parents. As some schools were sensitive about the impact of awareness-raising on prospective recruitment to the school it was also important to have LEA - wide publicity by preparing material for publication in the local press.
- The need to have practical strategies which were linked to the work of specific curriculum areas. This would allow areas to relate existing data concerning student-performance to appropriate strategies. It would also encourage commitment to and ownership of the work, as departments and teams were implementing and monitoring their own strategies. These strategies could be regarded as 'broad-brush' or 'macro' strategies, such as improving processes of feedback and monitoring of work within the department, or encouraging boys with their reading.
- The need to have strategies which modified ways of working within the classroom, modifying the way teacher and students related to each other

and to the range of teaching and learning strategies which could be created. Here, questions of classroom management, use of sanctions and rewards, and debates about grouping of students and learning style would be considered. Such 'micro' matters were generally regarded as being both difficult yet fundamental to address - often they were seen to involve challenging the 'taken-for-granted' assumptions of classroom life.

The three stages above have arisen through process of discussion with colleagues in school as a positive, sustainable and coherent approach to one aspect of managing educational change - managing the enhancement of the performance of boys in secondary school. Short-term gains will be measured in qualitative terms - improved interactions in lessons and improved motivation on the part of boys. The quantitatively-based measure of progress through improved GCSE results will, obviously, take some years to work through the system, but, even here, the schools' processes of formative assessment, through mid-year examinations and use of target grades should be accessible to early examination.

References

Alkin, M. C, (1987)   *Evaluation - Who needs it? Who cares?* **In** Murphy, R. and Torrance, H. (eds.) Evaluating education: Issues and methods. Harper and Row/OUP

Barber, M. (1994) *Young people and their attitudes to school. An interim Report.* University of Keele.

Boustead, M. W. (1989) *Who talks? The position of girls in mixed-sex classrooms* English in Education, **3**(3), pp.42-51.

Connell, R.W. (1989) *Cool guys, swots and wimps: the interplay of masculinity and education.* **In** Oxford Review of Education, **1**(3), pp.291-303.

Davies, B. et al. (1995) *Education Management for the 1990's.* Pitman Publishing.

Denzin, N.K. and Lincoln, Y.S. (eds.) (1994) *Handbook of qualitative research.* Sage.

D.F.E.E. (1995) *GCSE Results 1994-5. LEA and England Averages.* D.F.E.E.

Downes, P. (1994) *The gender effect.* **In** Managing Schools Today, **3**(5), pp.7 - 8.

Elliott, J. (1991) *Action research for educational change.* O.U. Press.

Everard, K.B. (1987) *Developing management in schools.* Blackwell.

Fitz-Gibbon, C.T. and Morris, L.L. (1978) *How to Design a Program Evaluation.* Sage.

Fitz-Gibbon, C.T. (1995) *Cross-age tutoring in Mathematics in inner-city schools.* Presentation at the C.S.C.S. Northern Conference, Chester.

Furlong, A. (1994) *A decade of decline. Social class and post-school destinations of minimum-age school leavers in Scotland 1977 - 1987.* In Frith, R. and Mahony, P. Promoting quality and equality in schools. Empowering teachers through change. David Fulton Publishers.

Harris, S. et al (1993) *School work, homework and gender.* In Gender and Education, **5**(1), pp.3-15.

Hill, J. (1994) *The paradox of gender: Sex stereotyping within statementing procedure.* In British Educational Research Journal, **20**(3), pp.345 - 355.

Hutchinson, B. and Whitehouse, P. (1986) *Action research, professional competence and school organisation.* In British Educational Research Journal, **12**(1), pp. 85-94.

Hymas, C. and Cohen, J. (1994) *The trouble with boys.* In The Sunday Times. 19/6/94. pp. 4.

Imich, A.J. (1994) *Exclusions from school: Current trends and issues.* In Educational Research, **36**(1), pp. 3-11.

Kirklees LEA (1992) *Gender issues in the curriculum.* Kirklees.

Kirklees LEA (1995) *Summary of results at age 16.* Kirklees.

Licht, B.G. and Dweck, C.S. (1983) *Sex differences in achievement orientations: consequences for academic choices and attainments.* In Marland, M. (ed.) *Sex differentiation and schooling.* Heinemann.

McNiff, J. (1988) *Action research. Principles and practice.* Macmillan.

Merriam, S.B. (1988) *Case study research in education. A qualitative approach.* San Francisco. Jossey-Bass.

Morris, L.L. and Fitz-Gibbon, C. T. (1978) *Evaluator's Handbook.* Sage.

Morris, L.L. and Fitz-Gibbon, C.T. (1978) *Program Evaluation Kit.* Sage.

Morris, N. (1990) *Understanding Educational Evaluation.* Kogan Page/CARE, University of East Anglia.

Murphy, R. and Torrance, H. (eds.) (1987) *Evaluating education: Issues and methods.* Harper and Row/O.U.P.

Nuttall, D.L. et al (1989) *Differential school effectiveness.* In The International Journal of Educational Research, **13**(7), pp.769-76.

Reason, P. (1994) *Three approaches to participative enquiry.* **In** Denzin, N.K. and Lincoln, Y.S. (eds.) *Handbook of qualitative research.* Sage.

Robson, C. (1993) *Real World Research. A resource for Social Scientists and Practitioner-Researchers.* Blackwell.

Sanderson, P. et al. (1992) *Cross-age peer tutoring in Science.* **In** School Science Review, **74**(266), pp.48-56

Somekh, B. (1995) *The contribution of action research to development in social endeavours: a position paper on action research methodology.* **In** British Educational Research Journal, **21**(3), pp.339-355.

Stenhouse, L. (1987) **In** Murphy, R. and Torrance, H. (eds.) Evaluating education: Issues and Methods. Harper and Row/OUP.

Swann, J. and Graddol, D. (1988) *Gender inequalities in classroom talk.* **In** English in Education, **22**(1), pp.48-65.

3 The teaching of literacy skills to eleven year old pupils with problems in reading, handwriting and spelling

Lynn Free

Abstract

This paper deals with the challenge of the Warnock Report and the subsequent Education Acts of the 1980s and 90s to the management of the teaching of reading, spelling and handwriting to a cohort of Year 7 pupils in the nine comprehensive schools of a West Yorkshire town who had a reading age below nine years. The study was prior to the introduction of the Code of Practice in 1994 and 1995. It was established that structured reading programmes were delivered to children on a withdrawal basis. Progress was significant.

Introduction

The inadequate levels of literacy amongst some adults has given concern for most of this century. There are many who have passed through the statutory educational system without being able to meet the demands of an increasingly industrialised, technological and socially complex nation because of a lower level of literacy.

Government legislation (from the 1981 Education Act to the 1993 Education Act) has given a lead, guidance and support to encourage local authorities and schools to develop policies, resources and strategies so that literacy can be achieved.

The aim of this case study was to examine what happened to Year 7 children who had lower levels of literacy and who entered the nine high schools in September 1993 in a West Yorkshire town. This was two years before the Code of Practice (CoP) (DFE, 1994) was fully implemented in September, 1995. The town, type of schools and their infrastructure, identification of Special Educational Needs (SEN) pupils, monitoring and evaluating of progress and the methods used in their teaching were investigated.

The case study

The West Yorkshire town is in an area of deprivation in terms of national statistics for wages, unemployment, physical and mental health, housing, life expectancy and degree of family breakdown. The nine schools surveyed varied from having very deprived to average catchment areas. Twenty-five percent of the pupils were of Asian or Afro-Caribbean origin. Children in the district may begin their schooling handicapped by the conditions within the family, the home, the workplace of the parent(s) and the region in which they live.

The town's high schools are all 11-16 co-educational comprehensive schools except for the Catholic-run school which also has a sixth form. There was a surplus of nearly 2,000 places, although some upturn in population had already reached the primary schools. All schools are within easy reach of each other and very accessible and near to the town centre. It would therefore be logical to follow government advice to rationalise the situation by the closure of possibly two secondary schools. This would produce significant savings financially without creating difficult travelling arrangements for displaced pupils. This would allow more money to be directed to the remaining schools which must benefit children at all levels of ability. Those with severe literacy problems could gain from increased resources.

The infrastructure within the schools for the teaching of pupils with low levels of literacy was well established.

All schools had at least one member of staff designated as a Head of Department for SEN (HoDSEN) and/or a SEN Co-ordinator. Only in one school was a Deputy Head specifically designated to assist SEN staff, the other HoDs were also the SEN Co-ordinator. Because of the cross-curricular nature of SEN and special provision combined with the statutory nature of much of that provision under recent Education Acts, it is desirable that a senior member of staff and a governor be directly involved in overseeing SEN work. This gives extra power when resources and time-tabling are under discussion. The SEN Co-ordinator should also be giving bulletins on SEN work termly to the staff and the whole governing body. This is not current practice presently within all the High Schools.

Until recently, training of SEN staff had been ad hoc - with the initiative for it coming from the teachers themselves - most of whom had acquired good relevant qualifications such as Master's degrees involving SEN, Diplomas in training dyslexic children and Certificates in teaching pupils with SEN. However, the LEA had funded for the last three years (and intends to continue doing so) the updating of any staff interested in SEN provision so that a SENIS (SEN In Schools) Certificate may be obtained. The future emphasis on providing a module in the teaching of reading is to be welcomed even if it is sadly belated as few teachers until recently have been trained in the teaching of literacy skills.

All high schools have moved away from the 'broom cupboard' image that was the image of accommodation for SEN resources and pupils. Each one had a base room and one had as many as three.

Financing for ongoing resourcing was adequate. There was a tendency for this to vary according to special bidding. This is satisfactory if there is a need to apply for monies for special projects being introduced but it would be better if every department could rely on a minimum figure every year so that ordinary demands on funding could be met with certainty (see Figure 1).

The LEA had been generous in distributing to schools staff to support pupils with a statement of SEN. Virtually every school had an extra qualified teacher (usually able to teach dyslexic children) to help with the Year 7 pupils who were the subject of the survey. It was very expensive as most were taught on a one-to-one basis and consideration should be given to the system seen in one school where a group of up to 10 working at the same level was taught in a more economic and social unit.

Also Non-Teaching Ancillaries (NTAs) were funded. The training of these, however, was minimal. A half day session was not enough. Courses had been provided but the take-up was voluntary, unpaid and unco-ordinated. The LEA's NTAs were mainly caring people who empathised with their SEN charges, explaining work and transcribing texts - but there needs to be more careful training so that pupils are not allowed to become dependent on their NTAs and are trained to think for themselves and work towards independence. There was not enough collaboration between NTAs, LEA funded staff and school staff. However, in one school there was a weekly meeting of all SEN staff. In another, the NTAs kept careful log-books on their charges so that the SEN Co-ordinator and parents could see what support was given and how the behaviour, attitudes and work level of the pupils were progressing. These methods could well be put into operation in all high schools.

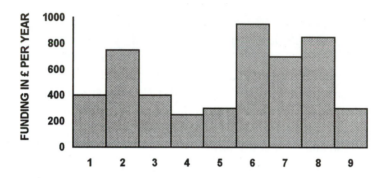

Figure 1 Funding for SEN department

The identification of SEN pupils should be the responsibility of the LEA and/or the schools.

The CoP states that

> The importance of early identification, assessment and provision for any child who may have special educational needs cannot be over-emphasised. The earlier action is taken, the more responsive the child is likely to be .....

The town's high schools followed a broadly similar pattern of information gathering leading to identification of SEN pupils which took a period of nearly 12 months spread over much of Year 6 and nearly a term of Year 7 (see Figures 6 and 7).

The monitoring and evaluation of the Year 7 pupils was found to be carried out in all schools but the overall picture was not satisfactory. Ron Dearing (1993) said

Assessments made over a period of time should be used to review and evaluate the provision made for the children during that time ... assessments form the basis for further assessment ... we use the knowledge we gain about children to plan the future

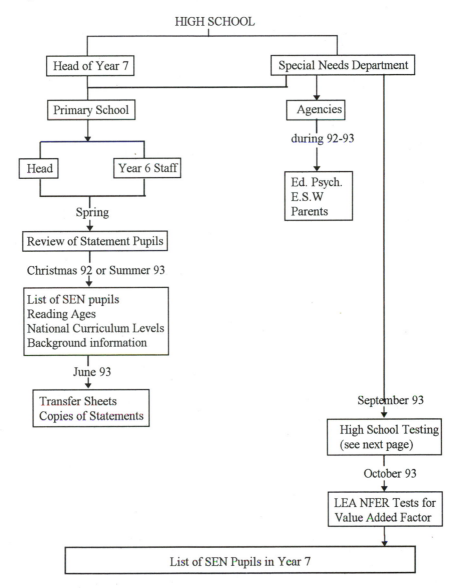

Figure 2 Identification procedures

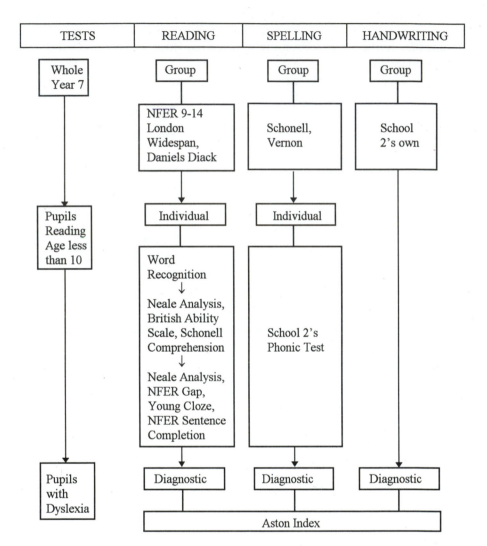

TESTS	READING	SPELLING	HANDWRITING
Whole Year 7	Group	Group	Group
	NFER 9-14 London Widespan, Daniels Diack	Schonell, Vernon	School 2's own
Pupils Reading Age less than 10	Individual	Individual	
	Word Recognition ↓ Neale Analysis, British Ability Scale, Schonell Comprehension ↓ Neale Analysis, NFER Gap, Young Cloze, NFER Sentence Completion	School 2's Phonic Test	
Pupils with Dyslexia	Diagnostic	Diagnostic	Diagnostic
	Aston Index		

Figure 3   Testing in the high schools

For it follows that the success of any literacy programme to be measured there must be 'before' and 'after' accomplishments to be noted. This can be achieved by re-testing using the same tests. Only half the schools returned the results of such an exercise and only half of these were able to show a proper monitoring - that was only in reading (which was shown to have attained significant success). Best practice in methods of improving literacy skills are impossible to assess without a fuller evaluation. It is important that all the high schools should follow a system of evaluation of the efficacy of reading, spelling and handwriting, detailing the extent of pupils' literacy, and the progress made after entry to school should be the core of annual, if not termly, reports to the governors.

In 1994, the move towards eradication of low literacy levels was seen, by the limited statistics provided by five out of nine high schools, to be achieving marked success. There was a 50 percent reduction in the number of low literacy pupils (i.e. pupils with a reading age of below 9) by the end of Year 7. The average rate of improvement had increased three times that achieved before entry to the high schools. If the rate of reduction could be maintained then by the end of Year 11 only 3 percent of the low literacy pupils that started Year 6 would be left. However, a reading age of 9 would not be deemed adequate for a 16 year old. Even so there would be a strong likelihood of a diminution in low literacy levels throughout Key Stages 3 and 4 in the town's high schools. If the rate of improvement could be maintained, low literacy would virtually disappear but evaluation over 5 years was not part of the study.

Programmes to combat low literacy were carried out in all High Schools all of whom tackled problems in reading as a high priority but the issue of 'withdrawal from' versus 'integration in' the classroom was paramount in determining methods to be used.

Eighteen percent of Year 7 children in the town had a reading age below 9. Literacy skills provision had to be made. This included the 7 percent who had profound difficulties (i.e. they had a reading age below 8). The dilemma for SEN Co-ordinators was to how, where and when this provision should be made.

Since the Warnock Report and the 1981 Education Act there has been a philosophy of integration of SEN pupils. Special schools were to be used only if absolutely necessary. Remedial departments in mainstream schools were also deemed to be isolationist with resultant social ills. Controversy has raged ever since. Tony Lingard (1994) addressed the problem and acknowledged that 'it is generally believed that secondary students with special needs should be given full access to the secondary curriculum' but observes that in contrast 'most literacy specialists claim that regular specific help is essential for young people with reading and writing difficulties'. This is confirmed by the clause in the provision section of most Statements that children needed either individual or small group teaching in basic skills and required methods that were not compatible with normal class teaching.

Jean-Pierre Vélis (1990, p.83) noted

When the pupils reach the age of 11, the reading differences in a single class have often become so extensive that in the long run special steps to aid the weakest readers are unavoidable.

Linguard notes with alarm that 'so many secondary schools have greatly reduced or even completely abandoned, small group teaching for low attainers'. SEN Co-ordinators have been moved by motives such as the belief that 'segregation is highly damaging to students' self esteem', or that their LEA through its Inspector of SEN and through OFSTED inspections indicated that the separation of pupils was not to be encouraged.

However, the LEA, through the statementing process, acknowledged that certain pupils required specialist help which in practice would mean such separation. All high schools used more withdrawal than for just the statemented pupils because they recognised that statemented pupils accounted for about 3 percent of their new intake but the actual amount of profound literacy problems as noted (below a reading age of 8) was 7 percent.

Since the survey the Code of Practice (1994) reminds schools that integration means to ensure that 'children with special educational needs engage in the activities of the school together with children who do not have special educational needs'.

This does not specify that 'wherever possible' means so. HoDSEN used their own judgement when they embarked on their various programmes to improve literacy. They chose to withdraw most pupils. Lingard proved that pupils with direct and separate help in basic skills 'achieved far greater progress with both reading and spelling' and that 'the low attainers in literacy who were taught within small mainstream mixed ability classes made very limited progress. The mainstream English curriculum was clearly ineffective in enabling them to overcome their learning difficulties'.

In one school, progress of the groups more severely and less severely affected by low literacy was monitored:

Withdrawal group of low literacy pupils:
Reading ages less than 8 in September 1993.
Average improvement by June, 1994 was 1.3 years which was above the progress made by an average child and was three times the pupils' progress in the primary school.

Supported group of less low literacy pupils in small mainstream classes: Reading ages of 8 to 9 in September 1993.

Average improvement by June, 1994 was less with an increase of 0.75 years which is still less progress than that made by an average child but was 1.25 times the pupils' progress in the primary school.

The first (weaker) group made 160 percent of the progress made by the (less weak) second group. This confirmed Lingard's conclusions about the benefits of withdrawal and denied the philosophy of in-class support which has been prevalent since Warnock.

Methods used to teach low literacy pupils

Three percent of Year 7 pupils were recognised as having profound learning difficulties and were subject to Statements. The LEA therefore acknowledged that special provision should be given to those pupils and funded extra teaching time with teachers qualified in dealing with dyslexia. Also two schools each had already employed such a teacher.

There are two main ways of teaching dyslexics - through the RSA course based on *Alpha to Omega*, Bev Hornsby (1988) or by using *Dyslexia: a Language Training Course for Teacher and Learners*, Kathleen Hickey (1977) which has been modified in recent years and is promoted by the Dyslexia Institute.

Hornsby states that her manual is 'a phonetic, linguistic approach to the teaching of reading, writing and spelling'. She stresses that 'as the ability to read the printed word and the ability to write down words are all part of language ability as a whole, all these areas should be taught and improved concurrently'.

The work is very tightly structured from simple letter sounds (with some letters having two sounds, e.g. s is (s) or (z) or x is (ks) or (gs) to consonant combinations (she, ch, etc.), short vowels, consonant blends (bl, cr, sw, etc.) and vowel diagraphs (ee, ar, oy, etc.). As each is introduced, it is given names and sounds and is then written in cursive script with exercises in all. This is called a multi-sensory approach as eyes, ears and hand co-ordinate to produce consolidation in the three areas of reading, spelling and handwriting.

This method of combining the senses for improving all areas of basic literacy is supported by the views of Cripps and Peters (1990). They say

... classroom practice based on the concept that spelling is a hand/eye skill ... obviously, phonological awareness is necessary and children must be able to hear and discriminate letter sounds ... But the two areas in which children are vulnerable as far as spelling is concerned are the motor and visual areas ...

Hornsby continues with long vowels and digraphs, hard and soft sounds, prefixes and suffixes and letter strings (eg. -tion). The exercises are supplemented by the use of games. These motivate the pupils and provide reinforcement through pleasurable practice. Only words and sentences are given to read and write - never whole stories written freely.

Each lesson of one hour has a clear objective and is discrete in that no lesson runs into another. However, revision is always part of the lesson so that the pupils build on previous experience only. If done twice a week, the course may be finished in two years.

However, unlike a primary school's daily diet of English, this was reduced to only 2 hours per week in secondary schools so that if other areas of the National Curriculum were to be covered, i.e. Speaking and Listening and Writing, time was needed to be taken from other subject areas for the above specialist English teaching.

Like the Hornsby method, Hickey's work has to be done at least twice a week for 2 years, is a very structured course and depends on a strongly multi-sensory approach. Townend (1994, p.21) says

Multi-sensory techniques are those which use more than one sensory channel for input of information ... the stronger channel is used to support the weaker, while the weaker channel is being trained and developed. Material presented in a multi-sensory way has a better chance of being retained.

and on p.22 she observes that

Multi-sensory techniques are employed to integrate the learning of the sound of a letter, its shape on the written page, and the feel of writing it in cursive script, so that a secure sound-symbol relationship is established for reading and spelling.

This approach links closely with the philosophy of Cripps and Peters mentioned earlier.

Like Hornsby there is an attack on 'single letters, consonant blends, consonant and vowel digraphs and the rules of syllable division, suffixing and prefixing'. Each small step, similarly takes one lesson; builds only with sounds and rules covered already and so the pupil is not confused with anything that has not been taught previously. On p.23 Townend stresses that 'about 85 percent of written English is regular and rule governed'.

Rack and Walker, (1994) said on their use of the programme 'During teaching, children progress at roughly twice the rate at which they were progressing prior to teaching'. This was for pupils in groups of one or two. One school achieved three times their primary school rate despite using Hickey with a group of 10 children all starting at the same time and keeping together throughout the year - incidentally it seems to have been a factor in high attendance. Those who showed their frustrations in other subject areas by bad behaviour were positive in their attitude to learning and conducted themselves well in the small group situation that offered rewarding and appropriate work.

There was a further 15 percent of Year 7 children in the town's high schools who were without statements and who needed provision within normal funding.

The Report on the LEA's survey in primary schools (1993, pp.20-21) said

> pupils with difficulty need to be helped in ways which do not infringe either their dignity in the eyes of themselves and their peers, or their access to their entitlement to the full National Curriculum in all subject areas. The less high profile withdrawal from the mainstream classroom takes place the better.

It also noted that

> Schools where the class teacher worked with those with problems, and any part-time teacher support or NTA time was directed at ensuring the continued orderly working of the main class group, were observed as achieving optimum returns within this survey.

This is the opposite opinion to Lingard and so posed a dilemma for high school SEN Co-ordinators who had to decide what to do with non-statemented low-literacy pupils.

Support in the English class was done in some cases - usually for pupils with relatively high literacy. The difficulty by eleven years old is that there is an increasing spread of ability in the class and the child has to be taught, for example, simple phonics when possibly the rest of the class may be immersed in learning about 19th century literature. This causes the problem that some of the main class work is missed. Another disadvantage is that support can only be spread thinly over the other classes in Year 7. See Figure 4 for time allocation.

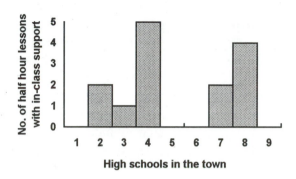

Figure 4   Provision of in-class support in English lessons

In order not to miss the core subject English curriculum, other times could be chosen when non-core subjects time could be used. This caused disruption to those lessons and to some extent, devalued them. School 5 took pupils out for 4 hours a week but took 1 hour each from different subjects and obtained parents' permission. School 6 did so for 3 hours a week from subjects such as music and drama but did receive parental complaints. School 1 took pupils out for 12 week blocks so only missed one third of the year. Within schools 7 and 8 - the withdrawal was in a setted situation in English so did not disrupt the rest of the English class (see Figure 5 for time allocation).

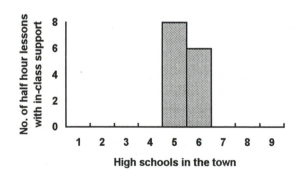

Figure 5   Provision of in-class support in other lessons

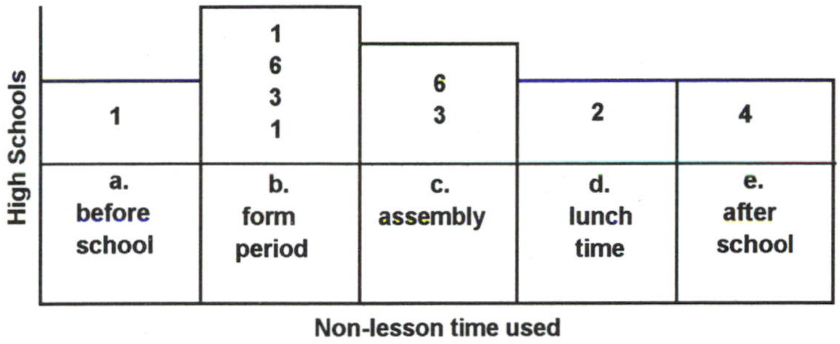

High Schools | Non-lesson time used

a. before school	b. form period	c. assembly	d. lunch time	e. after school
1	1 6 3 1	6 3	2	4

Figure 6   Schools 8 and 9 did not as they were fully catered for in (1)

In (a), (d) and (e) parental consent was required but in some cases caused problems for transport. Pupil co-operation was required and at times the motivation was not always there. Conflict with other demands e.g. from clubs, caused difficulty. The HoDs of SEN acknowledged that (i) was the least disruptive to the children's time-tables but felt it was the least productive so (ii) and (iii) were favoured despite their disadvantages.

The actual programme of work given to these pupils who were not statemented but needed support to overcome their problems of illiteracy were in three areas:

1   reading
2   spelling, and
3   handwriting.

Reading

In the LEA's Primary Survey (1993) it noted 'The tendency in most schools was to give the child who was behind in ... reading, an increase in the amount of it ... but with variable results'. However, in the high schools actual reading was made part of a varied and positive programme in some of four ways:

Reading schemes

Not one used a scheme as its core provision. Nearly all used them as a small part of their general resource or books. An exception was School 7 which did have one hour a week in English when the pupils of reading age 7-9.4 read Trend books and did exercises set on them.

Individual reading

All the high schools had a school library in which simpler books existed. In one school the library had a specially marked section from which books were voluntarily taken at lunchtime. It also had a special needs departmental library from which two books a week were taken for homework. It was the only school to have graded its readers in 6 months reading ages using teacher judgement or the SMOG Readability Formula (simplified) - given in *Make Reading Easier*, ALBSU (1992). This had the advantage of books being accessible to those pupils who had a reading age of that level and also the reward of the promotion to a different colour if the reading level of the child improved. The pupil saw the progress during the school year. This library used a mixture of real books and those from reading schemes.

Other schools used class displays of mixed books in the SEN Departments using schemes such as Fuzz Buzz, 123 and Away and Tim Books (which are more of primary age interest), Wellington Square and the Badger Reading Box (which are more suitable for secondary age).

Another school used a box, changed half-termly, of 60 mixed books in each form room - selected during PSE lessons. Also in English there was another box of 60 books.

Group reading of books was part of the provision at only one school. A group of up to four pupils read a sentence in turn (to reinforce what a sentence is and to note the punctuation involved). Decoding skills such as using clues from pictures, context (a form of close procedure) and from phonics taught in the Hickey scheme. The National Curriculum Reading Level 2 requirements such as 'Pupils show interest in and basic understanding of one of the characters and more than one event in the book and are able to describe them simply' and 'Pupils make simple connection between the passage and what happens later' could be met by discussion during the reading (which in turn helped with the English element of speaking and listening). The chief features in this whole exercise were of enjoyment and therefore motivation and above all success.

Except in the school libraries, there was little evidence of the 'quiet, comfortable, aesthetic book areas' that are required as recommended by the LEAD (1994) except one school with its departmental library - shelving, posters, indoor plants and rocking chair.

Paired reading

Topping (1988) former Educational Psychologist in the town's LEA, said that 'During the last ten years, it has become increasingly apparent that "learning to be literate" does not begin or end in the classroom. One developing area of educational interest in the 1980s is thus the involvement of parents in their child's reading development'. He also noted that 'The evidence from research reports is that Paired Readers progress at about three times normal rates in Reading Accuracy and about 5 times normal rates in Reading Comprehension'. It was an idea originally promoted by Roger Morgan in 1974 but Topping introduced it into the LEA's high schools in 1985. Schools later found success with pairings with other adults, within the peer group or across the age. Seven of the nine high schools used it in 1993-4.

There is only positive action in Paired Reading where the child chooses its own book and can reject it later if necessary, when a pupil fails on a word it is soon supplied, where there is praise during and at the end of each session and where the relationship (especially where parents are involved) is enhanced. This is not a case of reading 'yet more books' but reading them with pleasure and with success.

Corrective reading

The high schools all felt that pupils required more than just greater quantities of reading. Reading attack of a more intensive kind was required. Florek (1985) observed of secondary schools,

> The open and accessible first year pupil is all too quickly replaced by the increasingly cynical adolescent fourth year. This shortage of remedial time is also often compounded by the negative self-image of the pupils concerned who arrive at the big school expecting to fail.

Therefore it is most important to have an ameliorative programme which is positive, rewarding, motivating and successful. In 1985, Topping trained one school's staff to introduce Corrective Reading to its Year 7 SEN pupils. Funding for the expensive materials was shared between the school, the Advisory Service and the Educational Psychology Service. This method of Direct Instruction was developed primarily by Siefried Engelmann from the University of Oregon. It is structured step-by-step learning; group as opposed to individual instruction; continuous and controlled practice; sufficient time allocations for learning; immediate and corrective feedback; and questioning at a low cognitive level to ensure production of correct responses.

Six of the nine high schools were found to be using Corrective Reading despite criticism in 1987 by HMI at one of the schools. Also the town's special school was finding Direct Instruction very productive.

In *Direct Instruction - A Review, SRA* (1984), the criticism by some advisors that 'Scripted lessons detract from a teacher's personal influence or skills' was answered by teachers.

> scripted lessons allow them to concentrate more fully on the children, because they do not have to worry about what to do or say next. The children like it because they know what to expect; are answering questions and being praised. They learn more - meaning success for both child and teacher.

The scheme caters for different ages - Decoding B is for reading age levels 6.5-9.5. It is spread over 140 lessons and has a test to determine where the small group begins. The sounds covered are similar to Hickey and Hornsby - short and long vowels, suffixes and consonant and vowel digraphs and consonant blends. In addition, decoding stories are given which are 100-700 words long and interspersed in these stories are questions which are verbally answered. Points are taken off for mistakes, omissions, insertions and not stopping at the end of the sentence. The scoring for the whole group is dependent upon a target set so a story may have to be repeated. This is in addition to phonic work at the beginning and reading of individual words. The scores are charted by the child so that progress can be seen and the class teacher may set an extra ongoing rewarding system, e.g. 1 sweet for 100 points.

The work is periodically subject to a timed exercise. All the work fitted in well with the National Curriculum Levels 1, 2 and to some extent 3. However, spelling was only done indirectly through the phonic work. Handwriting is hardly used. The children were well-motivated, totally on task and learning to be co-operative and tolerant with each other during the lesson. They were delighted with their own and others' progress during the scheme's operation.

Because of the restraints of the complex high schools' timetables, the ideal of using the system daily was never reached, except for one school which used it for the whole of Year 7 during a blocked timetable. Corrective

Reading was the main core for attacking poor reading skills but was supplemented by some of the methods described previously.

Despite not meeting the conditions of working daily, all the participating schools felt Corrective Reading was very productive.

Spelling

When asked to define literacy, only two schools felt that weakness in spelling was an important factor if their pupils' spelling age was below 8. Yet when initial testing took place in September, 1993, four schools screened the intake for spelling. Two schools used the Schonell Test, one the Vernon Spelling Test and one the NFER Test. Where children were withdrawn for special provision, most schools included a programme for improving spelling.

The pupils had left the primary school where one class teacher had an overall view and handling of their education and had come to the high school with as many as 12 different subject teachers for each child. Cripps (1975) says 'The ability to spell should be regarded as part of the common responsibility for language development, which should be shared by teachers of all subjects'. This was rarely achieved as the skills needed, the whole school co-ordination and the time required did not exist.

There is also despair in high schools that spelling, by the age of 11 is very difficult to improve. Cripps and Peters (1970, p.15) say:

> There is evidence that if children by the age of 7-8 years fail to 'catch' spelling from the linguistic network available to them it is unlikely they will ever 'catch' it. Hence, from the earliest possible moment these children must be taught, and taught rationally and systematically.

The 'linguistic network' had certainly failed the SEN pupils who came to the high schools in 1993. Many were observed to be poor in oral language skills, were from families with little access to books or ownership of them and had not absorbed the enriched language teaching in their infancy. These children had not 'caught' spelling by 8 and indeed continued not to have 'caught' it by 11. The HoDs of SEN arranged programmes of remediation for this but have not generally evaluated their progress.

The provision was that pupils with statements and supported by LEA-funded teachers using the Hornsby or Hickey courses were very fortunate as these followed Cripps' ideal referred to previously where phonics, handwriting and spelling were complementary and dovetailed together so that the multi-sensory techniques used resulted in ear-hand-eye co-ordination that is essential to mastery of spelling. The school that involved other pupils similar to the statemented pupils and monitored them then and at the end of Year 7 had made significant progress (0.7 years - much better than experienced by the children previously).

The SRA Spelling Mastery Level B programme was found to be useful because, like the Corrective Reading which included attack on phonic cues, is very structured with pupils working on task, learning letter strings so that repetition and practice with reward created enough impact for them to retain the spellings. The teacher had no preparation to do and the programme could be administered very easily.

The Blackwell Spelling Kit was used. There are graded cards each with a particular letter string. Exercises are sentences with gaps into which the words from the card were inserted so the hand got used to the 'string'. Children worked individually and the work was marked easily.

'2 Way Spelling', from Arnold, consists of exercises in which words are slotted into a row of boxes unfortunately leading to the use of printed rather than cursive writing. Cripps feels the latter is essential for the hand-eye co-ordination as it reinforces the learning of the spelling pattern.

Murray's 'Phonic Reading Workshop' which allowed individual pupils to be placed at their own level helped with spelling.

Computer programmes were used so that pupils who generally enjoy using computers were motivated to spend time learning spelling patterns. There was a self-marking system and an instant reward for success. Cripps says that the role the use of computer plays is underestimated.

> 1. Spelling is predominantly a visual skill ... competent spellers check the correctness of their spelling by seeing whether the word 'looks right'.
> 2. Spelling is also a motor skill ... the typist becomes aware of the motor movement required for each particular letter sequence...

Various LEA programmes were used as well as the 'Reading Skills, Spelling and Punctuation - Phantom of Fleet St, Punk Man and Henrietta's Book of Spells' produced by Bangor Institute of Phonics.

From the graph it can be seen that schools used more than one scheme.
a. had the greatest involvement of ear, eye and hand (listening to sound, knowing the letter(s) to be used and actually writing it (them)), a.-e. needed involvement by a teacher but only f. could be done by the child itself often at times not linked to the time-table.

Only two schools had a whole-school policy of look, cover and write advocated by Cripps (1990, p.23) which was used in any subject. This was better than the traditional way of making the pupils copy the word out several times (which required no effort to memorise). Peters (1970) said '... in fact, three quarters of classes where most progress in spelling takes place ... is where rational teachers were drawing attention to 'hard spots' within the words'. This contrasted with 'three quarters of classes where least progress is made ... teachers demanding that children copy out each mistake three or more times'.

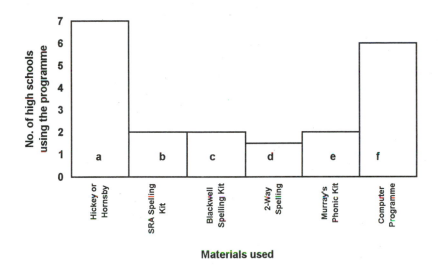

Figure 7   Number of high schools using specific materials

In one school, a vocabulary book was also kept so that any consistently difficult word could be entered - useful in subjects which have their own specialist words. Spelling, except in scheme a., took a second place to reading in SEN provision both in emphasis and in finding time to learn it. Hence the value of f. - the computer - to those children who devoted their own time to use the software available.

Handwriting

The modified National Curriculum produced under the guidance of Ron Dearing in 1994 states that during Key Stage 2 (at the end of which is the point of transfer to the high schools in this West Yorkshire town) 'pupils should be given opportunities to continue to develop legible handwriting in both joined up and printed styles ...'.

Of the high schools surveyed, only one school conducted tests to screen handwriting in pupils. A school-produced test was given so that both printed and cursive handwriting were examined with every letter in three positions (beginning, middle and end of word). Each letter shape was looked at, as well as whether the letters were on the line or not and as to the correct positions of the 'sticks and tails'.

Laterality tests were given as there is an effect on both reading and handwriting. This was done:

(a) by the child looking through a 'telescope' to see which eye was used,
(b) by looking at a distant object with both eyes through a ring made by finger and thumb and then closing each eye in turn to see which continued to see the object through the ring. These two tests gave the dominant eye.
(c) Handedness was checked by observing several tasks which included writing, kicking, throwing. If eye and hand were different, the children were said to be cross-lateral. In one school, of a group of SEN pupils, half were cross-lateral which was higher than the expected average of 10 percent.

Cross-laterality is important as seeing letters in a reverse way can result, eg. b. and d. Also, perception of all letters can be confused. In recent years at the school, two pupils, despite intensive tuition, laid out the alphabet from z to a and each letter was reversed! Only when repeatedly asked to check what they had done did they realise their mistake.

Left-handedness was also noted as some reversals of letters and words (eg. saw and was) may have been influenced by it.

Cripps (1990, p.24) says that 'The teacher must watch the child form letters correctly until the habit is established'. This had patently not been done previously - judging by the numerous errors in the printed shapes written by many new entrants to the high schools. The reason may well be the sheer size of reception classes (which will increase due to under-funding to LEAs). However, after six years of primary schooling where errors have been compounded, the high schools have great difficulty in breaking the old habits which have become ingrained. As there is a strong link between handwriting and spelling it makes the task more urgent. All but one high school addressed the issue. For pupils with statements or those taught with them who were taught by LEA-funded dyslexia teachers, handwriting was taught as an integral part of the multi-sensory approach which combined attacks on all three areas of low literacy - reading, spelling and handwriting. The latter was done cursively. Cripps (1975) said that:

> the disadvantage of printed script - not like the free scribble done as small children is that it is another break to 'joined-up' writing. Many revert to disconnected letters. Without the joining strokes the child can't space letters.

The two latter defects could be seen in most high school entrants but particularly in SEN pupils. Some pupils had lap-top computers provided by the LEA which helped with clear writing but was disconnected from spelling. Also, typing skills were not taught prior to their use. Other children (non-statemented) were given exercises from a variety of sources which enabled them to feel the correct shapes, to position the letters and to join them up. However, this was done separately from spelling in most cases, thus losing that 'feel' for letter strings which facilitates spelling. Other materials were:

A Hand for Spelling - Cripps } *both combined handwriting*
A Handwriting for Spelling - LDA } *and spelling*
A Second Chance - LDA
Sheffield Structure - Margaret Crombie

Three schools rewarded good handwriting - in one school there was a competition in all of Year 7 (as a result of a whole school approach on handwriting as part of the School Language Policy). Two winners were rewarded from each class. Handwriting was seen by the high schools to be important but lack of time or of a co-ordinated policy prevented the teaching of the full mastery or cursive script. This led to the pupils at Key Stage 3 being unable to perform as described in the National Curriculum 1994 'to use different forms of handwriting for different purposes, e.g. print for labelling maps or diagrams; a clear, neat hand for finished, presented work; a faster script for notes'. Accessibility to the National Curriculum was therefore severely impeded.

Conclusion

In managing the development of literacy skills in Year 7 of the high schools in a West Yorkshire town in 1993-94, changes had been made in order to identify pupils, monitor and evaluate their progress (which proved to be significant) and use methods which in most cases were structured programmes delivered controversially in a withdrawal situation. The context of the town and the type and infrastructure of the schools provided the setting for the pupils.

A highly complex and wide-ranging attack on acquiring better skills in reading, spelling and handwriting in order to improve pupils' literacy from the merely basic level they started with was implemented. Its merits were that all areas of literacy skills were addressed, that maximum use was made of time, a mixture of compulsory and voluntary activities were used and the programme was very varied.

The Code of Practice became fully operational in September, 1995 and hastened and formalised this management of pupils with SEN.

References

Cripps, C. (1975) *A Language for Life*. London: Harcourt Brace Jovanovitch. (Recommendation 131)

Cripps, C. and Peter, M.L. (1990) *Catchwords, Ideas for Teaching Spelling* (National Curriculum ed.). London: Harcourt Brace Jovanovitch.

Dearing, R. (1993) *The National Curriculum and its Assessment*, Final Report. London: SCAA.

DFE (1994) *Assessment Arrangements*: a Statement by Sir Ron Dearing, Chairman Designate of SCAA. London: DFE.

DFE (1994) *Code of Practice on the Identification and Assessment of Special Education Needs*. London: Central Office of Information.

DFE (1995) *English in the National Curriculum*. London: HMSO.

Dyslexia Institute (1994) Dyslexia Review Dyslexia Review. 5(2). Staines.

Englemann, S., Carnine, L. and Johnson, G. (1978) *Word-Attack Basics - Teacher's Book, Corrective Reading Decoding B*. USA: SRA.

Florek, A. (1985) *The Old Lag's Tale - Direct Instruction at Connah's Quay High School*. Direct Instruction Scene.

Hickey, K. (1977) *Dyslexia: a Language Training Course for Teachers and Learners*. London: Kathleen Hickey Publications.

Hornsby, B and Shear, F. (1980) *Alpha to Omega: the A-Z of Teaching Reading, Writing and Spelling*. London: Heinemann.

Kirklees Education Authority (1993) *First I have to read it in my head* - a Survey of Reading in Kirklees Primary Schools, KEA Inspection and Monitoring Service, Huddersfield. November.

Kirklees Metropolitan Council Education Service (KMCES) (1994) *The Teaching and Learning of Reading 3-11* - a Kirklees LEA Curriculum

Policy Statement, KMCES Curriculum Policy Document No.13, Huddersfield.

Lingard, T. (1994) The Acquisition of Literacy in *Secondary Education*, **24**, p.4, December.

Mercer, N. (ed.) (1988) *Language Literacy: from an education perspective*, **2**, in Schools, Chapter 3.5 Parental Involvement in Reading Scheme by Keith Topping. Milton Keynes: OUP Press.

Peters, M.L. (1985) *Spelling: Caught or Taught? A New Look*. London: Routledge, Kegan and Paul.

Rack, J. and Walker, J. (1994) Does Dyslexia Institute Teaching Work? *Dyslexia Review*.

SRA (1984) *Direct Instruction - A Review*. New York: SRA.

Townend, J. (1994) *Understanding Dyslexia: a teacher's perspective*. Staines: Dyslexia Institute.

Vélis, J-P (1990) *Through a glass darkly: functional illiteracy in industrialised countries*. New York: UNESCO.

4 Transforming teachers' practice through Action Learning

Stephen Billett

Abstract

This chapter examines the potential of Action Learning as a professional development strategy for teachers. Using a case study of a professional development program which prepared teachers to become industry consultants, the chapter examines the potential and impediments of this approach to managing change in educational practice. The chapter commences with a brief commentary on change from cognitive psychology and change theory perspectives. Next, the case study is described and findings from an evaluation are discussed. Finally, some deductions from the case study are provided about how an Action Learning based approach to educational change might be best managed.

Introduction

Currently, vocational educators are being asked to confront and adopt change with increasing frequency. Much of this change results from vocational education being seen by governments as central to achieving national policy goals, such as economic competitiveness. Therefore, this change often has its origins within decision-making processes that are remote from the practitioners who are expected to implement it with fidelity. Moreover, there appears to be a belief among stakeholders associated with this centralised decision-making that teachers will uniformly implement innovations as directed. Yet such a view denies current understanding about the way that teachers think, act and decide how to deploy their energies in the effortful activity of changing their practice (Billett, 1995). The motivation and interest of individuals plays a key role in underpinning engagement in such effortful activity and unless they hold a belief about benefits accruing from such activity that their engagement is likely to be, at best, superficial. Furthermore, this superficial engagement will probably focus on public aspects of practice (Logan, 1988) thereby indicating compliance, rather than the ability to implement the innovation within their teaching practice. This situation leads to questions about how best can educational change be managed to engage teachers and provide the means for them to become committed to the change.

This chapter describes and discusses a case study in which an Action-learning based program was used to develop vocational teachers' industry consultancy skills. It is claimed in this chapter that the management of change is not just about getting teachers to superficially adopt changes in practice arising from policy innovations. Rather, it is held that change management should be concerned with developing teachers' capacities and dispositions to successfully implement these innovations. Therefore, processes which aim to foster change should be focussed on teacher learning and development if they are to be successful. It is this focus that is likely to underpin the successful adoption of change. An assumption within this chapter is that these innovations are worthwhile and justifiable, which may not always be the case. Ideologically-driven initiatives, such as Competency-Based Training, may well founder on their own inadequacies as teachers reflecting on the implementation of such initiatives are likely to discover the source of inadequacies are in the initiatives themselves. The problems associated with these types of initiatives are outside the scope of this short chapter.

What is advanced here is that gaining teachers' commitment to educational change is premised on their ability to be successful with the implementation of the innovation, thereby resulting in the adoption of the innovation. However, what is meant by commitment needs to be articulated as it provides goals for the change process. Commitment is more than enthusiasm for a particular innovation because it includes a belief on the part of teachers that the innovation is worthwhile and can assist with their practice (McLaughlin & Marsh, 1978). Underpinning this belief is the possession of the concepts, procedures and dispositions necessary for the successful implementation of the innovation. It is these attributes which provide - the ability to function in the changed circumstances - that is generative of commitment (Guskey, 1986). Hence, the management of change requires more than briefing sessions, it necessitates the provision of opportunities for teachers to construct the forms of knowledge required for successful performance with the innovation. So, in considering approaches to managing educational change, arrangements which permit the development of the requisite forms of knowledge to successfully implement the innovative practice should be favoured.

Moreover, as adopting change is the product of individual learning and development, it is posited that even innovations aiming to transform institutions need to view change as ultimately an intimate and personal process involving individuals' competence and well-being (Fullan, 1985). Change has been described as 'little deaths' by Kindler (1979), with transformational change causing the greatest concerns to those effected by it. This is because it takes individuals away from the very circumstances which underpin their confidence. Therefore, deliberations about the management of institutional change must also see individuals' learning and development as the primary source of change. This is not to say that the individual is impervious to the influence of the social practice in which they engage, because it is clear that physical and social factors influence cognition (Rogoff, & Lave, 1984; Wertsch, 1993). As will be argued below, the close and more distant forms of guidance provided by social practice are essential to the construction of the knowledge required to successfully implement innovations. However, fundamental to the change process are the changes to individuals' ontogenies, their life histories, which are constructed through participating in ongoing and overlapping social practice. The focus in this chapter is therefore on the management of individual change through learning and development.

The structure of this chapter is as follows. Firstly, conceptions which underpin a view of the adoption of change being premised on individuals acquiring the requisite forms of knowledge are advanced. Next, the quality of Action Learning as a staff development methodology is discussed. Following this, a case study of Action Learning being used for the development of vocational educators is described and the findings of an evaluation advanced. A discussion about managing Action Learning as a staff development methodology is advanced next. The chapter concludes by arguing that the management of change is premised on the provision of learning and development for teachers.

61

Management of change

Goals of development process

It has been advocated above that processes aiming to change educational practice need to address the further development of individuals' knowledge including their dispositions (values, attitudes and beliefs) appropriate for the change. Cognitive processes and structures provide the internal mechanisms for thinking and acting. Cognitive processes are the array of cognitive activities deployed by an individual when engaged in any type of goal-directed activity (thinking, acting or learning). This includes both routine and non-routine activities, with the latter potentially transforming knowledge and the former reinforcing that knowledge through ongoing application. Cognitive structures, which comprise levels of propositional (*knowledge that*) and procedural knowledge *(knowledge how)* are also primary elements within this framework (Anderson, 1982). Propositional knowledge comprises information, facts, assertions and propositions, whereas procedural knowledge comprises techniques, skills, ability to secure goals (Stevenson, 1991). The characteristics of experts' propositional knowledge is acknowledged in terms of deep conceptual understandings within a particular domain of knowledge. It is these understandings which inform the educational practitioner, which of a number of options is the most appropriate for the particular situation. Experts also possess robust procedures within a domain. Procedural knowledge has a hierarchy from specific autonomous procedures to higher orders of procedural knowledge, which are postulated to have an executive role in organising and transferring knowledge and understandings (Stevenson, 1991).

The role that 'non-cognitive' dispositions, such as value and belief, play in thinking and acting is being acknowledged in recent research. Pea (1987), for instance, advocates transfer as being interpretative and being constructed by individually orientated perceptions and representations. So, rather than seeing transfer and adaptability in purely cognitive terms, he argues that values and affect play a major role in cognitive activities and development. Values also determine the quality of action. For example, they determine whether individuals do a thorough job or a shoddy job, or determining what level of work is required for a particular situation. As Goodnow (1990) suggests, people not only learn to solve problems, but also what problems are worth solving.

Learning and cognitive development

Learning is increasingly being held to be a constructive process with individuals actively acquiring knowledge and understanding through interaction with the world they experience (von Glasersfeld, 1987). This constructive process is initially idiosyncratic being founded on the unique personal history (ontogeny) of the individual (Rogoff, 1995). However, through social mediation that knowledge becomes commonly understood and communicable (Newman, Griffin & Cole, 1989). Learning is therefore conceptualised as a process of constructing meaning and making knowledge viable through a process of engaging in activities within social practice. The nature of understanding is interpreted by individuals as they seek to make their knowledge base viable, that is to successfully apply that knowledge. In essence, the individual seeks to make sense of the things they experience by either assimilating into existing structures or by extending those structures to accommodate new stimuli and experiences, as Piaget would say. That 'making sense' involves individuals comparing their existing knowledge base with what they experience and then extending that knowledge as they seek to understand and progress. This raises a key issue within adult learning theory - the need to extend existing cognitive structures. If the learning process encourages assimilation, by attempting only to link all new stimuli to existing cognitive structures, the outcomes are likely to be weaker than if accommodation is achieved by pressing the individual into generating new structures. The latter process is far more effortful and demanding than the former. So the adoption of an innovation, may require changes to practice and belief which may be a difficult and effortful transformation. This effortful transformation is unlikely to occur if the teacher remains unconvinced and lacks the ability to successfully implement the initiative.

A view which suggests learning is a matter of construction, rather than instruction, poses significant questions for educational practitioners. Recent innovations and approaches to instruction such as Reciprocal Teaching of Comprehension (Palinscar & Brown, 1984), Cognitive Apprenticeship (Collins, Brown & Newman, 1989), Apprenticeships Instruction for Real-World Tasks (Gott, 1989), Apprenticeships in Thinking (Rogoff, 1990), Legitimate Peripheral Participation (Lave & Wenger, 1991) and Guided Participation (Rogoff, 1995) emphasise the importance of close social interaction (proximal guidance) in the construction of knowledge, and place learners in a role in which they are pressed to take responsibility for constructing meaning, albeit guided by more expert others.

Consequently, the instructional role becomes one of organising and guiding the learners' experiences to permit them to construct appropriate knowledge and understanding. Such a proposition extends the concept of good teaching practice of 'making sure the learners are doing the thinking', to making sure that their thinking is guided towards the effective organisation of viable knowledge, through social mediation. This change in emphasis of the instructional role is underpinned by von Glasersfeld's (1987) notion of reinforcement. Reinforcement is usually associated with external statements of endorsement or rewards by teachers or experts, as portrayed in behaviourism. Rather, it needs now to be equated with the learner achieving a satisfactory organisation of knowledge, a viable way of dealing with some sector of experience, with the rewarding consequences of a fit being found within the individual's cognitive structures (von Glasersfeld, 1987). Hence, learners experience satisfaction with the viability of their knowledge. This does not negate the value of extrinsic rewards, such as verbal reinforcement, but suggests that this is secondary to the inherent rewards that the learner enjoys from reinforcing and extending their viable knowledge base. This view of learning has a range of implications for the further development of vocational educators. Such a view of learning also provides an evaluative framework to assess Action Learning as a methodology for teacher development.

Given these views about learning and cognitive development, a useful way to describe and evaluate instructional processes is to consider them in terms of activity and agency. Activities, are what learners do, and agency the support of a direct or indirect nature that is provided to learners. In the following section a brief overview of Action Learning as a developmental methodology is advanced. Action Learning is then investigated further using agency and activity as units of analysis. This investigation draws upon a range of empirical research from cognitive psychology, cultural psychology, and sociology.

Action Learning

As its title implies Action Learning is characterised as a highly active learning process with the learner engaging in projects with the supportive mediation of peers in learning sets and, in some cases, external facilitators or content experts. The focus of the learning process is to secure goals relevant to the project and then reflect upon the learning process to extend their knowledge further. Action Learning has been defined as 'a means by which people learn with and from each other by attempting to identify and then implement solutions to their problems/issues/opportunities' (Revans, 1982:65). Originally conceived as an approach to develop management skills after the Second World War in British industries that were short of experienced managers, Revans had recognised the ability of people to work together productively and effectively in times of common concern. Consequently, he developed an approach to learning based on the development of responsible risk-takers who asked of themselves and their peers a series of questions about their problems. The questions were used to clarify problems and to determine likely solutions that were not bound by existing expertise or theory.

Action Learning is aligned to the interpretivist perspective aiming to provide participants with a reflective process to improve their practice. It is a practical strategy that might question assumptions about practice, but which is primarily concerned with pragmatic and instrumental goals associated with improving practice by allowing them to stand outside of their work and examine it in a relatively objective way. This reflective process is important because it presses learners beyond assimilation towards accommodation. Significantly, much of earlier views about adult learning (e.g. Knowles, 1984) emphasised the assimilatory aspects of learning by granting primacy to the protection of learners' self esteem in building upon what they already know, thereby failing to emphasise the need to transform existing cognitive structures. Hence, critical reflection is necessary (even in its non-emancipatory form) to extend and transform experientially based learning arrangements. Without such transformational activities experientially-based learning remains just that - building upon existing knowledge rather than the development of new cognitive structures. Therefore, this process of reflection or questioning insight, as Revans called it, is central to Action Learning as it converts a specific experience learning process into one which extends understandings and efficacy of practice. Action Learning features processes that are largely the responsibility of the learner who engages in activities to secure goals, albeit goals established by others. However, the activities of the learners are mediated by peers, experts and the requirements of the task which provide a quality of indirect guidance which is often under-acknowledged.

Consequently, in seeking to evaluate Action Learning from a current view of learning it is claimed that Action Learning focuses on activity and mediation. Both of these contributions are sympathetic to promoting constructivist views of learning and cognitive development.

Activity and mediation

The interaction of activities and mediation is a central consideration for developmental processes. Dewey (1916/1970), suggested that the most central significant event in learning and performance are mediated experiences and events related to their adaptive function. This suggests that internal mental processes interacting with tangible purposes or functions are central to effective learning. Or, put more succinctly, the activities individuals engage in influence and organise their thinking - activity structures cognition (Rogoff, 1990).

The notion of activity permits an examination of Action Learning, its project orientation and its autonomous nature (Passfield & Billett, 1995). Key distinctions between experts and novices include the ability to monitor and self-regulate performance, within a specific domain of knowledge (Chi, Farr & Glaser, 1982). Learning arrangements which place the participants in the active role of initiating, planning and managing their learning are conducive of developing these attributes. For example, in contrasting the learning outcomes between theory and practical classes, in Technical and Further Education (TAFE) colleges, it has been found that the latter engages learners in activities which are conducive of self-regulation and monitoring (Stevenson & McKavanagh, 1991). It is proposed that when learners are pressed into taking responsibility for their learning they develop and organise knowledge effectively, and learn to manage the use of that knowledge.

If activities structure cognition, then the quality of those activities becomes important. In developing competence in an area of vocational practice it is highly desirable for staff to access authentic activities, that is those which are the same as those in which the targeted knowledge is deployed, not substitute of simulated activities. Consequently, projects which provide the participant with an authentic activity in which they can develop procedures that are authentic are likely to be purposeful for constructing knowledge associated with that activity (Billett, 1992, 1993a & 1994b). It is becoming increasingly accepted that the activities are embedded in socio-cultural practice (Brown, Collins & Duguid, 1989; Lave & Wenger, 1991; Rogoff & Lave, 1984). One of the problems with learning arrangements that are substitute, (eg. training room activities), is that they tend to generate knowledge and understandings based on the requirements of the training room rather than practice and as such may not transfer to practice (Billett, 1994b; Raizen, 1991). That is, forms of knowledge are shaped by particular circumstances and do not readily transfer to circumstances and situations which are remote from those in which the knowledge was acquired. Access to authentic activities minimises this transfer problem (Billett, 1994a). However, activity alone is not sufficient. The mediation of the learners' experiences by others, expert others and the context are essential ingredients of learning arrangements (Collins et al, 1989).

It is becoming almost commonplace to accept a social basis within cognition (Goodnow, 1990). This implies that guidance of a direct nature (others and expert others) and an indirect nature (the social and physical context) are important for the construction of knowledge. Recent research and theorising has increasingly focussed on the role of external factors and, particularly, the social and cultural contributions to learning (Brown et al, 1989; Collins et al, 1989; Lave & Wenger, 1991; Rogoff, 1995). Rather than being solely the product of internal mental activity the development and organisation of these cognitive processes and structures are influenced by external factors such as social interaction and cultural practices. Within Action Learning social mediation is evident in the contributions of others in the learning set, expert others external to the set and the facilitative actions of set advisers.

So, in summary, constructivist views of learning which emphasise the importance and authenticity of activity, social mediation, engagement in social practice and reflection appear to be partially addressed by Action Learning. Therefore, on its own terms this approach to learning and development appears to offer an array of attributes by which teachers' knowledge can be extended to accommodate and implement innovations.

A case study of teachers' participation in an Action Learning program is described and evaluated in the next section. The evaluation provides a basis for considering the efficacy of this approach to learning and how its potential might be fully realised.

Case study: industry training development program, Victoria, Australia

This section provides a descriptive overview of the Industry Training Development Program (ITDP) followed by deductions from data about the efficacy of this program's use of Action Learning as professional development strategy, during a formal evaluation (Dickie, Passfield & Billett, 1995).

Background

The ITDP was an Action Learning based development program used in the TAFE system in Victoria, Australia. The program aimed to prepare practising TAFE teachers for a role as industry consultants working in a fee-for-service role, providing educational services and consultancies to enterprises. The program was conducted in 1989, 1990 and 1991 during which time approximately 100 staff from metropolitan and non-metropolitan TAFE colleges participated. Due to financial constraints the program has not been offered since 1991. The need for industry consultants within the Victorian TAFE system arose as a response to a changing demand for skill acquisition processes within industry, which resulted from industrial award and industry restructuring. These initiatives are part of governmental micro-economic reforms. These reforms which focussed on transforming workplace activities included linking skills acquisition to increased remuneration in an attempt to enhance productivity. There was also an interest in the consultants deriving revenue for their host colleges by seeking to capitalise on fee-for-service opportunities being presented within a more open and user-pays training market place. Therefore, these industry consultants were being prepared to work in industry and generate funds for their host colleges.

Program structure and design

Induction to program and Action Learning

The program's induction phase comprised a two week workshop. This was designed to prepare participants by providing information about their role, the industrial environment and introduce them to Action Learning. In addition, information about the procedures that the participants would have to acquire to become effective consultants was stated, as goals for their self-development. These procedures included project management, costing a project, presentation of a project and business planning. The arrangements for development, beyond the induction phase, were based on group learning processes or 'sets' organised by regional locations. These groups, the project, support from mentors and senior consultants, and the quality of arrangements provided by participants' colleges were perceived as being key variables which determined successful participation in the program.

The participants' role included: (i) attending weekly meetings with their support group; (ii) participation in activities determined by the group; (iii) completing a learning contract; (iv) working on a designated project for two days a week, and (v) liaising with the college mentor. When the program commenced in 1989 there were few experts available to mentor participants because consultancy was not being undertaken in any significant way within the TAFE system. Some later groups had access to colleagues or mentors who had enjoyed success in the program, and gone on to successfully manage industry training projects.

Release from duties

ITDP participants were selected by their host college. During their participation, they were released from normal work duties for 3 days a week, over a period of 20 weeks. On one of these three days the participants met as a group to discuss issues and arrange access to expert advice. This advice was usually provided by a content specialist external to the group. Each group was furnished with a budget to secure these services. The other two days were taken up within projects. During the later part of their release, the participants worked for the entire three days per week on the project. Not all participants were able to secure complete release and some reported having to balance a range of commitments, particularly teaching duties, with their participation in the ITDP. Some participants also reported that projects were not readily available or provided. These participants sometimes had to canvass for and locate their own projects within industry.

Support for participants

Support was available at two levels during the twenty-week program. Each participant was under the guidance of a senior TAFE consultant who had a 'regional' responsibility for a group of participants from a number of colleges. The consultants' role included: (i) monitoring the total group and individuals within the group; (ii) bringing in extra (specialist) assistance; (iii) to be a point of reference and (iv) to meet with the group one day per week. Access to these consultants and their attributes were frequently reported as being a key determinant for successful participation within the ITDP. Each participant also had a college-based mentor. The role of the mentor was designated as: (i) providing practical advice and assistance; (ii) guidance and support; (iii) monitoring participants' progress and performance with projects, and (iv) meeting with senior TAFE consultants and the project manager as required. It was recommended by the organisers of the program that the college-based mentor have fee-for-service experience. However, as stated above and particularly in the first program, not all mentors possessed appropriate experience or expertise in consultancy activities. Other support processes were utilised when either the content or process skills of the mentor were not viewed positively by the participants. Typical amongst these was a reliance on peer support within the set and advisory processes.

Learning contract

Participants in the later programs were also to be asked to develop a learning contract in conjunction with their college-based mentor and senior TAFE consultant. A number of these participants reported that the learning contract was difficult to negotiate and achieve because of uncertainty with projects and the unknown qualities of the project work being undertaken. Some respondents noted that the contracts were 'forgotten about', because they were unrealistic or perceived as being inappropriate accountability measures.

Evaluation of the Action Learning methodology

During a formal evaluation of the Action Learning as an approach to staff development data was elicited from ITDP participants and mentors (Dickie et al., 1995). The focus of the evaluation was to assess the outcomes of the Action Learning process for the participants and determine what was useful about the learning methodology. The questions elicited information about: (i) the essential conditions for the successful use of this methodology, (ii) what would inhibit its success; (iii) why this methodology would be used in preference to another approach and (iv) when it would not be useful. Respondents accessed in the evaluation were ex-ITDP participants and some mentors. Both face-to-face and telephone interviews were conducted with individuals and groups of participants from TAFE colleges. In particular, telephone interviews were conducted with non-metropolitan participants in the program to determine if their relative isolation influenced participation and success in the program.

Both common and different views were evident in perceptions about the Action Learning process. The differences included views in the levels of readiness of participants, the processes to select participants, the support given by sponsoring colleges, the quality of mentors and also individual perceptions of the usefulness of the methodology. These responses provided a basis for delineating strengths and weaknesses of the methodology for its use in educational settings, and furnished some overall propositions about the efficacy of Action Learning as a teacher development methodology.

Although continuing to use an Action Learning methodology, the developmental strategy of the program was transformed over the three year period of its offering. Both participants and mentors reported that, over this period, the developmental process moved from being less-structured to being highly structured. This change was apparently in response to two disparate demands. Firstly, the administrative system's demand for accountability and the need to consider formal recognition, influenced the nature of the program with a growing emphasis on formalised written assessment items. Secondly, the design of the program was, in part, dependent upon the preferences of the participants who for a range of reasons appeared to demand greater structure in the second and third years of the program. Reasons advanced by observers for this change include a 'less-ready' group of participants; demands of formal assessment and also the increased homogeneity of the participants. Of particular importance in the findings was the readiness of participants to engage in a self-directed forms of learning and development.

Summaries of the data which pertained to the outcomes, utility, conditions for success and those inhibiting success, and the limits of Action Learning are provided in the next section. These categories were the focus of the questions in the evaluation.

Outcomes of Action Learning for the participants

Respondents stated that different types of knowledge had been generated through participation in the process. It was claimed that propositional knowledge (factual information or *knowledge that* such as knowledge about industrial relations; award restructuring; networks; contacts, college system; concepts about consultancy; etc.) had been acquired through the Action Learning process. Moreover, activities which privileged access to procedural knowledge (means of securing goals and completing tasks or *knowledge how*) had also been undertaken. Consequently, procedures such as: writing skills and writing proposals; consultancy skills; transferability of existing skills; participating in group decision-making; project management; basic costing; 'people skills'; and communicating with different groups of individuals were acquired. When comparing the types of knowledge accessed it seems that procedures were associated with more transferable or robust outcomes than the propositional knowledge accessed. Moreover, dispositional attributes associated with consultancy were also claimed to be generated through participation. These attributes included: confidence to go and talk to clients; changed attitudes to responsibility for learning; and valuing group support.

These responses indicate that a range of knowledge types were developed by participants. What the data indicates is that low-level propositional and forms of procedural and dispositional knowledge appeared to be accessed by participants. This is perhaps not surprising for an activity-based approach to learning such as Action Learning. A combination of all these types of knowledge are required for skilled practice. It would be expected that learning processes restricted to the formal learning setting would have privileged the development of propositional knowledge, possibly at a cost to the types of procedures and dispositions required for successful consultation activities. While development of the three knowledge types is positive, there remains the concern that without reflection on practice the development of the propositional base may be neglected.

Utility of the Action Learning process

The utility of the Action Learning process has been characterised as providing involvement, activities, reflection, group processes, self-evaluation and relevance in the data. The consequences of these factors are summarised in Table 1.

Table 1   Perceptions of the utility of Action Learning

Factor	Consequence
Involvement	• engaged learners into activities and pressed them into problem solving • allowed the learners' stage of development or readiness to be addressed, and allowed progress determined by learner • encouraged risk taking • made learner responsible for own decisions and actions
Activities	• relevant, practical and challenging • authentic demands • achievement related to activities
Reflection	• provided a basis for reflection • required participants to look at themselves
Group Processes	• support of group valued - learnt from others - discussions • everyone was equal in groups

Self-evaluation	• had to be self-monitoring - flowed from motivation and enthusiasm • allows for continual checking of progress
Relevance	• the learning activities were highly relevant

The perceived utility of the Action Learning approach adopted in this program is depicted in this table. In doing so it yields an account of the potential of its approach to engage learners in authentic socially-mediated learning activities.

Conditions to make Action Learning successful

The responses to this item were classified under the categorises synthesised from the data. The conditions which contribute to the categories are summarised in Table 2 and emphasise participant qualities, skills of mentors and qualities of the learning experiences.

Table 2   Conditions to make Action Learning successful

Categories	Conditions
Participant Qualities	• self-directed • analytical ability • ability to make and use judgements • action orientated
Skilled Facilitators	• experienced - available - willing - encouraging • knowledge of tasks to be learnt - able to present alternatives • non-directive in style • able to provide a range of support • empathetic with role
Management of Action Learning Process	• selection of participants - inform them of their role and expectations • support with project - provision, guidance and feedback • clear expectations and reporting mechanisms - specify outcomes - agreed objectives - agreed time lines • senior management support
Learning Experiences	• support with project - back up when undertaking project

73

	• access to project - ideal project would have beginning and attainable end • foster responsibility

It appears that a number of TAFE colleges have utilised their ITDP participants effectively within specialised commercial or industry training units. However, it was reported that some participants have not utilised or have not been able to practise the skills developed during the ITDP. So just as not all mentors had the full complement of skills and experience, not all host institutions provided the opportunities for the participants to engage in the types of activities and enjoy the sort of support which enabled them to develop their knowledge of consultancy.

Conditions which inhibit effectiveness of Action Learning

The conditions likely to inhibit successful participation in Action Learning are summarised against each category in Table 3. Again, the responses to this item have been classified under categories synthesised from the responses.

Table 3   Conditions which inhibit Action Learning

Categories	Conditions
Participants	• may come from a culture which has not encouraged: risk taking, critical reflection, innovation, and entrepreneuralism • lack of critical skills • dependency on highly structured approach to learning Inappropriate selection: • lack of readiness • lack of motivation
Organisation	• lack of support • unavailability of project • lack of sponsorship - arrangements made so participation can occur • lack of strategic vision
Pressure from participants	• requests for too much structure in learning process • overly specific framework may inhibit the sort of outcomes desired from Action Learning

College Culture	• not conducive to change or support of change
Mentors	• quality of mentors - content knowledge and process skills

Although reflecting similar concerns depicted in Table 2, the data here provides a basis for considering the importance of selection, barriers within educational institutions and the demands of participants which may need to be addressed.

Preference for Action Learning against other approaches

In support of Action Learning as a preferred approach to teacher development, the responses to this item emphasised the active, authentic and engaging nature of Action Learning. It was claimed in the data that this preference was attributed to:

- learning by doing - 'you cannot learn to be a consultant by just listening - its not the same as being involved';
- the only way to develop the skills is to make it all interact;
- requiring you to think and become more actively engaged;
- its being a highly active process;
- turns theory into a practical exercise.

These statements of preference emphasise acquisition of procedural knowledge through participation in goal-directed activities associated with the goals of the developmental program.

Limits of Action learning

The final item determined the limits of Action Learning as an approach to learning. The data emphasised that if there was a lack of guidance/support that participants might find themselves in situations that resulted in negative outcomes for them, thereby inhibiting further development. Moreover, the development of some forms of propositional knowledge through the program, which require didactic type approaches of instruction were not accessible, thereby failing to secure those forms of knowledge. The respondents suggested the following list of circumstances which would make the use of Action Learning inappropriate. These circumstances are when:

75

- factual (conceptual) information is privileged;
- risks are too great to warrant experiential learning;
- other methods better to provide information; and
- the environment is all wrong.

So this set of evaluatory outcomes has provided a basis for considering the potential and limitations of this approach to Action Learning as an approach to managing the effective development of teachers. In the concluding section, some key issues are teased out and conclusions offered.

Concluding comments and discussion

From the evaluation of ITDP, it is held that Action Learning has, with careful management and some change, the potential to provide access to and assist with the development of the types of knowledge that are required for the continuing development of teachers. The reflective process, if used effectively may provide a basis for strong individual conceptual growth and makes the learning process transformational. To what degree it is possible to construct reflective activities as a structured component of the Action Learning process remains unclear. However, as a learning process which features guidance from either peers or mentors while engaged in authentic tasks associated with work practice, it has a range of benefits to offer in the development of professional expertise. Some key areas emerging from this case study which will require careful management, yet which are important for developing the types of knowledge required to be successful in adopting innovations, follow. These areas focus on the readiness and guidance of participants, their access to authentic activities and institutional and group support.

Selection/induction

While it is not necessary for participants to be familiar with Action Learning it would seem that selection and induction processes need to acknowledge the autonomous nature of the learning arrangements and prepare participants for this role. Ideally, participants should be asked to justify their inclusion in a developmental program and being part of a socially-mediated process. Such an approach would assist with choice of participants most ready and prepared to learn in the self and group-directed manner demanded by Action Learning. Ultimately, learning is a highly individualised process and the interests and motivations of the learner are key determinants. A strong focus in the induction phase about the nature of autonomous learning and its responsibilities may be facilitiative. This might include the benefit of seeking and securing appropriate support and guidance.

Institutional-based support

The support and sponsorship of the participants' host college was a key determinant. Participants from colleges where supportive arrangements were in place reported benefiting from access to projects, interest by senior staff, access to mentors and had clear and practical goals to achieve. These colleges had clear intentions for the use of the consultants and had planned the integration of the participants in their strategic directions. The converse of all the above was also true when colleges disinterest about their nominee's engagement and support resulted in the outcomes for the participant being limited.

Readiness and support

As the readiness of individuals to participate in the Action learning model of development is likely to be quite different, support is necessary. Participants will respond quite differently to the challenges of autonomous or group learning arrangements. The degrees of support available are likely to be differentiated according to the readiness of participants. While differentiation is required, it is still necessary to maintain the principle of giving the participants a task within their overall capability, yet one that will push them to the limits of their capability and will require action, thereby extending the learner and providing a basis for reflection. So the key principles of Action Learning should not be compromised, rather the management of learners' readiness needs to be taken into account in induction procedures to build a level of guided support which, over time, extends the participant to achieve the program's goals. The support of mentors is, therefore, crucial. An appropriate model for guided learning to be considered by mentors is that of the apprenticeship model of modelling, coaching, scaffolding and fading (Billett, 1993c; Collins et al., 1989).

Group activity - the learning set

The degree that group activity will play a major role will be determined by the preferences of participants and access to other forms of support. However, at its most modest level group support for the learning sets will probably provide the most practical and realistic form of reflection on action.

At its greatest potential it will provide a forum for modelling, comparing development, clarifying socially-determined knowledge and making it congruent.

It can be seen from the theoretical discussions advanced initially and the data from the evaluation that followed, that Action Learning provides a basis for extending the individual existing knowledge in order to adopt innovations if managed in the ways indicated above. Yet some additional emphasis may be required within the Action Learning approach. It seems that a weakness of Action Learning in pushing the learner into accommodation, is the access to more expert others and reflection. If the social mediation is only through the learning set this may have limitations in terms of the access to experts who are able to make accessible what is hidden and may remain unknown through experiential learning. Moreover, an expert can provide a sophistication of guidance which is beyond that which can be acquired through peers. This is particularly the case in making accessible that conceptual knowledge which would be otherwise accessible. It would seem that Action Learning may privilege the development of procedures over concepts. So, while the experiential and shared nature of 'learning sets' is important, they are likely to be enhanced by access to particular expertise. There is a danger here that a purely experiential approach may lead to assimilation rather than accommodation as expert guidance and reflection are likely to be salient in the generation of new cognitive structures. This is more likely to be the case if reflection is also without social source and mediation. Therefore, it is held that close guidance by more expert others be considered to complement the social mediation of the learning set.

In conclusion, from a constructivist perspective Action Learning, although instrumental, provides an array of attributes (e.g. authenticity, social mediation, engagement) which are conducive of the development of cognitive structures that are robust within a domain of knowledge. The major emphasis on guided learning also recommends this approach and posits it within current views about how individuals' construct knowledge. What has been advanced in this chapter is that managing change is primarily concerned with the development of those who are asked to implement change. Without the development of teachers' ability to succeed with innovations, it would seem that they will likely remain as policy goals. At the centre of even the most instrumental approach to the management of educational change is learning and the development of teachers' knowledge because ultimately it is the teachers who are the curriculum makers.

Notes

It is necessary to thank the National TAFE Staff Development Committee for funding the research referred to in this chapter. Also the participants who contributed in this research deserve thanks. Finally, to my colleague Ron Passfield with whom I worked on this project go thanks and acknowledgement for his contribution.

References

Anderson, J.R. (1982). Acquisition of Cognitive Skills. *Psychological Review,* **89** (4) pp.369-406.

Billett, S. (1993a). What's in a setting - learning in the workplace. *Australian Journal of Adult and Community Education,* **33**(1) pp.4-14.

Billett, S. (1993b) Authenticity and a culture of workpractice. *Australian and New Zealand Journal of Vocational Education Research,* **2**(1) pp.1-29.

Billett, S. (1993c). *Learning is working when working is learning - a guide to learning in the workplace.* Centre for Skill Formation Research and Development. Brisbane, Australia: Griffith University.

Billett, S.R. (1994a). Searching for authenticity - a sociocultural perspective of vocational skill development. *Vocational Aspects of Education,* **46**(1) pp.3-16.

Billett, S. (1994b). Situated Learning - a workplace experience. *Australian Journal of Adult and Community Education,* **34**(2) pp.112-130.

Billett, S. (1995). Constructing the curricula: national curricula, teachers' practice and change. *New Horizons in Education,* **92** pp.30-45.

Brown, J.S., Collins, A. and Duguid, P. (1989). Situated Cognition and the Culture of Learning. *Educational Researcher,* **18**(1) pp.32-34.

Chi, M.T.H., Glaser, R. and Farr, M.J (1982). *The nature of expertise.* Hillsdale, NJ: Erlbaum & Associates.

Collins, A., Brown, J.S. and Newman, S.E. (1989). Cognitive Apprenticeship: Teaching the Crafts of Reading, Writing and Mathematics. **In** L.B. Resnick (ed.) *Knowing, Learning and Instruction, Essays in honour of Robert Glaser.* Hillsdale, NJ: Erlbaum & Associates.

Dewey, J. (1916/1970). *Democracy and Education.* New York: The MacMillan Company. pp.179-192, 279-285, 410-417. Reproduced in Cahn. S.M (ed.) *The philosophical foundations of education* (pp.201-261). New York: Harper & Row.

Dickie, K., Passfield, R. and Billett, S. (1995). *Applied Principles.* Action Learning in Vocational Education and Training Vol 3, Chadstone, Victoria: The National Staff Development Committee for Vocational Education and Training.

Fullan, M. (1985). Change Process and Strategies at the Local Level. *Elementary School Journal,* **85**(3), pp.391-421.

Goodnow, J.J (1990). The socialisation of cognition: what's involved?. *Cultural Psychology.* (ed.) Stigler, J.W., Shweder, R.A., and Herdt, G. (pp.259-86). Cambridge: Cambridge University Press.

Gott, S. (1989). Apprenticeship Instruction for Real-World Tasks: The Coordination of Procedures, Mental Models, and Strategies. **In** Rothhopf, E. Z. (Ed) *Review of Research in Education*, Washington, DC: American Educational Research Association.

Guskey, T.R. (1986). Staff Development and the Process of Teacher Change. *Educational Researcher,* **15** (5), 5-11.

Kindler, H.S. (1979). Two Planning Strategies - Incremental and Transformational Change. *Group and Organisational Studies,* **8**, pp.476 8.

Knowles, M. (1984). *Andragogy in Action.* San Francisco: Jossey-Bass.

Lave, J. and Wenger, E. (1991) *Situated learning - legitimate peripheral participation.* Cambridge: Cambridge University Press.

Logan, L. (1988) A note on School-Based Inset. *British Journal of In-service Education,* **14** (3), pp.160-61.

McLaughlin M. W., & Marsh D. D (1978). Staff Development and School Change. *Teachers College Record,* **80** (1), pp.69-94.

Newman, D., Griffin, P. and Cole, M. (1989). *The construction zone: Working for cognitive change in schools.* Cambridge: Cambridge University Press.

Palinscar, A.S. and Brown, A.L. (1984). Reciprocal Teaching of Comprehension - Fostering and Comprehension - Monitoring Activities. *Cognition and Instruction,* **1**(2), pp.117-175.

Passfield, R. and Billett, S. (1995). *Action Learning as a process: Theoretical Foundations.* Action Learning in Vocational Education and Training Vol 2, Chadstone, Victoria: The National Staff Development Committee for Vocational Education and Training.

Pea, R.D. (1987). Socializing the knowledge transfer problem. *International Journal of Educational Research,* **11** (6), pp.639-663.

Raizen, S.A. (1991). *Learning and Work: the research base.* Paris: OECD.

Revans, R.W. (1982). What is Action Learning? *Journal of Management Development,* **1** (3), pp.64-75.

Rogoff, B. (1990). *Apprenticeship in thinking - Cognitive Development in Social Context.* New York: Oxford University Press.

Rogoff, B. (1995). Observing sociocultural activity on three planes: Participatory appropriation, guided participation, apprenticeship. **In** J.W. Wertsch, A. Alvarez and P. del Rio, (eds.). *Sociocultural studies of mind* (pp.139-164). Cambridge: Cambridge University Press.

Rogoff, B. and Lave, J. (eds.) (1984). *Everyday Cognition: Its development in social context.* Cambridge, Mass: Harvard University Press.

Stevenson, J.C. (1991). Cognitive structures for the teaching of adaptability in vocational education. In G. Evans (ed.). *Learning and teaching cognitive skills.* (pp.144-163). Victoria, Australia: ACER.

Stevenson, J.C. and McKavanagh, C. (1991). Cognitive Structures Developed in TAFE Classes, a paper presented at the *1991 Conference of the Australian Association for Research in Education.* (Gold Coast) November 1991.

von Glasersfeld, E. (1987). Learning as a constructive activity. **In** C. Janvier (ed.). *Problems of representation in the teaching and learning of mathematics.* Hillsdale, NJ: Lawrence Erlbaum.

Wertsch, J.V. (1993). *Voices of the mind: A socio-cultural approach to mediated action.* Cambridge, Mass: Harvard University Press.

5 The challenge of distance education for community nurses: managing the learning process through student empowerment

Ros Carnwell

Abstract

This chapter addresses the changes needed in developing and delivering distance learning opportunities to community nurses. The challenges facing distance educators are discussed including: facilitating independence in students; designing materials in a manner which is responsive to student needs; and changing the power base in order to empower students to take charge of their own learning. The chapter concludes with the need to adopt a dialogic, constructivist approach to the development and delivery of distance learning.

Introduction

Nurse education has undergone unprecedented changes during the past few years. The inception of Project 2000 (UKCC, 1986) resulted in nurses being educated at diploma level with the subsequent transfer of courses into institutions of higher education. These dramatic changes led to the need to consider the educational needs of community nurses which were addressed in The Future of Professional Practice (UKCC, 1994). This report dictated that all community nursing would be taught at degree level, thus allowing academic progression for qualified Project 2000 nurses.

This decision created a knowledge deficit for traditionally trained nurses who do not possess diploma level credits but wish to embark on a career in community settings.

One way of responding to this problem has been to develop distance learning programmes which provide diploma level credits in relevant subjects. This has provided both an opportunity and a challenge to community nurse educators. However, the need to respond quickly to student demand may lead to the development and implementation of distance learning programmes which do not cater for the individual learning needs of students.

This chapter will address this challenge by considering three types of change evident in the provision of distance learning opportunities for community nurses. First, students will need to change from being dependent to independent learners. Second, learning materials need to be designed in a manner which promotes student empowerment. Finally, opportunities for dialogue need to be exploited in order to change the balance of power. Before these three changes are discussed the chapter will consider the nature of distance learning in relation to community nursing.

The nature of distance learning in relation to community nursing

Distance education can be defined as education that takes place at a distance from the institution at which the student is registered. As such it comprises certain characteristics: separation of teacher and learner; influence of an educational organisation; use of technical media to unite the teacher and learner; provision of two-way communication enabling either teacher or learner to initiate dialogue and the possibility of occasional meetings (Keegan, 1980). Evans and Nation (1992) believe that institutions maintain the distance in the teaching and learning relationship by 'reconstructing the relationships between the places students occupy and the place(s) occupied by the institution' (p.9). This system embraces the notion of student autonomy through negotiation of learning needs and intentions allowing both staff and students to enter a deeper learning process (O'Reilly, 1991). Thus, institutions deliver distance education programmes in a manner which assumes that students are autonomous learners. For community nurse educators this assumption represents a major dilemma because nurses who have followed a traditional training programme tend not to be autonomous learners.

Autonomous learners are, by definition, self-directed and mature enough to use their personal experience rather than material taught by the teacher. They are assumed to direct their own study through their own motivation and a problem solving approach (Knowles, 1980). Although nurses, as mature, professional students are often motivated and are familiar with problem solving processes, they will not necessarily wish to direct their own study. As Pratt (1988) points out, not all adults wish to engage in self-direction and it should not be assumed that collaborative learning methods are always appropriate. This argument is supported by various studies into learning styles and preferences which will be discussed later in this chapter.

Nevertheless, as Jennett (1991) argues, the personal commitment required of self-directed learning increases the likelihood of producing health professionals who are more willing to alter practice patterns and to impact on patient care. Adult nursing students are, therefore, ideal candidates for the self directed learning approach implicit within distance learning programmes. They have the requisite maturity and a rich source of experience on which to draw, as well as possessing the relevant problem solving skills (Carnwell, 1995).

Advantages and limitations of distance education

Distance education has several advantages. It allows students the flexibility and autonomy to begin and finish courses and submit assignments as they wish (Holmberg, 1989). It creates freedom in relation to time and place restrictions, selection and entry qualifications; curriculum choice; goal selection and evaluation (Rumble, 1989; Keegan, 1985 and Wedemeyer, 1977) and the potential for higher-quality learning and effective outcomes (Jennett, 1991). The materials present information in varied forms which draw on life experiences thereby arousing emotional responses normally only occurring in private (Stainton-Rogers, 1986). Stainton-Rogers suggests that this process facilitates 'mindful' acquisition through actively engaging students and allows both in-depth study as well as broader analysis of certain issues. Thorpe (1979) asserts that distance education extends beyond text materials to an interaction between students, tutors and the course team, whilst Daniel and Marquis (1979) remind us that no other medium is sufficiently flexible to be carried around and consulted with the same ease.

Most disadvantages of distance education are concerned with curriculum control, materials design, and assessment practices. Concerns surrounding curriculum control centre around the control of the curriculum by institutions who are seen as the holders and regulators of expert knowledge so that the teaching role is depersonalised, making it harder for students to question the value given to knowledge and to gain power over it (Chesterton, 1985; Tait, 1988; Snell, 1987).

Materials design has been criticised for encouraging rote learning due to its demand for respect for the printed word and the necessity to regurgitate such material in assignments (Perraton, 1985). Since materials are produced for an unknown audience they become 'sterile' and tightly packaged (Chesterton, 1985) subordinating the individual needs of students to the package and allowing little opportunity to challenge course objectives, content and outcomes (Sewart, 1987). Students are thus reduced to passive consumers who must adapt to a curriculum content which may or may not meet their individual needs (Harris, 1976; Sewart, 1976).

Assessment practices in distance education have been criticised for being 'closed' allowing little opportunity for students to demonstrate their engagement with course materials in an active and creative way, specific measures of success being dictated by others (Chesterton, 1985; Evans and Nation, 1989). Unlike attendance students, distance education students have fewer opportunities to ascertain what is expected of them and to read work submitted by others (Thorpe, 1987). Cropley and Kahl (1983) also argue that in distance education there is a delay between response and feedback resulting in the absence of an important set of reinforcing stimuli. Distance learners have less opportunity to use the teacher as a role model or to learn by identification with the values and beliefs of the teachers. The authors acknowledge that distance education does avoid some undesirable effects of teacher/learner relationships but is also unable to capitalise on the moment by moment student feedback and non-verbal communication evident in face-to-face teaching. Thus, according to Cropley et al didactic activities and materials are the greatest strengths and weaknesses of distance education, being both well organised and clear but impersonal and rigid. Conversely, evaluation and feedback in distance education allow students more control over what to send in for evaluation thus encouraging greater exploration, autonomy and independence, unlike face-to-face tuition in which evaluation partly measures the ability to fit into the organisation's goals (Cropley and Kahl, 1983).

In spite of these limitations distance education does have the advantage of removing the student from classroom restrictions in which individual needs are subservient to the mean of the two extremes of the group (Sewart, 1985). However, distance education students have no one against whom they can measure their performance, relying purely on the comments from their tutor. It would appear then that distance education has the advantage of meeting students' individual needs but achieves this at the expense of the support and interaction gained from being part of a student group.

Facilitating change from dependence to independence

In order to promote independence in distance learners in the community nursing discipline it is important to understand some of the personal characteristics of students, including their learning style preferences, their cognitive processing styles and their orientation to study. Knowledge of learning styles and preferences have proved useful in education in considering how people learn in educational or training situations (Kirby, 1979), how they collect, organise and transform information into useful knowledge (Conti and Welborn, 1986) and how this influences their choice of learning setting, learning content and approach to learning.

Learning preferences can be sub-divided into instructional preferences models like Canfield's (1980) LSI which deals with preference for structure, pace of learning, and relationships with teachers and peers; and information processing models such as Kolb's LSI which refers to aspects of information processing such as concrete experience, or critical questioning of content.

Instructional preference

Canfield's (1980) model identifies four conditions (need for affiliation with peers and tutors, need for structure, need for achievement and need for eminence); four content areas of orientation (number, words, inanimate and people); and four modes of learning (listening, reading, iconics and direct experience). The model reveals that nursing students have significantly lower preferences for the structure, direct experience, affiliation and iconic scales and significantly higher preferences for the reading scale (Merritt, 1983). Moreover, Ostmoe's (1984) study of 92 baccalaureate nursing students showed that nursing students 'prefer learning strategies that are: traditional, teacher-directed, denote student passivity, and are highly organised'. Furthermore, preference for non-traditional learning does little to improve student's perceptions of these methods and therefore indicates that positive perceptions of non-traditional methods may arise from personal characteristics rather than experience.

Nursing students clearly have a preference for well organised, traditional, teacher-directed learning, and this preference may persist throughout time. Distance learning, although normally well organised, is neither traditional nor teacher-directed, therefore nurses may not adapt easily to this method. The use of strategies of teaching and learning which facilitate the transition from traditional learning to distance learning therefore need to be considered. Canfield's LSI is an important measure of student preferences which could diagnose future learning preferences. Such considerations may have an impact on performance (Conti and Welborn, 1986). Conti and Welborn found that students achieved highest when their tutors used a collaborative mode and conclude that learning efficiency might be fostered by making students aware of their learning styles and by providing counselling sessions to enable them to adapt their learning style to the course content.

Canfield's modes of learning are of particular importance for distance learning. Of the four modes (listening, reading, iconics and direct experience) reading is clearly the mode that is used most frequently in distance learning. The use of Canfield's (1980) LSI will reveal some important preferences of distance learners. For example, if most students prefer working in different conditions, content areas and modes than those provided by the distance learning experience then curriculum developers will need to consider methods of delivering distance learning experiences in a more appropriate manner; or will need to prepare students more effectively to either adapt their preferences to the distance learning experience or to select a mode of learning that is more suited to their instructional preference.

Cognitive learning style

Kolb (1976) defines learning style as a preferred way of processing information from the world. For example, people may process information in either an abstract or a concrete manner. The reflection versus active experiment dimension of Kolb's model refers to transformations of experience. Reflective thinkers are said to transform experience intentionally by internal reflection whereas active thinkers transform experience extentionally by actively manipulating the environment. Kolb designed a

Learning Style Inventory (LSI) to measure these information processing styles in students.

Kolb's LSI comprises a four stage cycle which is based on the premise that concrete experience is the basis of reflective observation which will be used to form abstract conceptualisation of the meaning of the learning experience. Abstract conceptualisations are used to generate theories and hypotheses which are tested in new situations, and active experimentation using existing theories to sole problems. Two polar opposites are evident in the cycle, with concrete experience being the polar opposite of abstract conceptualisation and reflective observation being the opposite of active experimentation. From these dimensions, as well as research and clinical observation, Kolb (1976) identified four statistically significant learning styles - convergers, divergers, assimilators and accommodators.

Divergers favour both concrete experience and reflective observation. They have great imaginative ability and are able to view concrete situations from a variety of perspectives. They prefer concrete, people-orientated learning experiences in which they can generate new ideas through 'brain storming'. In distance learning situations one may expect them to desire concrete examples in the text as well as through face-to-face tuition. Tutorials would also provide them with a people-orientated learning experience which would enable them to generate ideas from a variety of perspectives.

Assimilators ascribe to reflective observation and abstract conceptualisation. They are orientated towards theoretical models and inductive reasoning and preferred learning experiences which require symbolic thought. Their lack of interest in people may make them natural distance learners. One may also expect that they would require little more than text materials which they would reflect upon and analyse.

Convergers prefer abstract conceptualisation and active experimentation. They are good at testing out theories in practical situations, problem solving, and prefer learning situations requiring the search for a single correct answer. They tend to be unemotional, uninterested in people and have narrow technical interests. As distance learners one would expect convergers to focus only on parts of the text which can be applied to practice and provide answers which they are looking for. In group tutorials they will require a single solution to problems and will be less interested in discussion of theories or group support. Such students may therefore be instrumental and assessment orientated in their learning and may restrict their reading of distance learning materials to information which will enable them to answer an assignment.

Accommodators prefer concrete experience and active experimentation and excel at carrying out plans and seeking new experiences. They are less analytical than others and trust their instinct in problem solving situations. Their greatest strength lies in carrying out plans and getting involved in new experiences. They solve problems in an intuitive trial-and-error manner, relying heavily on other people rather than their own analytic ability. One would expect them to be well organised and systematic in distance learning situations although their competence in using concrete experience and their lack of analytical skills may result in a need for tutorial support.

A summary of different styles and their implications for distance learning is indicated in Table 1.

Table 1   The impact of different learning styles on distance learning

STYLE	PREFERENCE/ CHARACTERISTICS	IMPACT ON DISTANCE LEARNING
Diverger (Concrete experience - Reflective observation)	Concrete, people-orientated. Good at generating new ideas, view from different perspectives.	Need concrete examples in text. Opportunities for group discussion and case studies.
Assimilator (Reflective observation - Abstract conceptualisation)	Theoretical models, inductive reasoning. Prefer thinking symbolically. Less interested in people.	Probably natural distance learners. Would enjoy reflecting upon and analysing DL materials.
Converger (Abstract conceptualisation - Active experimentation)	Test theories in practice, solve problems. Prefer learning situations requiring the search for a singly correct answer.	May focus only on parts of the text which can be applied to practice and provide answers which they are looking for. May be instrumental and assessment orientated in their learning.
Accommodator (Active experimentation - Concrete experience)	Carry out plans and seek new experiences. Less analytical than others and trust their instinct in problem solving situations. Rely on others in problem solving.	Well organised and systematic in distance learning situations. Desire for concrete experience and lack of analytical skills may result in a need for tutorial support which will also provide support from others to solve problems.

Kolb and Wolfe (1981) further developed Kolb's theory in relation to learning *environments*. They describe four different learning environments which emphasise different *competencies* resulting in the creation of a 'learning press' on the learner. This means that in order to succeed in a particular learning *environment*, the learner must possess the relevant *competencies* for that environment. For example, Kolb (1976) found that human service disciplines were found to have concrete learning styles and learning environments associated with these disciplines were perceived to have a concrete/affective environmental press. Kolb also found that individuals whose styles matched the predominating learning demands of the discipline were more satisfied with their career choices and expressed stronger commitment. Those whose styles did not match the learning environment scored higher on alienation and lower on satisfaction. Laschinger and Boss (1989) apply this concept to nursing students and the nursing environment, and argue that the structure of nursing knowledge creates a concrete environmental press and that nursing learning environments have resulted in concrete learning styles among nursing students. Thus, they argue, learning opportunities requiring abstract learning styles will be incongruent with the current environmental press of nurses. They conclude that learning experiences which promote abstract learning competencies may result in a more positive attitude towards theory-based practice. Distance learning, if provided in a manner which responds to students' existing learning styles may provide such a learning experience.

Kolb's LSI has been the subject of at least two literature reviews relating to the nursing discipline (Spence-Laschinger, 1990; DeCoux, 1990). Spence-Laschinger (1990) concluded that the most consistent finding from research is the predominance of concrete learning styles in nursing students. One of the important characteristics of learning style is its capacity to influence student's perception of different learning experiences (environmental press) as well as their ability to process information which is presented in a manner which is incongruent with their learning style (Spence-Laschinger, 1990).

Of particular interest is the impact of learning style on distance learning which is addressed by research into self-directed readiness using the Guglielmino Self Directed Learning Readiness Scale (SDLRS) (O'Kell, 1988). O'Kell found that divergers and accommodators scored significantly lower on self-directed learning readiness than convergers and assimilators. She concluded that because convergers and assimilators are less concerned with people than divergers and accommodators, they may be happier 'doing their own thing' and studying on their own. This was supported by

Laschinger (1987) who found that concrete learners preferred small group discussions and 'hands on' practical methods, whereas abstract learners preferred reading and lectures from experts. Since concrete learning styles are prevalent among nurses, then distance learning may not come naturally to them due to the lack of practical activity and opportunity for discussion.

The challenge for curriculum developers in distance learning is to capture the imagination of students with different learning styles, both in the production of distance learning materials and in the provision of tutorial provision and support systems. Given that most students rank independent study low on their list of preferences (Wells and Higgs, 1990), and that the 'learning press' of distance learning may be incongruent with distance learning, text materials need to provide concrete examples within the text which can be readily applied to practical situations. The use of case studies and activities throughout the text also responds to the learning needs of concrete learners. However, it is important to point out that although most studies suggest that nurses are concrete learners, they have been found within all four quadrants. Thus, it is possible that materials designed in the manner described above could frustrate and alienate learners with abstract learning styles, and in particular assimilators.

Curriculum developers may use this information to provide distance learning programmes that match the learning style of the participants. Students may also be given advice and information about the importance of learning style in relation to the experience of distance learning so that they can adopt the learning style most conducive to successful learning. Highfield (1988) points out that students are more successful when they know their learning style, and when their style is matched with a teacher style and a learning situation compatible to their learning style. Distance education is unlikely to match teaching style with learning style preference, except for perhaps in terms of personal tuition. The distance learning environment may however, successfully match learning styles with distance education provision.

Orientation to study

Despite the potential impact of students' personality characteristics which are reflected in their learning preferences, their success as distance learners could be determined by something much more pragmatic. As adult, mature students with professional roles and multiple responsibilities their motivation to engage in a distance learning programme may be complex.

Orientations to study are defined by Taylor, Morgan and Gibbs (1981) as

> all those attitudes and aims that express the student's individual relationship with a course.... it does not assume any psychological trait or state belonging to the student. It is a quality of the relationship between student and course rather than a quality inherent in the student.

Morgan et al (1982a) examined four crucial factors influencing learning: personal, vocational and academic orientations to study (enhanced job prospects, personal development); development as learners (transition from learning as accumulation of knowledge to learning as an active process); approaches to studying and relationship to learning outcomes (progression from surface-level to deep-level approaches to learning); and demands of learning materials (use of student directed project work to facilitate deep-level approaches to learning). The authors concluded that attempts to improve learning should include: the development of students' concepts of learning by student-centred facilitation of self awareness; the development of flexibility of students to adopt appropriate learning strategies; and the requirement within the course design for students to take responsibility for their own learning.

Taylor's (1981) study of 29 Open University students revealed that the most frequent orientation was personal, described as both widening horizons and compensating for previous deprivation of opportunity. The second most prevalent orientation is vocational, characterised by pursuit of future job prospects or promotion as well as training. When compared with students from a traditional university, Open University students had a much greater personal orientation. The authors conclude that orientations to study will influence their approach to learning, a personal orientation suggesting openness to change and willingness to apply content to personal experience resulting in understanding meaning (Marton and Saljo, 1976). Students orientated towards compensation are likely to be assessment conscious and may have a tendency to reproduce material rather than understand its meaning (Marton and Saljo, 1976). A study of community nurses (Carnwell, 1995) revealed that orientations were partially determined by whether the student wished to gain access to degree level study or to use distance learning to convert an existing community nursing qualification to diploma level. Students studying to gain access to the degree were more orientated towards enhanced job prospects, with personal development being second most important to them. Students wishing to convert their qualification were more orientated to personal development, the desire for an academic qualification being their second priority. According to Taylor and Morgan (1984) the most successful students had a personal growth orientation, as well as the need for a secondary qualification related to job prospects. However, Strange (1987) found that not all students with an apparently helpful orientation were successful learners since they used a 'surface' level approach to memorise as much as possible, rather than understanding and reflecting on the process of learning. Strange (1987) therefore suggests that it is more important to ask what it is that motivates students than how much motivation each one has.

It is evident that the production and delivery of distance education is far more complex than the need to deliver learning materials at a distance from the institution in order to free students from the restrictions of traditional teaching. Community nurses have several characteristics arising from professional experienced, personality and family life which may impede their development as distance learners. Hence, distance learning materials need to be designed in a manner that facilitates this development.

Designing distance education materials for student empowerment

It is the contention of this chapter that the facilitation of independent learning within the nursing discipline requires a constructivist approach to learning which empowers students to take charge of their own learning through dialogue. Although most distance learning materials are designed in a manner that promotes interaction between the author and student, this interaction is one-way. Thus, opportunities for students to construct their own meaning from written text are limited by the lack of interaction with others. A constructivist approach to education is relevant to distance education because this view perceives knowledge as directly known only when it has been conceived, perceived and construed by the learner. The objective facts, as presented in text materials, are only important if they are construed by the student. Constructivists like Kelly (1955) believe that each person construes the world and uses this construct as a template to fit over various realities as they occur in order to make sense of the world. We therefore constantly test our constructs against those of other people who have experienced that same 'reality'. For this reason, it can be argued that distance education should not be conducted in isolation.

Garrison (1993) uses a constructivist approach to argue that much distance education design and delivery has been based on behavioural learning which is not conducive to achieving complex ill-structured subject areas. Garrison (1993) argues that pre-packaged learning materials are prescriptive in nature affording little flexibility over the negotiation of learning goals, collaborative learning decisions, or for learners to assume responsibility for constructing meaning for themselves. The first objective is to pass the examination or complete the assignment 'correctly', not to analyse the content critically for meaning (Garrison, 1993). The emphasis is on producing materials that are so complete that learners should not need much contact with a tutor (Garrison). For Garrison, the constructivist learner actively constructs meaning, not in isolation, but through dialogue with oneself and others. New information is then integrated into existing knowledge structures. Thus knowledge can only be created by the learner, the teacher's role being to monitor the learner's cognitive processes and challenge unclear perspectives. It is this dialogue between teacher and learner that results in the development of complex knowledge structures, rather than the dissemination of prescribed information to a passive uncritical learner. Drawing on the views of Holmberg (1989), Garrison argues that although the learner is ultimately responsible for learning, educationally the quality of learning is established through the proactive interaction and guidance of a teacher. It is therefore the transaction between the teacher and learner that makes learning educational. The challenge for the designers of distance learning materials is the creation of opportunities for dialogue within the package.

Garrison believes that the solution is a paradigm which involves technologies that support interdependence of mind and thought which can only be achieved through two-way communication in which scepticism and assumptions are challenged and modelled. Although Garrison suggests that such models should include audio-teleconferencing and computer-mediated communication, it must also be recognised that some students will not have access to the necessary technologies. Therefore, written materials should also be designed in a manner which promotes dialogue. Intext devices may include questions designed to enhance students' understanding, although they have been found in experimental studies (Marton, 1975) to cause students to fixate on the explicit requirements of the question so that the learning task is narrowed and trivialised. Gibbs, Morgan and Taylor (1982) conclude that

> ... attempts to induce deep level processing may interfere with or 'technify' student learning.

Such activities can also be completed in isolation with little opportunity to use one's construction of meaning as a template to test against other students. Group-based activities should therefore be included within text materials, together with discussion points and alternative explanations and competing theories. These could also include debates in which students are encouraged to argue in favour of competing arguments and to defend their position against others. In nurse education the use of practical examples, exercises and case studies may by an additional way of bridging the learner knowledge gap.

Difficulties associated with assessment may be overcome by negotiated assessment and self assessment requiring the student to analyse and synthesise material rather than merely regurgitate it; and by directing students to extensive reading lists on which assessment is partly based. Tait favours a development orientation (Boot and Hodgson, 1987) in which tuition and counselling would be critical in enabling the student to use knowledge to attribute meaning to the world.

Managing the distance learning experience through dialogue

The importance of facilitating dialogue within the design of distance learning materials has been discussed. However, of equal importance is the management of the distance learning experience. It is not sufficient to provide students with packages and then leave them to their own devices. This argument is supported by the theories already discussed in this chapter as well as research findings which suggest that adult, professional students need opportunities for dialogue with both their tutors and other students (Ostmoe, 1984; Carnwell, 1995). What makes learning educational is the transaction between teacher and learner. The teacher is not an optional resource in an educational transaction because the teacher communicates social values and knowledge (Garrison, 1993).

Tutor-student interaction is also viewed as important by Sewart (1985) who argues that support and group interaction forms part of the 'essential facet of the teacher' in conventional teaching which cannot be adequately replaced by a package, students' needs not being wholly related to the subject being studied. Although Holmberg (1989) believes that distance education is based on motivational deep-learning as an individual activity, Garrison asks whether it 'is reasonable to expect motivated deep-learning from individuals studying in private' because 'few students by themselves have the ability to analyse their current knowledge and beliefs critically, to assume responsibility for constructing new meaning, and to act upon the understanding for purposes of confirming its usefulness and long-term assimilation'. Although interaction, albeit not of a social nature, may occur when a solitary and silent student mulls over the 'knowables' in a text he is reading (Daniel and Marquis, 1979) integrating, elaborating, and restructuring concepts are 'more likely when one is required to explain, elaborate, or defend one's position to others, as well as to oneself (Brown and Palinscar, 1989).

A constructivist approach to the delivery of distance education in community nursing would require the facilitation of dialogue between students and tutors. As suggested earlier, this could be provided to some extent by teleconferencing and computerised technology. However, dialogue between students and tutors is of more importance because it 'involves the idea that humans in communication are engaged actively in the making and exchange of meanings, it is not merely about the transmission of messages' (Evans and Nation, 1989). Dialogue would therefore serve various functions. First, through personal interaction with students, tutors would compensate for some inappropriate course designs (Burge, 1988). For example, course writers may assume that students understand certain concepts and knowledge at course entry, students not possessing such knowledge may be able to make progress with course materials without some clarification from a tutor. Second, in order for students to feel able to discuss their academic problems with a tutor, a rapport between them must first exist. Thus, the warmth and expression generated through dialogue enables a rapport to develop between student and teacher, allowing the teacher to check the students' progress and understanding of the methods of presentation (Perraton, 1985). Third, as Stewart suggests, the advice and support offered in distance education embraces the inclusion of knowledge into the student's own peculiar framework and this enables the student to construct new meaning. Finally, dialogue

> opposes potential of distance education for totalitarian practice where a monopoly on what is allowed as knowledge can be enshrined in the course units (Trait, 1988)

and therefore prevents education becoming indoctrination (Perraton, 1985).

Dialogue between tutor and student appears to be the most important facet of a successful distance education programme in community nurse education. Carnwell (1995) found that the most consistent finding in a survey of distance learners was the need for more interaction with and support from a tutor. This includes the need for more personal and group tutorials as well as more telephone availability of tutors. This certainly emphasises the distance between course teams producing content and the adult student with individual learning needs attempting to make sense of difficult concepts in isolation from those who have produced them. One of the basic tenets of androgogy is respect for the life experiences of adult learners and how these may contribute to their experience of learning. If no attempt is made to generate dialogue with students this opportunity may be lost.

In view of the importance of dialogue it is proposed that distance educators providing nurse education programmes should consider alternative methods of providing contact between tutors and students. The value of technology-based learning must not be underestimated, but neither should it be used to replace human contact. Many nurses, and particularly those who have undergone traditional nurse training, are dependent in their approach to learning. This means that, not only will they need personal contact with a tutor to increase their confidence, but they may not possess the necessary skills in self-direction to be successful distance learners - particularly during the early stages of their distance learning experience. Distance educators therefore need to be committed to dialogue as a means of creating independent learners who will need less support as they progress through their learning experience.

Using a constructivist, dialogic approach to the delivery of distance education programmes should therefore facilitate the transition of students from dependent to independent learning. However, tutors providing distance learning materials also need to take into account the personal factors that may inhibit opportunities for dialogue and the construction of meaning.

Conclusion

A dialogic, constructivist approach to distance learning is undoubtedly the most effective way of designing and delivering distance learning programmes. However, as pointed out earlier the personal characteristics of nurses may impact on the opportunity for and perception of dialogue. In particular, nurses tend to have concrete learning styles as well as an environmental press which is not conducive to distance learning. In addition, their learning preferences are for traditional, teacher-directed, highly structured learning experiences and their orientation for study is often a complex web of factors determined by various personal, work and family commitments. Therefore, the major problem for distance educators is the delivery of distance learning materials which cater for individual needs of students whilst facilitating a transition from dependent to independent learning.

Methods of creating independent learners include diagnosis of learning style, preferences and orientations to study; and the use of dialogue to empower students to take control over their own learning. The use of LSI scales such as Kolb's, as well as Canfield's learning preference inventory would make students aware of personal barriers that they need to overcome in order to become successful distance learners. A discussion of their orientation to study would also illustrate motivating forces, their perception of the value of knowledge and any personal commitments which may impact on their learning experience. An analysis of these factors and discussion with students concerning how they can best manage their learning experience necessarily involves the use of dialogue.

Through dialogue students can be empowered to diagnose their own learning needs and take control over the learning process. The various functions of dialogue discussed earlier include: clarification of concepts, the development of a rapport, advice and support and prevention of indoctrination. Implicit within these purposes is the need to create an independent learner through the use of support and this involves transferring the control of the learning process from the tutor to the student. Control refers to the opportunity and ability to influence, direct and determine educational decisions which can only be achieved by striking a balance between independence, power and support (Garrison and Bayton, 1987). The teacher role as support is paramount in enabling the student to assume autonomy and emotional independence. Independence, according to Garrison and Bayton (1987), is the freedom to diagnose one's own learning needs and to formulate one's own learning goals. Power is the ability to draw on requisite intellectual ability, study skills and motivation in order to assume responsibility for the learning process. Support refers to the learning resources that students may access including materials and teachers. These three dimensions are fundamental to the concept of control since

> to be fully in control of the learning process the student must have freedom to explore possible learning objectives, the power to handle a learning activity, and the support necessary to complete the educational experience (Garrison and Baynton, 1987).

If any one of the components is missing the degree of control over the learning process would be diminished. It may be assumed then, that support, independence and power are the means by which students become autonomous learners. Chene (1983) questions how

> learners know that a resource is adequate or an objective realistic or an anticipated result is pertinent if they have not completed the learning process. How can they insure that everything necessary for success is done without having to confirm their judgement with someone else? (Chene, 1983).

This is particularly pertinent for community nurses working at a distance and feeling unsure about whether the progress they are making is acceptable. Without reference to a tutor the education progress becomes nothing more than trial-and-error learning with the inevitable disappointment if concepts and guidelines were misunderstood.

Tutors, then, have a crucial role in empowering students to shape their own learning. They need to provide sufficient dialogue to support students towards their quest for independence, power and autonomy.

References

Boot, R.E. and Hodgson, V. (1987) Open Learning. Meaning and Experience. **In** Hodgson, V, Mann, S and Snell, B. (eds.) *Beyond Distance Teaching Towards Open Learning*. Open University Press. pp.5-15.

Brown and Palinscar (1989) Guided, cooperative learning and individual knowledge acquisition. **In** Resnick, L.N. (ed.) *Knowing, learning and instruction: Essays in honor of Robert Glaser*. Hillsdale, NJ: Lawrence Erlbaum.

Burge, L. (1988) *Beyond Androgogy: Some Explorations for Distance Learning Design*. Journal of Distance Education 3(1), p.5-23.

Canfield, A.A. (1980) *Learning styles inventory manual* (2nd ed.) Ann Arbor: Humanics Media, 1980.

Carnwell, R. (1995) Empowering Distance Education Learners - an Ethnographic Study. Presented at *Vocational Aspects of Education Conference, Research and Change in Further and Vocational Education*. University of Greenwich. 19-21 July, 1995.

Chene, A. (1983) *The Concept of Autonomy in Adult Education: a Philosophical Discussion*. Adult Education Quarterly, **34**(1) Fall, 1983, pp.38-47.

Chesterton, P. (1985) *Curriculum Control in Distance Education*. Teaching at a Distance, 26, pp.32-37.

Conti, G.J. and Welborn, R.B. (1986) *Teaching - Learning Styles and the Adult Learner*. Lifelong Learner **8**(8), pp.20-24.

Cropley, A.J. and Kahl, T.N. (1983) *Distance Education and Distance Learning: some psychological considerations*. Distance Education **4**(1), pp.27-39.

Daniel, J.S. and Marquis, C. (1979) *Interaction and Independence: Getting the Mixture Right*. Teaching at a Distance, 14, pp.29-43.

Decoux, V.M. (1990) *Kolb's Learning Style Inventory: a review of its applications in Nursing Research*. Journal of Nursing, **29**(5) pp.202-207.

Evans, T. and Nation, D. (1989) *Dialogue in Practice, Research and Theory in Distance Education*. Open Learning **4**(2) June, pp.37-42.

Evans, T. and Nation, D. (1992) *Theorising open and distance education*. Open Learning, June 1992, pp.3-13.

Garrison, D.R. and Baynton, M. (1987) *Beyond Independence in Distance Education: the Concept of Control*. The American Journal of Distance Education **1**(3), pp.3-15.

Gibbs, G., Morgan, A. and Taylor, E. (1982) *A Review of the Research of Ference Marton and the Goteborg Group: a Phenomenological Research Perspective on Learning*. Higher Education 11, pp.123-145.

Gugliolmino, L.M. (1977) *Development of the Self-directed Learning Readiness Scale*. Dissertation, Athens, GA: University of Georgia.

Harris, D. (1976) 'Educational Technology at the Open University: a short history of achievement and cancellation'. British Journal of Educational Technology, 71, p.44. In Rumble, G. (1989) *Open Learning, Distance Learning, and the Misuse of Language*. Open Learning, June 1989, pp.28-36.

Highfield, M.E. (1988) *Learning Styles*. Nurse Educator, **13**(6), pp.25-33.

Holmberg, B. (1989) *Theory and Practice of Distance Education*. London: Routledge.

Jennett, P.A. (1991) *Self-Directed Learning: a Pragmatic View*. Journal of Continuing Education in the Health Professions, **12**, pp.99-104.

Keegan, D.J. (1980) *On Defining Distance Education*. Distance Education, **1**(1), pp.13-36.

Kelly, G.A. (1955) *The Psychology of Personal Constructs, volumes 1 and 2*. New York: W.W. Norton.

Kirby, P. (1979) *Cognitive Style, Learning Style and Transfer Skill Acquisition*. National Centre for Research into Vocational Education. Columbus: Ohio State University.

Knowles, M. (1980) *How do you get people to become Self-directed Learners?* Training and Development Journal, May 1980, pp.96-99.

Kolb, D.A. (1976) *Learning Style Inventory Self Scoring Test and Implementation Booklet*. Boston: McBer and Company.

Kolb, D.A. and Wolfe, D.M. (1981) *Professional Education and Career Development: a cross-sectional study of adaptive competencies in experiential learning*. Lifelong Learning and Adult Development Project, Final Report. Cleveland, Ohio: Case Western Reserve University.

Laschinger, H.K. (1987) *Learning Styles of Baccalaureate Nursing Students and Attitudes Towards Theory-based Nursing. A validation study of Kolb's theory of experiential learning*. Unpublished doctoral dissertation. Ottawa: University of Ottawa.

Laschinger, H.K. and Boss (1989) *Learning Styles of Baccalaureate Nursing Students and Attitudes Towards Theory-based Nursing*. Journal of Professional Nursing, 5(4), pp.215-223.

Marton, F. (1975) *On Non-verbatim Learning: II: the erosion effect of a task induced learning algorithm*. Reports from the Institute of Education, University of Goteborg, No. 40.

Marton, F. and Saljo, R. (1976) *On Qualitative Differences in Learning I: outcome and process*. The British Journal of Educational Psychology, 46, pp.4-11.

Merritt, S.L. (1983) *Learning Style Preferences of Baccalaureate Nursing Students*. Nursing Research, November December 1983, 32(6), pp.357-372.

Morgan, A., Taylor, E. and Gibbs, G. (1982) Understanding the Distance Learner as a Whole Person. In Daniel, J.S., Stroud, M.A. and Thompson, J.R. (eds.) *Learning at a Distance: a world Perspective*. Edmonton: Athabasca University.

O'Kell, S.P. (1988) *A study of the relationship between learning style, readiness of self-directed learning and teaching preference of learner nurses in one health district*. Nurse Education Today, 8, pp.197-204.

O'Reilly, D. (1991) *Developing Opportunities for Independent Learners*. Open Learning, November 1991, pp.3-13.

Ostmoe, P.M., Van Hoozer, H.L., Scheffel, A.L. and Crowell, C.M. (1984) *Learning Style Preferences and Selection of Learning Strategies: Consideration and Implications for Nurse Educators*. Journal of Nursing Education, **23**(1), January 1984, pp.27-30.

Perraton, H. (1985) A Theory of Distance Education: **In** Sewart, D, Keegan, D. and Holmberg, B. (1985) *Distance Education: International Perspectives*. Beckenham, Kent: Croom Helm.

Pratt, D.D. (1988) *Androgogy as a Relational Construct*. Adult Education Quarterly, **38**(3), pp.160-172.

Rumble, G. (1989) *Open Learning, Distance Learning and the Misuse of Language*. Open Learning, **4**(2), June 1989, pp.28-36.

Sewart, D. (1976) *Introduction: Learning from a Distance*, No. 4, pp.1-4.

Sewart, D. (1987) Limitations of the Learning Package. **In** Thorpe, M. and Grugeon, D. (eds.) (1987) *Open Learning for Adults*. Harlow, Essex: Longman. pp.31-37.

Snell, R.S., Hodgson, V.E. and Mann, S.J. (1987) Beyond Distance Teaching Towards Open Learning. **In** Hodgson, V., Mann, S. and Snell, B. (eds.) *Beyond Distance Teaching Towards Open Learning*. Milton Keynes: Open University Press. pp.161-172.

Spence-Laschinger, H.K. (1990) *Review of Experiential Learning Theory Research in the Nursing Profession*. Journal of Advanced Nursing, 15, pp.985-993.

Stainton Rogers, W.S. (1986) *Changing Attitudes Through Distance Learning*. Open Learning, November. pp.12-17.

Strang, A. (1987) The Hidden Barriers. **In** Hodgson, V., Mann, S. and Snell, B. (eds.) *Beyond Distance Teaching Towards Open Learning*. Milton Keynes: Open University Press. pp.20-40.

Tait, A. (1988) *Democracy in Distance Education and the Role of Tutorial and Counselling Services*. Journal of Distance Education, **3**(1), pp.95-99.

Taylor, E. and Morgan, A. (1984) *Students' Open University Careers*. Study Methods Group Report No.15, IET, Open University, Milton Keynes (mimeo).

Taylor, E., Morgan, A. and Gibbs, G. (1981) *The 'Orientation' of Open University Foundation Students to their Studies*. Teaching at a Distance, 10. Vol 1 Winter, pp.3-12.

Thorpe, M. (1979) *When is a Course not a Course?* Teaching at a Distance, 16, pp.13-18.

Thorpe, M. (1987) Student Assignments, **In** Thorpe, M. and Grugeon, D. (1987) *Open Learning for Adults*. Harrow, Essex: Longman Open Learning.

United Kingdom Central Council for Nursing, Midwifery and Health Visiting (1986) Project 2000: *A new preparation for practice - document of the United Kingdom Central Council for Nursing, Midwifery and Health Visiting*. (UKCC), London.

United Kingdom Central Council for Nursing, Midwifery and Health Visiting (1994) The Future of Professional Practice - the Council's Standards for Education and Practice following Registration.

Wedemeyer, C.A. (1977) Independent Study. **In** Knowles, A.S. (ed.) *The International Encyclopaedia of Higher Education*. Boston: CIHED.

Wells, D. and Higgs, Z.R. (1990) *Learning Styles and Learning Preferences of First and Fourth Semester Baccalaureate Degree Nursing Students*. Journal of Nursing Education, **29**(9), pp.385-390.

6 Development of a resource-based learning centre: a case study

Helen Trayers

Abstract

In this chapter the author examines the background economic situation which has brought about the rapid development of more open types of learning in colleges of further education. She describes the results of her research firstly into the understanding of the different terminology used to describe these various forms of learning, and then into the use and development of a Learning Resource Centre at the college of further education where she works. She examines the attitudes of staff to the introduction of resource-based learning and describes how these have changed during the period of sixteen months over which the research was carried out. There is an analysis of the number of students, their ages, and the times when they use the Centre, together with an overview of the courses on offer. Finally there is a description of the ways in which Learning Centre staff and vocational colleagues have worked together to try to make the centre a success.

Introduction

Large-scale unemployment in the 1970s and 1980s forced the government to examine ways of upgrading workforce skills and of providing opportunities for personal and community development. Fulton (1981) said that it should be the policy of government and of higher education institutions to encourage the participation of adults in courses of further and higher education at all levels, and to make appropriate provision for their special needs. The White Paper 'Employment for the 1990s' emphasised the need to assess and meet training needs locally and 'A Strategy for Skills, 1991-93' stressed the importance of ensuring that all our people including those who need particular help because they are at a disadvantage in the job market, have the opportunity to fulfil their potential. The changes in education proposed by the White Paper 'Education and Training for the 21st Century' (1991), also aim to improve participation and increase levels of achievement. A person's desire to participate in an educational programme is often the result of a changing personal, social or vocational situation. Consequently programmes must be designed to satisfy the interests of the participants. Personal choice education should be available to all who can benefit from it and with the effort for wider access goes a need to adapt the curriculum practices to meet the needs of those seeking it.

Mcdonald (1984) commented that attempting to fit mature unemployed people into the existing education system only served to highlight its inadequacies and that they were being expected to fit into courses designed for eighteen-year olds. Shortly after this the Further Education Unit (FEU, 1985) warned of the dangers of trying to fit as diverse a group as the unemployed into the existing framework and said that they should not be categorised into administratively convenient groups. It was becoming obvious that new methods both of improving access for more mature students and new methods of learning appropriate to their specific needs must be designed. Since 1988 £25 million has been given to further education for development and support of open and flexible learning and is aimed at reducing the traditional barriers of time, place and pace, and hoping to widen access for many hitherto neglected potential students. The money was made available through support grants from the Department of Education and Science. The use of open and independent forms of study can greatly enhance the efficiency of learning and nowadays most further education institutions have an open learning workshop but as yet only a few integrate open learning into all their courses.

The recent reform in qualifications and the advent of more competence-based assessment, the setting of national education targets and lifelong learning targets, the development of the credit framework and the accreditation of prior learning, mean that colleges of further education are no longer tied to one method of operating through set syllabuses and courses. Additionally, colleges of further education have become independent of local authorities (April, 1993) and the major part of the college financing from the Further Education Funding Council (FEFC) now results from provision which leads to academic or vocational qualifications, provides access to higher education, or to higher levels of further education, enables learners to acquire basic skills, or skills in English for speakers of other languages or caters for adults with special educational needs. This new system also means that the colleges are under great pressure to expand since the method of funding is tied to expansion and those institutions which do not recruit extra students will be penalised. There is additionally the concept of achievement-led funding as outlined in 'Resourcing Tomorrow's College', Field (1994), which stresses the importance of the learner's achievements and encourages the development of openness and flexibility by valuing it through the funding mechanism. He says that it offers potential for strengthening the links between non-traditional methods of learning and college-based routes to achievement. The concept of achievement does not just mean the achievement of a paper-based qualification; it can cover such elements as 'value-added' in terms of 'distance travelled', personal development and the attainment of core skills. It fulfils the requirement of the Further and Higher Education Bill in that it relates funding to quality. This is one of the driving forces behind the decision to expand the open learning centres.

This implementation of incorporation and the imposition of Further Education Funding Councils (FEFC) financing has additionally caused many colleges of further education to examine the way in which their courses are structured. The FEFC definition of a full-time student as 'one who receives 15 hours or more class contact over 30 weeks' has caused the college on which this study is based to rethink its previous policy of 21 hours of class contact per week for each full-time student. As there is to be no additional money forthcoming for these extra hours of class contact then financial constraints dictate that they are reduced. The FEFC has also decreed that an extra allowance will be available for each student undertaking additional learning support. This is the second factor which has brought about the decision of Academic Board of the College of Further Education where this research was carried out, hereafter known as the College, that over a period of two years, class contact hours would be cut to 15 and an additional element of open learning would be introduced into each course. This was foreseen by Cottle (1993) when he said that open learning must be used more in further education in order to provide the economics required and to maximise the use of staff resources.

The college where this research was undertaken was established in 1928 largely to meet the increased demand for education and training for the coal industry. Over the years it has developed steadily despite the decimation of the industries on which its vocational work was originally based. Mining and engineering have virtually disappeared and the college now offers a much broader curriculum which includes a range of vocational programmes as well as mature access provision, retraining programmes, GCSEs and A levels and some higher education programmes. New developments have affected the college continuously from the early impact of the Manpower Services Commission through to European funding and the college has participated in many areas of development including the Technical and Vocational Education Initiative (TVEI), European funded retraining programmes such as the Iron and Steel Employees Re-adaptation Benefits Scheme (ISERBS), Community Outreach programmes, the Equal Opportunities project and the development and pilot of the local Open College Federation. It has an extensive network of adult education and outreach venues in the neighbouring villages. The college has developed an open-access learning centre which provides a range of flexible learning opportunities for those who cannot attend classes or who require additional support in the core areas of Communication, Numeracy and Information Technology.

The Learning Resource Centre (LRC) at the college was established in 1989 as a direct result of an Open and Flexible Learning Project funded by the local Education Authority. It was originally known as the Open Learning Centre and was initially centred around learning support but by January 1994 when the first study was undertaken it had developed to offer open access to word processing, computer facilities and support in Communications/English and Numeracy together with a range of courses offered on an open/flexible learning basis including Sociology, Health Studies and Accounting. Additionally pre-course support for students wishing to enter the police or nursing professions or higher education was also on offer and proved to be very popular. At this time it was known as the Resource-based Learning Centre. It provided drop-in support in areas such as curriculum vitae preparation and job applications. During the academic year 1994-95 the name of this flexible learning centre was changed to the Learning Resource Centre, a term which was thought to encompass open, flexible and resource-based learning all of which to a greater or lesser extent would be on offer there.

The introduction of resource-based/flexible learning demands changes in approach by teachers. It requires more co-operation with other colleagues both in actual teaching and in course design. It means that the teacher has to teach students rather than subjects and so needs a much greater flexibility in learning approaches than is perhaps required in a classroom. Teaching has moved from being teacher-centred to student-centred and the central role of the teacher has changed to be that of a facilitator. Instead of lectures there are now student packages and much more time and effort may have to be spent on producing individual learning packs. It means greater use of criterion referenced assessment and more rigorous evaluation procedures. There will be a greater need for accurate tracking of student performance in a situation where every student may have his/her individual learning programme. Assessment, instead of being at the end of the period of learning, is usually continuous and new methods of assessment may well have to be devised. It implies individual learning and student autonomy. There could well be an increased emphasis on educational technology and this is an area which holds terror for those teachers who may not be as computer literate as many of their students. All this requires a large input in terms of staff development.

The research

Over a period of two years, the author has undertaken several short research projects to investigate different aspects of open learning. From the onset it was clear that there was considerable confusion and ambiguity about the terminology used to describe this and similar concepts. Many programmes have been developed in recent years which aim to increase student autonomy and remove the traditional barriers which until now have prevented access to education for many people. These programmes have many characteristics in common. Students take the responsibility for their own learning, they study at a pace to suit their own needs on a course of their own choosing probably using specially designed materials; and they often study alone in a place determined by themselves but may come together in small groups. The learning is student-centred although help is available from a tutor. The programmes have been variously described as open-learning, distance-learning, resource-based learning and flexible learning. The author has personally delivered the same programme in the same manner, using the same materials to individual learners in two different colleges. In one establishment it was called open learning and in the other, resource-based learning. The problem was highlighted in a recent article by a librarian (Carr, 1995), who said that confusion over terminology such as open learning, flexible learning and resource-based learning caused panic amongst students and reduced them to tears because they were unsure what was expected of them.

Should the terms open learning and flexible learning be regarded as generic terms which encompass all other learner-centred methods of delivery? Is it more appropriate to consider that these concepts describe an approach to learning rather than a method of delivery? The definition of open learning given by the Manpower Services Commission in 1984, for example, concentrates on the empowerment of the learners - putting them in charge of their own learning. A further consideration could be that one essential feature of both these 'generic' terms is that they emphasise learning and not teaching, ie. they concentrate on the outcomes. Resource-based learning and distance learning on the other hand concentrate on the process and the way in which it works.

In order to investigate the range of understanding of the different terminology by the writer's colleagues and students, she undertook an investigation, by means of structured interviews and questionnaires, into the perception of these different, but closely related concepts. She also sought to ascertain the views of colleagues on the introduction of resource-based learning. The author interviewed colleagues from several vocational areas (Engineering, Health and Social Care, Business Studies and generalists as well as a colleague who works in the LRC), who would be responsible for the delivery of the RBL sessions or who would have the task of incorporating RBL into their course programmes. She also obtained the views of senior managers who are concerned with policy making. Thus an assistant principal with the overall responsibility for curriculum was interviewed together with the senior lecturer in charge of the LRC and learning support. The library plays a vital role in the delivery of resource-based learning and therefore the views of the college librarian were also sought. In this way it was felt that a representative section of staff who might reasonably be expected to be involved in implementation of RBL was covered.

The results of this research were interesting in that they displayed a wide difference in the perception of the different concepts not just between staff or students but also amongst colleagues there was a wide range of interpretation of the different terms. However from the responses the author was able to compile the following definitions.

Open learning was perceived by staff to be an approach which gives students control over their own learning, allowing them to study in a way which suits their own learning style and at a pace which is suitable for them.

This is very similar to the view taken by students who see it as a means of enabling them to study at a time suitable to themselves rather than suiting their individual learning style.

Distance learning was thought by staff and students to be a flexible method of learning which enables students to study at a place of their own choosing. Staff also consider that it gives students some degree of control over their learning; students themselves see it as a means of allowing them to study at their own pace.

Resource-based learning was regarded by staff and students as an independent learning method which uses resource materials. Students feel that it promotes active learning whilst staff regard it as a flexible learning programme.

The importance of flexible learning to both staff and students was perceived to lie in the fact that it provides individual learning programmes which students can study at times convenient to themselves. Students view it as allowing them to study at their own pace whilst staff regard it as being student-centred.

The above analysis also made it possible to identify those characteristics which are felt to be unique to each learning concept. Open learning enables students to study in a way which matches the student's own learning style. Distance learning permits students to study in their own homes and can be effective across huge distances. Resource-based learning involves the students in active learning using resource materials and flexible learning is the only one which the respondents thought allowed students to follow individual learning programmes.

It is clear to the writer that these unique features are not, in themselves sufficient to describe each concept - we do not want such narrow definitions which in themselves are ambiguous: distance learning, for example, has itself been described as 'flexible' by both staff, and students. We need sufficient information contained within each definition to enable us to accurately define each concept meaningfully, that is if in fact we do believe that the concepts are themselves sufficiently unique to warrant separate definitions. Or should we be thinking in terms of generic definitions which Thorpe and Grugeon (1987) describe as the 'umbrellas' which encompass a whole range of student-centred options? Whatever we decide, there is a need for students to know exactly what each concept means and what is expected from them. (The choice of name for the college open learning/flexible learning/resource-based learning has neatly avoided this ambiguity.) Therefore to avoid

111

needless stress on the part of the reader, the definition of resource-based learning used in this paper is that given by Dorrell (1993):

> a broad heading covering open learning, distance learning and flexible learning in which the use of learning resources is the main thrust of any scheme developed.

At the time of the initial research, most staff were very apprehensive about the increased use of resource-based/flexible learning methods. Many held a very narrow view that the LRC is a place where students go to work, mainly on their own, to complete a learning package. The majority had little or no experience of it and were unfamiliar with both the new methods of delivery and learning materials which have been developed (Lewis, 1993).What became immediately apparent was the divergence of colleagues' perception of resource-based learning from it being 'one-to-one learning by using packages given out to students which they work their way through' to 'a base where they (students) can come where there is a wealth of resources to use, and staff'. Many were concerned about their jobs and saw the LRC as a threat - 'they won't need us any more' whilst others thought it was a management ploy to replace lecturing staff with cheaper technicians. Staffing was seen as a major issue and the appointment of 'appropriate' staff was deemed to be crucial. All colleagues interviewed thought that the LRC was inappropriately staffed with some staff being assigned to the centre mainly because they had spare hours on their timetables and not because they were the most suitable people to work there.

Some staff looked forward to the change but others were less enthusiastic. They feared the loss of contact with their students and thought that they would be losing control of the learning process. The majority felt that they had not the skills to develop learning packages, incorporate RBL into their programme or facilitate students in the LRC. One colleague thought that the traditional class teacher would have greater difficulty in adjusting to the requirements of RBL saying that if one approached an LRC student with a 'classroom' head on then you would 'lose it'. Two colleagues stated their dislike of bought-in packages and almost without exception expressed concern at their perceived lack of information technology skills. All felt that much staff development needed to be undertaken.

There was concern that an LRC centre was not suitable for everyone and that some students worked better in a group. This does not mean that group work is excluded from resource-based or flexible learning and one colleague with some experience in this area said that she actively encouraged this. It was felt by most staff that most students do not possess the basic skills to work in a LRC centre. It was thought that they would need special help to work effectively and take control of their own learning and that this would be a gradual process. Many students particularly the school leavers, came into college lacking fundamental skills such as the ability to find information in the library. A lot of additional time would be needed to be spent on acquiring these basic study skills.

The LRC at the college is a small unit although it does offer a fairly wide range of learning programmes. As part of the initial student induction programme which every new full-time student undergoes, screening tests are administered to the students in order to identify any area of Numeracy or Communication skills where the student may need support from staff in the LRC. A large proportion of LRC students are mature individuals who attend either to develop their basic communication skills (the college has a very successful Basic Adult Education unit which channels students into the LRC) or come as part of their Access to Higher Education/University Foundation Course in Combined Studies in order to take the GCSE English and Mathematics examinations. Other students are referred to the LRC by their course tutors who have diagnosed an area of specific need usually in Communication Skills and occasionally in Study Skills. A further small group of students use the computing facilities in the LRC in order to complete the assignments set as part of their normal course work. Finally there are those students who wish to study other courses such as Sociology or Book-keeping which the college offers in the LRC for those unable to attend during 'normal' class times.

The population of students at the college at the time of the initial questionnaire was 670 full-time students and 3,500 part-time students. 5,179 students used the workshop in 1993/94 and of these 247 were enrolled specifically as open learning students. Sixteen months later the college has a total student population of 3,700 of which 1,002 are full-time and 532 have enrolled into the LRC.

At the time the initial questionnaire was carried out 36 percent of the students attending the LRC were male and 64 percent female. The corresponding figures 16 months later were 37.5 percent and 62.5 percent respectively. This is significantly different from the proportion of males and females in the population as a whole (48 percent male and 52 percent female) and from the local area where according to the 1991 census figures, the proportion of males to females is 48.8 percent to 51.2 percent. The author suspects that there is a high proportion of female one-parent families in the area which the college is helping to bring back to education by means of its broad Outreach Programmes based on the poorer local communities. Currently there are 3,584 one-parent families in the local borough of which 3,314 are female lone-parents and this figure, according to the Community Care plan is expected to rise.

The following table shows the age range of students in the LRC compared with the percentage of the local population calculated at the 1991 census.

Table 1   Age range of students in the LRC

Age group	Census figures (percentage)	Time of initial survey (percentage)	16 months later (percentage)
16-19	8.7	25.0	38.0
20-44	57.0	61.0	50.0
45-64	34.3	14.0	12.0

The majority of students fall within the 16-25 years age groups and the increase in the percentage of 16-19 year olds between the two surveys is mainly as a result of the incorporation of core-skill support, i.e. Communication, Numeracy and Information Technology, for the GNVQ courses being given in the LRC by LRC staff. There is perhaps an unexpectedly high number of mature students in the age group 20-44. The college would appear to have more than the 'national' percentage of students in the age range 17-44 as given in the Guardian Education Adult Education Survey of May 1995-86 percent and 88 percent compared with the national figure of 46 percent. This could reflect the area's high unemployment rate of 16.5 percent compared to the national figure of 10 percent and so one might expect that more adults would be attending education/training courses. Young people under 25 formed one third of the unemployed. Three-quarters of the collieries have closed and associated industries have suffered as a result. Production in the steel works has also declined drastically in recent years. These were some of the reasons for the decision by the college Senior Management Team to expand and widen the flexible/open learning provision in order to improve access for these mature students which experience showed were beginning to look at continuing their education in order to increase their employment prospects or to proceed to higher education. The college is now making positive efforts to recruit redundant miners onto its courses, in particular onto the Access to Higher Education course and University Foundation courses in Combined Studies and in Electronics. In addition the college is participating in the Return to Work scheme whereby persons who have been unemployed for a minimum of 12 months can return to study up to 21 hours per week without a reduction in their unemployment benefits.

The most popular course in the LRC during the period of the initial survey was GCSE English followed by GCSE Mathematics. Sixteen months later the situation has changed and now the Mathematics workshop is the most popular programme with 21 percent of students enrolling on this programme closely followed by the English Support workshop (18 percent). The Information Technology workshop was an area which the principal was most eager should expand and many more students have now enrolled for this compared with 16 months ago. Many new programmes have been introduced and students can now choose from a wider range of GCSEs and A levels. Other courses on offer which were not available to students previously include the AAT Foundation course, Book-keeping and Accounts, English Support (ESOL), the Food Hygiene IEHO Certificate, Environmental Studies and programmes for supervisors and first line managers. Many of these programmes have been validated by the local Open College and are available at different credit levels. TDLB units will shortly be available through the LRC. Currently 53 percent of the students enrolled on specific LRC programmes are full-time students on other courses and are attending either for core study support or additionality, e.g. the NVQ Catering students are completing their studies for the Basic Food Hygiene Certificate in the LRC. Drop-in support is also on offer to students on all the college programmes together with help in Study Skills, job applications and interviews and preparation for further or higher education. 88 percent of the LRC's drop-in students are enrolled on other full-time college programmes.

Initially 36 percent of LRC students attended between 9-12 am; another 36 percent between 12-6 pm and 28 percent students attended in the evenings between 6-9 pm. Sixteen months later the pattern of attendance for LRC students enrolled on specific courses was 53 percent in the morning, 32 percent in the afternoon and 15 percent in the evening. Of those LRC students enrolled for drop-in support, 33 percent attended in the morning and the remaining 67 percent in the afternoon and evening. Analysis of the students on specific programmes showed that 27 percent of all attendances were on a Wednesday, closely followed by Thursday (26 percent), and Monday (25 percent). Fewest attendances were on Fridays (8 percent), and Tuesdays had 15 percent of the total attendance. (NB. Some students attended on more than one occasion.) Mornings were more popular than afternoons and the fewest students, 15 percent, attended in the evenings. Friday afternoon, as might be expected, was the least popular session. (There is no evening session on Fridays.)

When asked for their reasons for choosing to work in the LRC rather than attending 'conventional' programmes, all respondents rated personal development, attendance at times to suit your needs and pace of work to suit yourself as being most important. Individual tuition was not thought to be a very important reason for their choice. When asked to give their desired outcomes from the programmes in the LRC, those listed as being most important by the majority of students were gaining qualifications, as an entry to other educational courses and to help you get a job. Less important were making friends and gaining self-confidence. Keeping up with technology was rated unimportant by all but one respondent.

Over the period of research, staff perceptions have undergone a change. Colleagues who previously were very apprehensive about integrating resource-based learning into their programmes are now more enthusiastic, some extremely so. The LRC is no longer seen as a place where the students go to complete paper packages. This, the writer feels is the result of much positive action to increase liaison between staff working in different areas and a determination on the part of all colleagues to make the system work. Much consultation has taken place between programme staff and LRC staff who in fact are now considered to be members of the programme team and they work together designing learning programmes and course assignments which integrate the core units into the vocational programme and assessing and recording them. The areas where this co-operation is felt to be most successful is where the same colleague who delivers the core units in the course programme is also providing support for these areas in the LRC. Co-operation on a wider scale has also begun and cross-college teams, eg. for GNVQ and NVQ programmes now meet regularly. As a result of these meetings it was decided to form a College Core Studies team in order that the delivery of these units could be made uniform across the college. It also enables common strategies to be put in place and the best practice implemented across college. Much material has been bought in - some of it excellent - but it is left to the programme teams as to how this should be used. Despite initial protestations that staff were unconfident about producing their own materials, much has been produced, often using ideas from the bought-in material, but also some of it innovative. This has certainly overcome the earlier complaint that colleagues were never sure what they (the packages) were aiming at.

As a result of staff pressure much staff development has been offered in the area of Information Technology and colleagues are now, in general, feeling more confident of their abilities. Other development sessions have been held for the LRC staff some of whom have now been appointed on permanent contracts and it is no longer the cry that LRC is used to top-up the timetables of 'weaker' members of staff. It is seen as a specialised area which requires specialised staff who have very specific skills particularly in the areas of communication and motivation. It is essential that they are able to empathise with the students and their problems. One colleague commented that the type of person employed was more important than their subject speciality. The initial fear that staff might be replaced by 'cheaper' technicians has not materialised. Many staff who hitherto had no experience of working in the LRC centre have, after having expressed a desire to work in the LRC, been given the opportunity to do so for a few hours per week and are thoroughly enjoying the experience developing their skills in new areas. Not all staff, however, appear to be able to make the adjustment from being a classroom teacher to being a one-to-one facilitator and as far as possible efforts have been made to ensure that staff are placed where they feel most comfortable. A few difficulties have been experienced where there has been disagreement between the management of the LRC centre and staff who appear to wish to deliver programmes in the traditional manner. Most colleagues would agree with the sentiments expressed by Jack (1988) when he said that RBL is a state of mind rather than a method with particular characteristics. Management and staff are determined to surmount these problems and with continued goodwill feel that the difficulties will soon be resolved.

Conclusion

There has been considerable expansion in the role of the LRC centre over the past 16 months. The number of programmes on offer has expanded and along with this the number of students across the whole age range has grown. More staff are becoming involved in delivering LRC programmes or running programmes which incorporate resource-based learning either in a supporting role or for the attainment of subjects seen as being additional to the main student programme. Much hard work has been undertaken to ensure that the co-operation between vocational and LRC colleagues is successful and that there is a proper integration of all elements of the programme. This is an ongoing process and is being supported by cross-college teams who meet regularly to ensure the cross fertilisation of good practice. As resource-based learning plays a greater part in the programmes of full-time students more and more are becoming aware of the opportunities it offers and new programmes are constantly being suggested, considered and implemented. It is obvious to anyone entering the LRC that it is successful. It is a thriving learning centre buzzing with activity and enthusiasm. Comments from one group of 16-year-olds previously 'reluctant' learners include 'Why wasn't maths like this at school?' Given that the current financial strictures are likely to continue for the foreseeable future, resource-based learning is here to stay and we can expect to see the LRC going from strength to strength.

References

Carr, L. (1996) What is a Learning Package in *EDUCA - The Digest for Vocational Education and Training*. No.153.

Central Statistical Office (1992) *Regional Trends No.27*. London: HMSO.

Confederation of British Industry (1989) *Towards a Skills Revolution*. London: CBI.

Confederation of British Industry (1991) *World Class Targets*. London: CBI.

Cottle, P. (1993) Open Learning: a case study in *TFH Journal*, Summer 1993.

DE (1988) *Employment for the 1990s*. London: Department of Employment.

DES/DE (1991) *Education and Training for the 21st Century*. Department of Education and Science/Department of Employment (2 vols). London: HMSO.

Dixon, K. (1987) *Implementing Open Learning in Local Authority Institutions*. London: FEU.

Dorrell, J. (1993) *Resourced Based Learning*. Maidenhead: McGraw-Hill.

Field, J. (1994) Open Learning and Consumer Culture in *Open Learning* 9 (2).

Fulton, O. (ed.) (1981) *Principles and Policies in Access to Higher Education*. Society for Research into Higher Education, Surrey University.

Further Education Unit (1985) *Adult Unemployment and the Curriculum: a Manual for Practitioners*. London: FEU.

Further Education Unit (1994) *Managing the Growth of College Learning Resource Services*. Coombe Lodge Report, Blagdon, **24** (2).

Further Education Unit (1994) *New Developments in Open Learning*. Coombe Lodge Report, Blagdon, **24** (4).

HC (1991) *Education and Training for the 21st Century*. House of Commons Select Committee on Education, Science and the Arts, 6th Report. London: HMSO.

HMSO (1992) *Social Trends 22*. London: Government Statistical Office.

Lewis, R. (1993) The Progress of Open Learning in *Education and Training*, **35** (4), pp.3-8.

Manpower Services Commission (1984) *A New Training Initiative*. Sheffield, MSC, p.7.

Manpower Services Commission (1987) *Ensuring Quality in Open Learning: a Handbook for Action*. Sheffield: MSC.

Mcdonald, J. (1984) *Education for Unemployed Adults*, DES. London: HMSO.

Tait, A. (ed.) (1992) *Key Issues in Open Learning*. Harlow: Longman/Open University.

Thorpe, M. and Grugeon, D. (eds.) (1987) *Open Learning for Adults*. Harlow: Longman.

Training, Education and Enterprise Directorate (1990) *Flexible Learning - a Framework for Education and Training in the Skills Decade*. Sheffield: TEED.

7 Negotiating the metamorphosis: collaborative change management in initial teacher education

Pauline James

Abstract

This chapter focuses on the potential of collaborative research with students to provide profound insights into learning and cultural change. A problematic situation and its resolution in initial teacher education is briefly described, together with the study which was instigated to improve classroom processes and outcomes. Recommendations for managing change in such circumstances are made and problematic elements that are apparent within this kind of work are explored. It is argued that, in these days of externally imposed change, collaborative research may well be vitally necessary in maintaining practitioner empowerment and sense of professionalism, as well as in enhancing student learning and meeting institutional requirements.

Introduction

Fullan (1991) following Louis and Miles (1990), notes that: 'Management involves designing and carrying out plans, getting things done, working effectively with people'. Leadership, on the other hand: 'relates to mission, direction, inspiration'. Yet, where change is involved, he explains, both leadership and management are intimately linked. This opinion is strongly supported by Karpin (1995) who, in a rather scathing indictment of Australian managers, urges that management should no longer relate to control, but rather to coaching, supporting and enabling action by others. It is in this latter sense that management is used in this chapter.

The need for managing educational change successfully has never been greater. Following world-wide trends, the last few years have seen considerable changes at all levels of Australian education. For example, the move towards a National Curriculum (Francis, 1993) and school-to-work programs in the senior years (Carmichael, 1992) are likely to modify dramatically the direction and focus of secondary education, and the vocational education and training system generally is undergoing massive restructuring. Many commentators (for example, Marginson, 1992) argue that such reshaping is driven almost exclusively by economic forces. Yet, some of these changes are likely to stimulate much productive rethinking about the purposes and processes of education (Sweet, 1994; Symes, 1995), as well as evoking fears of a take-over of education by business and industry in the name of efficiency and effectiveness (Lovat and Smith, 1995).

Lovat and Smith (1995) note that promotion of genuine educational change usually requires a shift in practitioner perceptions, beliefs and practices. Such change is only likely to be brought about through active discussion and the opportunity for professional development and ownership of change by all parties involved within the process. Yet, the dramatic re-orientations in education described above have, for the most part, been externally imposed. Time frames for implementation have often precluded the possibility of the 'normative/re-educative strategies' that seek to develop 'explicit and shared perceptions of the problem, and/or clearly identified and shared reasons for the change' (Lovat and Smith, 1995, p.219). Under such circumstances, modified behaviours may not be matched by concomitant changes in values and commitment and considerable resistance may be exhibited. Useful innovations may be grudgingly adopted but without proper investigation within a specific context, or poorly conceived ideas may be instigated regardless of consequences. In addition, any educational change is likely to be accompanied by strong feelings of insecurity, and conflict of some kind is probably inevitable (Lovat and Smith, 1995). They suggest that the provision of support through the transition is essential and conflict management recognised as a necessary accompaniment to the change process.

Thus, it appears that enabling practitioners to engage in the management of change in their own organisations is crucial. Under these circumstances, externally imposed 'innovations', over which practitioners do have little control, might be accommodated in ways that continue to serve the needs of students, as well as the values of justice and participatory democracy. A number of curriculum models (for example, that of Reid et al, 1989) incorporate classroom research as an important part of the process of innovation. Action research provides a methodology for undertaking such research and, as Sanger (1995) explains in relation to an appraisal system, it may be possible to bring action research into the mainstream to encourage critical reflection among practitioners to serve the needs of the institution as well as its students.

It is in this context, that I describe the management of collaboration within an action research study (Kemmis and McTaggart, 1988; Elliott, 1991), to promote and manage educational change on a number of levels and involving a group of beginning secondary teachers in an institute of education. Firstly, I discuss the problematic situation which confronted me and reasons for adopting the collaborative approach to managing (and resolving) it I subsequently took. Secondly, a theoretical framework for such collaboration is presented and I recount and explain very briefly what appeared to occur during the study (details of this have been presented elsewhere, for example, James, 1995, 1996). I also explore the problematic nature of collaboration in such circumstances and yet how and why the collaborative approach taken was crucial to the subsequent success of the project. Lastly, implications drawn from the study for managing change through collaboration are elaborated. Indeed, I argue that, given the nature of externally imposed educational change, collaborative processes among practitioners (and students), even if they appear quite difficult and unsuccessful at times, are vital, in empowering and maintaining a sense of well-being among practitioners, together with enabling just and effective improvements in educational provision.

The need for cultural change

A few years ago, I was asked to become an Educational Psychology lecturer for groups of beginning, mature-age, technology studies teachers. Participants in these all-male groups spent three days a week employed as teachers in secondary schools and two days a week undertaking an initial teacher education course in an institute of education. Such groups had, over the years developed something of a reputation for their resistance to academic learning and for sexist and racist humour, apparently useful for disrupting institute classes and in bonding the group against any challenge from their lecturers (Mealyea, 1989). In the schools, their mentors were often tradesteachers, many of whom had resisted the curriculum change to technology studies (Ministry of Education, 1988), introduced in the mid '80s into Victorian schools (perhaps a not well-managed change), and had produced an integrated culture, geographically and social separate from that of 'academic' teachers, based on their previous industrial experience and identity. This culture was characterised by a rhetoric of authoritarianism and 'toughness' (Gleeson, 1994) that often provoked rebellion in students and seemed particularly detrimental to the girls in their classes, as Rechter (1994) so vividly and passionately describes. Thus the need for change both at the Institute and in the schools was paramount. Indeed, an important aim for their total programme, according to a Hawthorn Institute Reaccreditation Submission Document (1987), was to develop teachers able and willing to learn for themselves to have positive attitudes towards change and the flexibility to adapt to new procedures, curricula and environments.

The Educational Psychology course (taught in two semester length units) is a practical, participatory subject, informed by humanistic and critical values, in which assistance is provided in coping with the transition to teaching; communicating with students, particularly in situations of conflict; developing an understanding of and strategies for working with adolescents; and enabling student learning and social and personal developments (James, 1995, 1996). A major aim of the course is to help people acquire a reflective stance to their own and others' practices in schools (Zeichner and Liston, 1987), based on discussion of real situations encountered in their classrooms and workshops. I concur with Beyer and Zeichner (1987) who argue that:

> ... we need to develop programs that self-consciously foster in students the commitment to becoming active, informed critics of their own experiences and situations, rather than merely passive respondents to their professional and occupational circumstances.

In addition, while contributing many new ideas for people to explore in practice, the course is presented as a collaborative learning venture in which group members participate in the construction of knowledge, based on an integration of theory and practice, somewhat along the lines that Hollingsworth (1994) describes, though in a different discipline area. The course had been developed over a number of years, in response to the needs of beginning teachers at the Institute.

Such a programme might appear to be highly meaningful and useful. However, resistance developed, similar to that described by other lecturers, and punitive attitudes towards students prevailed within the group. Indeed, it was not until the middle of the second unit that attitudes appeared to change and productive learning proceeded. While there were always a few participants, keen and interested throughout, to display this openly was usually to invite derision or hostility from others.

Thus, a number of aspects of educational change needed to be facilitated and subsequently managed. Participants required assistance in reflecting on their beliefs and assumptions about teaching and producing a culture that supported and encouraged such reflection; acquiring a positive stance to the rigours and uncertainties of personal learning and exploration; and becoming agents of change in the schools, sufficiently empowered to adopt new ways of working with students and to encourage their colleagues to do likewise. Similarly, I required a better understanding of what obstructed course participants' learning, developing more appropriate ways of enabling personal and professional change within the groups. Thus, although the course had not been imposed upon me, some aspects of its content and processes were sorely in need of revision - for these particular beginning teachers.

Collaborative action research

While there are many versions of action research (see, for example, Lomax, 1991; Smyth, 1991; Zuber-Skerritt, 1992; McNiff, 1993), essentially, this methodology in education involves 'trying out ideas in practice as a means of improvement and as a means of increasing knowledge about the curriculum, teaching and learning' (Kemmis and McTaggart, 1982). Such research involves a number of cycles of action, observations, reflection and planning for further strategic action, based on the understandings obtained in the process.

Many argue that collaboration is an essential component of action research because of the need for group members to challenge and critique an individual's constructions of events (Ewert, 1991). Thus, the ideal of a 'critical community' is presented, in which all have equal 'voice' and engage in rational 'dialogue', in the pursuit of 'truth'. In addition, a group often has the power to effect change where an individual cannot, and the processes leading to empowerment through reflection are said to be particularly potent when engaged within a group of 'critical friends', who may affirm or challenge one's reflections (Rappaport, 1986).

Certainly, for the improvement of a course dedicated to reflection and professional and personal change, a collaborative action research methodology appeared to be the most appropriate approach. The values of the Educational Psychology course would resonate with those of democratic participation and respect for people as *subjects* rather than *objects* in the evolving research process. They could collaborate with each other and with me, both in elucidating the processes in the Educational Psychology class and in learning appropriate strategies for working with their own students. Indeed, I thought the research process itself could contribute substantially to reflection and learning, people becoming more aware and understanding of their own practices and beliefs, as these became clarified as part of the research. Similarly, they could assist in elucidating aspects of my own practice that created barriers to their progress, helping to identify where difficulties within the course might lie. Together, we could discuss, at an appropriate level, any theoretical formulations emerging from the study resulting, one might hope, in improved insight and empowerment for all of us.

The study was ultimately undertaken with three consecutive groups of participants (A, B and C) before I was totally convinced that genuine improvement as a result of the strategic actions had taken place. Subsequently, I have taught three other groups with similar results. It may appear that this study has little to say about externally imposed educational change, in which practitioners are compelled to adopt a particular curriculum or organisational arrangement within an institution. Yet, for these participants, new learning apparently *was* an imposition of change, deeply felt and vigorously resisted. Thus, the problematic process of engaging people in a collaborative project to explore how change might be effected less painfully, but with justice and with more enjoyment, does, to some extent, find parallels with situations of externally initiated 'innovation'.

A theoretical framework for collaboration

Crawford (1995) notes the importance of sociocultural approaches to psychology, in focusing attention on the group of people who can share their several skills and insights in the process of constructing knowledge in action research. Such work can be both individually and culturally transformative and, in describing collaborative action research between academics and workers, Shuttleworth et al (1994) provide the cultural learning theories of Vygotsky as a conceptual framework for understanding the power of the processes involved. Vygotsky (1978) writes of the zone of proximal development, or the distance between the actual developmental level of a child as determined by independent problem-solving and the developmental level as exhibited under the guidance of a mentor or more capable peers. Bruner (1986), also drawing on Vygotsky's work, writes of a 'loan of consciousness' being provided (but not imposed) by others, to enable further understanding to develop. Similarly, through Lave and Wenger's work (1991), the powerful, holistic learning engaged through the processes of participating together within a community of practice can be readily understood.

A theoretical framework for collaboration

A proposal for collaboration

I wanted each group to join with me in exploring: what helped them to learn in Educational Psychology; what hindered their learning; what together we might change; and what I might enact in subsequent classes to provide improved conditions for empowerment and learning. While these themes were, of course, of direct relevance to group members, when the invitation to participate was actually proffered, they were my concerns alone. Kemmis and McTaggart (1988) do emphasise the importance of the *group* task, in action research, of developing a thematic concern together, providing ownership of an enterprise of mutual benefit, rather than merely 'involving' people in the agendas of others (McTaggart, 1989). Yet, clearly, in many situations, someone is needed to initiate the research (Heron, 1990) and power required to establish the 'co-operative'. I was also a mentor from whom they could learn both about research and the potential difficulties of their situation and, in this study, it seemed particularly necessary to launch the project from the beginning of the course, rather than delay until a group had already lapsed into disillusionment.

Therefore, after the introductory activity in the first session, I presented a 'research proposal' to each group. I asked if they were willing to assist me in improving the course, through the strategies described below.

1 Providing regular, anonymous feedback on reflective sheets (Powell, 1985) at the end of each session, reporting on what had interested them, what they had learned and how they felt about it, with reasons.

2 Discussing with me, regularly in class (and privately if necessary) what was occurring in the group and undertaking joint problem-solving if necessary.

3 Writing, in assignments, reflective commentary on the course and describing the usefulness of the material discussed for their work in schools, giving specific examples of the strategies employed. Written work was seen as difficult by some people but the requirement to express thoughts and feelings in writing is likely to result in highly valuable personal insights that might otherwise be unavailable. As Diamond (1991, 1992) argues, through our writing we can explore a number of different versions of our pedagogical selves and become empowered in the process. Only pass or fail grades were assigned and a failing assignment would be returned with feedback as to how it might reach the required standard.

4 Evaluating during the last session of each unit, small groups reporting their deliberations back to the whole group in a plenary and individuals writing their own anonymous comments.

5 Taping whole class discussions so that I could monitor carefully my own communication with group members, as well as accurately recording their spoken contributions to the class. This was agreed to, with the proviso that the recorder might be switched off at any time, if anyone preferred a conversation not to be taped. It seemed important to maintain such a record generally, since in the haste of decision-making, important points might be forgotten or neglected and subsequent interpretations distorted.

6 'Member-checking', towards the end of the course when, having analysed the 'data', I would write a detailed report for each group and ask for their opinions and comments on my 'conclusions'. This would bring us into a collaborative conversation once more.

I explained ways in which the 'data' would be used, that only I and a research 'auditor' (and potentially other researchers) would have access to the raw material and that the study was part of a PhD project.

Groups A and C were generally happy to proceed, though some concerns about confidentiality and anonymity being preserved in reporting the study were expressed in Group A. Members of Group B were somewhat more suspicious. I had been asked to introduce an 'observer' to the group, ostensibly to provide an alternative perspective, as well as enhance the research's credibility. Yet, the notion of a collaborative group settling their own concerns seemed to be compromised by her presence. There was much initial tension, some rather cynical comments made, such as: ' ... seems you need us to do your research', and a concern for being 'dissected' expressed. They felt they were under scrutiny, rather than the group processes in which I was also a key protagonist. Much explanation and assurance was required before agreement to proceed was reached and, subsequently, conditions under which the observer remained became a focus for joint problem-solving and conflict resolution.

Throughout the study, I wrote an observational and reflexive journal, which reported what I saw and heard in the groups and explored my own thoughts, feelings and actions in relation to these observations. In a methodological journal, I also examined, reflexively, by emerging constructions of events and my own investment ' ... in a variety of often contradictory privileges and struggles' (Lather, 1989).

Thus, I 'observed' the groups' responses to the course, while reflecting on my own practices and experiences. Similarly, group members presented views, observations and reflective comments, all constituting the 'data' of the study. From these we could reflect on implications for future strategic action. In addition, to assist my reflection and emerging interpretations, I discussed my work 'informally' with 'critical friends' and gave several papers on work-in-progress, both at the Institute and elsewhere.

Unit one: 'Lifting each other's spirits'

In Group A, unfortunately, resistance to the course developed once more. Analysis of feedback sheets showed positive people speaking together about professional concerns and feelings of stress. Yet, most people were negative, displaying a stance of 'toughness' associated with gender and occupational identity (Mealyea, 1989) that resulted in the 'silencing' of reflective voices through ridicule. Honest discussion, then, could only occur when the group was divided into small 'working parties', assigned to undertake role-plays or particular reflective and problem-solving tasks. Still, for the positive people, support from these small groups through the process of change appeared crucial and they were, apparently, learning substantially from the course.

However, for the majority, this avenue of support was closed, and negativism predominated as a coping strategy (Breakwell, 1986), providing temporary relief from anxiety, but precluding reflection and change. Numerous conflicts arose between myself and group members. These were managed in the short-term, by listening and acknowledging their position, while presenting other possibilities for consideration. Yet, the major issue of a cultural clash of values between those of their former occupation and those of academia was difficult to address without arousing considerable defensiveness. How was it possible to collaborate across such differences when our aims about what constituted good teaching and communication seemed so diametrically opposed?

Support through the change process appeared to be vital, though highly problematic, given the constraints of their culture. They also enjoyed story-telling and, in assignments, emphasised learning from, as one person expressed it, 'past experience and advice to formulate an opinion or reaction to an immediate problem'. So, I decided to write a short narrative, describing the trials and tribulations of a beginning technology studies teacher, his accompanying emotions and sense of disillusionment, in relation to his professional and personal life, at home, the Institute and his school. People could then discuss 'another', even if reluctant to reveal their own experiences. The story might help them understand the uncertainties of change more clearly, than when provided only with 'theoretical' explanation.

In fact, the 'case-study' accomplished far more than this. It appeared to bring about a breakthrough, in creating conditions for a genuinely collaborative group, as the change process, or 'metamorphosis', as one person described it, became a legitimate topic of conversation among them. Thus, reflectively, such discussion also accelerated the change process. The narrative apparently provided a 'loan of consciousness' and a language for expressing their concerns, thus creating conditions of intimacy under which support could be obtained. As a member of one of the groups wrote:

> These discussions allowed students to share both the troublesome and successful events experienced at practice schools. Thus we felt we were not alone [in] time of self-doubt ... And we could lift each other's spirits with the humorous and jubilant incidents.

Indeed, cultural change occurred; no longer were people 'silenced'; views were discussed and challenged in a spirit of friendship; 'perspective transformation' (Mezirow, 1991), through reflection, was encouraged; positive attitudes prevailed and new strategies were explored in practice in the schools. A community of practice dedicated to the improvement of teaching had been created.

Unit two: 'Becoming more confident'

Even Group A's culture underwent considerable change, though the unit started inauspiciously, with disruption and negative comments. Deciding to confront this, I explained that negativism not only affected individual learning but also created an unpleasant atmosphere for others. I invited them to assist me in creating a group culture which would foster rather than inhibit learning. Briefly describing what had occurred in Group B, I suggested that we had to work *as* a group rather than just *in* a group. They agreed, and my comments appeared to have inspired the positive people into more active leadership within the group. As one person wrote in his journal:

> I feel that it is up to those with positive attitudes to find out what is bothering others in the group and try to influence their views so that time can be spent more productively during lectures.

In addition, many people had, with experience, begun to recognise the disadvantages of authoritarianism and the usefulness of the constructs of stress and anxiety in understanding and, indeed, changing ways in which they experienced events. Another important influence on group attitudes was a collaborative learning exercise in which small groups were formed, each to research a chosen topic for a presentation to the rest. Thus, collaboration between people of different views began to occur. Positive people emerged as group leaders and, although this produced some sharp interchanges on occasions, they had each begun to listen to one another more carefully than in the past. As one previously rather negative person commented in class about those who had always appreciated the course:

> ... they were more confident and that might have reflected why there was more positive discussion in the second unit - or whatever - and there were more personality clashes with that, and that's probably the positive and the negative coming into battle.

There was polarisation; there was conflict. Yet, in spite of this, communication continued, and reflection and personal renewal appeared to be the norm.

Interestingly, but unfortunately for Group B, supportive group feeling dissipated in the second unit, in response to the external imposition of a grading system and an increased workload. People became individualistic and competitive and only after an intense 'heart to heart', in which people

131

spoke of their difficulties, was a renewed commitment made to work together in a collaborative spirit. Once accomplished, though, the quality of learning and reflection in the group improved considerably. In Group C, on the other hand (and for all other groups taught subsequently), in spite of some conflicts, collaboration and support were reasonably well maintained. As they and I came to understand the importance of managing the change process quite explicitly so, reflexively, the culture of the groups increasingly accommodated and promoted new ideas, while providing support and assistance to participants.

Collaborative management of change

Much has been written about the problematic nature of the concept of 'critical community' and the processes of collaboration and dialogue within action research (for example, Gibson, 1986; Holly, 1987; Ellsworth, 1989). There are no clear conventions for collaboration (Somekh, 1994), only a need for constant vigilance while 'writing' one's own procedures. This story serves to illustrate some of these difficulties in a number of important and interrelated areas, while illuminating potential possibilities for surmounting them.

The question of equality and the use of power within the collaborating group arises, with implications for enabling change that is owned and to which commitment is given by all concerned. A group may use its power to suppress the innovative ideas of individuals and resist change. Alternatively, a major power differential within a group may lead to the imposition of new ideas that are neither fully understood nor accepted by the majority. As Somekh (1994) notes, of teachers and academics working together:

> Collaboration is always fraught with difficulties and complete equality is probably impossible to achieve in any partnership.

For example, early in the life of Group A, positive and reflective voices were suppressed and my own voice dismissed as irrelevant to the world of the majority. Yet, as their lecturer, I had considerable power, illustrating the multiple and often contradictory positioning of people within a group (Ellsworth, 1989). (I take up issues associated with the relationship between a female lecturer and an all-male, adult group in James, 1994.) Lewis (1990) distinguishes between the power to enable democratic conditions to prevail within a group, that is, 'to liberate', and the power to suppress them, that is, 'to subjugate'. Indeed, in Group A's second unit, I *was* able to use power as their lecturer successfully, to mitigate the effects of the negative voices. Yet, this is a process fraught with difficulty and I was well aware of the dangers of intervention appearing alienating and oppressive. As one person commented in his journal, such actions 'could have the consequences of exacerbating the overall group problem'.

I was also concerned about imposing my version of 'truth' upon the groups, based on having a privileged perspective. After all, I alone had access to what they each of them wrote (Miller, 1990, reported a similar dilemma), when it would be more consistent with fully participatory action research if each group member also had access to this information. I was concerned about the situation contributing to a sense of disempowerment. Thus, before teaching Group B (after my experience with Group A), I wrote in my journal:

> The resistance to open self-disclosure in the group/the pressures put upon people in the sub-groups is a constraint under which this research and the people seem destined to labour.

I noted my preference for the voluntary exchange of feedback sheets and assignments, as people became increasingly open and trusting of each other. However, I recognised that this process could not be imposed because it: 'would be too threatening and reduce openness, or produce a new breed of data: those designed to impress or entertain the group'. In the event, I was unduly pessimistic, as all groups, eventually, did become open and supportive. Group members also discussed my construction of events very honestly during member-checking and (except for Group A in unit one) throughout the course. However, lack of understanding of each other's position was an initial constraint in the processes of collaboration, while ever a stance of 'toughness' and bravado was sustained.

Somekh also described (1994) the two 'castles' of the school and the academic, arguing that differences should be 'celebrated' and each identity strengthened while, at the same time, developing knowledge of the other so that movement between them is 'pleasurable, challenging and mutually empowering'. However, she comments (Somekh, 1994) that:

> True collaboration is only possible if there is an *intention* and *belief* that both partners will make an equal but different contribution to the action research process, and each will change as a result of the collaboration.

Yet, this presupposes mutual respect for each other's position and willingness to reflect on oneself. In my study, the clash of values with Group A appeared irreconcilable. The identity of technology teachers, as constituted, precluded movement towards the insights of academia and, while empathising with their situation, there was a limit to which I could accept, uncritically, certain culturally-derived values and practices. Change was required *before* collaboration was possible.

Waters-Adams (1994) describes the many forces working against collaboration among teachers in educational institutions: group hierarchies, mistrust, insecurity, defensiveness in facing problematic aspects of practice and different value systems. He highlights the intensely personal nature of reflexive action and the, at least, short-term demoralisation that may accompany group reflection. Strauss (1995) argues that support through such processes is essential and, in describing critical pedagogy, Lather (1989) also affirms the importance of making explicit for her students the likely emotional responses of anger and hopelessness experienced, to prepare them when confronted by new ideas and values. However, she acknowledges that for some people change may be too painful. In addition, Johnston (1994) suggests that narrative enquiry in which people explore each others' stories, and which emphasises 'connectedness', may be a more appropriate approach than group critique for encouraging an examination and understanding of practice. Similarly, Winter (1994), drawing on the back of Belenky et al (1986) notes the importance for women (and most probably for working class men) or engaging in a 'form of understanding derived from empathy that arises from collaborative conversation, rather than from the "judicious" imposition of abstract categories'. Rather than theoretical explanation, a story of experience can not only provide understanding of one's circumstances, but bring people together into a collaborative and open relationship.

Indeed, it appeared that the discussion of the narrative case-study, used with Group B and other groups subsequently, did provide the necessary conditions for 'connection', intimacy and support. The process reduced stress by demonstrating that 'everyone is in the same boat' and made critical reflection and change far less threatening and demoralising. Non-judgemental attitudes towards people prevailed, even though views and reported practices might be challenged and critiqued, and the balance of power was maintained within the group, through mutual self-disclosure, including mine. Thus, once conditions for genuine collaboration were established, the course and research could both proceed successfully and minor differences of opinion be addressed constructively. Miller (1990) suggests that the struggle to reach towards the ideal of a 'critical community' seems an important part of the reflection-action process itself, with the potential for considerable learning for everyone involved. Ellsworth (1989) recommends highlighting power relations within a group to assist in this process, a strategy I also occasionally employed. However, the major insight emerging from *this* study concerns the potential contribution of culturally-specific narrative, for enabling conditions for collaboration to be realised within these groups. In other contexts, different ways of providing such conditions may need to be investigated.

It also became apparent that collaboration was not only essential for the effective conduct of research and for the management of the changes that occurred, but also, as the work of Lave and Wenger (1991) and Vygotsky (1978) would suggest, for providing a powerful source of learning. Through collaboration, learning occurred about the processes of working with and understanding others, communicating and resolving conflict, providing and receiving support and developing self-insight. The research and course itself became intimately intertwined. As one person reflected on his learning: 'I also learnt about the group, which is the course. We evolved together', cultural and individual transformation occurring simultaneously.

Conclusion

It appears from this study (and the accompanying literature) that genuine educational change is likely to involve perspective transformation for individuals and cultural change for communities and groups. However, such changes may be highly threatening and anxiety-provoking, potentially leading to stress, conflict, negativism and resistance to the changes envisaged. Cultures are constantly being produced or reproduced (Willis, 1981). Yet, it may still be necessary to focus such changes in ways that lead to the productive learning of new skills, practices and discourses, requiring significant modification of beliefs, values and attitudes. It is argued in this paper that collaborative processes, if informed by critical values (Zeichner, 1993, 1994), are most likely to ensure that such change occurs along productive lines. Although problematic at times, genuine collaboration has the potential for addressing many of the above difficulties. Thus, the effective management of change requires that:

* the processes of and emotions often evoked by change are made explicit to all concerned, so that people feel empowered to take charge of events themselves and, reflexively, enhance further productive change;
* support through the processes is provided in some way; in this study, this was particularly problematic because of the 'macho' culture of course participants; nevertheless, once open discussion was facilitated through narrative, the problem became less salient, as the 'tough' and anti-academic stance was abandoned;
* conditions for open reflection on beliefs, values and practices are created, so that defensiveness is reduced and threat diminished; in this study, one support was provided with recognition of common difficulties, reflection could be engaged; through affirmation and challenge, people could then feel empowered to explore new approaches;
* people are given equal 'voice' within a democratic community of practice; in this study this was particularly problematic, in that certain powerful members of Group A would silence others; my privileged position as their lecturer also had the potential to suppress; these problems became less important once an open and reflective culture was established; I could then be a mentor, working in partnership with them, in constructing knowledge relevant to their classrooms, based on illustrative stories and theoretical insight;
* avenues for the resolution of conflict are provided; differences can be accommodated and even 'celebrated' as long as group members share certain common goals and values; in this study, problem-solving over research and course issues occurred frequently within a collaborative framework; and
* the opportunity for people to participate actively in learning new and unfamiliar material is provided; in this study, there were times when people learned how to resist (Lave and Wenger, 1991), rather than acquiring relevant knowledge; however, once cultural change occurred, this problem diminished considerably.

Thus, collaborative action research can provide a powerful methodology for engaging people in promoting and managing educational change in directions appropriate to their institutions. As Winter (1994) notes, it is possible through collaborative action research to reconcile:

> ... the intensity of subjective experience and commitment with the power of objective analysis, a power which always threatens to be external and oppressive but which *can* be 'harnessed' and assimilated.

Through such processes, insights may be acquired, improvements made and changes managed in educational institutions, in the best interests of the people they serve.

References

Belenky, M.F. et al (1986) *Women's Ways of Knowing. The Development of Self, Voice and Mind*, New York: Basic Books.

Beyer, L.E. and Zeichner, K. (1987) 'Teacher Education in Cultural Context: Beyond Reproduction', in Popkewitz, T.S. (ed.), *Critical Studies in Teacher Education. Its Folklore, Theory and Practice*, Philadelphia: The Falmer Press.

Breakwell, G. (1986) *Coping with Threatened Identities*, London: Methuen.

Bruner, J.S. (1986) *Actual Minds. Possible Worlds*, Cambridge: Harvard University Press.

Carmichael, L. (1992) *Australian Vocational Training Certificate System*, report of the Employment and Skills Foundation Council, Canberra: NBEET.

Crawford, K. (1995) 'What do Vygotskian Approaches to Psychology Have to Offer Action Research?', *Educational Action Research*, 3(2), pp.239-247.

Diamond, P.C.T. (1991) *Teacher Education as Transformation. A Psychological Perspective*, Philadelphia: Open University Press.

Diamond, P.C.T. (1992) 'Accounting for Our Accounts: Autoethnographic Approaches to Teacher Voice and Vision', *Curriculum Inquiry*, 22(1), pp.67-81.

Elliot, J. (1991) *Action Research for Educational Change*, Philadelphia: Open University Press.

Ellsworth, E. (1989) 'Why Doesn't It Feel Empowering? Working Through the Repressive Myths of Critical Pedagogy', *Harvard Educational Review*, 59(3), pp.297-324.

Ewert, G.D. (1991) 'Habermas and Education: A Comprehensive Overview of the Influence of Habermas in Educational Literature', *Review of Educational Research*, 61(3), pp.345-378.

Francis, D. (1993) 'Not the National Curriculum', *EQ Australia*, 1, pp.4-7.

Fullan, M.G. (1991) *The New Meaning of Educational Change*, (2nd ed.), New York: Teachers College Press.

Gibson, R. (1986) *Critical Theory and Education*, London: Hodder and Stoughton.

Gleeson, P. (1994) 'Cultural Differences in Teachers' Work: An Ethnography', *South Pacific Journal of Teacher Education*, 22(1), pp.5-18.

Hawthorn Institute (1987) Submission for Reaccreditation: Diploma of Teaching (Technology), Melbourne: Hawthorn Institute of Education.

Heron, J. (1990) 'Communication', *Collaborative Inquiry Newsletter*, 1, pp.3-4.

Hollingsworth, S. (1994) 'Feminist Pedagogy in the Action Research Class: An Example of Teacher Research', *Educational Action Research*, 2(1), pp.49-70.

Holly, P. (1987) 'Action Research: Cul-de-sac or Turnpike?' *Peabody Journal of Education*, 64(3), pp.71-100.

James, P. (1994) 'Reconstructing Masculinity in Teacher Education: A Story of Cultural Change', in Cooper, M. (ed.), *Voicing our Agendas: Gender and Teacher Education Conference Papers - Ubud, Bali*, Melbourne: University of Melbourne.

James, P. (1995) 'Models of Vocational Development Revisited: Reflecting on Concerns', *The Vocational Aspect of Education*, 47(3), pp.289-308.

James, P. (1996) 'Learning to Reflect: A Story of Empowerment', *Teaching and Teacher Education*, 12(1).

Johnston, S. 91994) 'Is Action Research a "Natural" Process for Teachers?', *Educational Action Research*, 2(1), pp.39-48.

Karpin, D.S. (1995) *Enterprising Nation. Renewing Australia's Managers to Meet the Challenges of the Asia-Pacific Century*, report of the Industry Task Force on Leadership and Management Skills, Canberra: Australian Government Publishing Services.

Kemmis, S. and McTaggart, R. (1982) *The Action Research Planner*, Victoria: Deakin University Press.

Kemmis, S. and McTaggart, R. (1988) (eds.), *The Action Research Planner*, 3rd ed, Victoria: Deakin University Press.

Lather, P. (1989) 'Staying Dumb? Student Resistance to Liberatory Curriculum', paper presented at the Annual Conference of the New Zealand Association for Research in Education, Wellington.

Lave, J. and Wenger, E. (1991) *Situated Learning: Legitimate Peripheral Participation*, New York: Cambridge University Press.

Lewis, M. (1990) 'Interrupting Patriarchy: Politics, Resistance and Transformation in the Feminist Classroom', *Harvard Educational Review*, 60(4), pp.467-488.

Lomax, P. (ed) (1991) *Managing Better Schools and Colleges. An Action Research Way*, Bera Dialogues 5, Clevedon: Multilingual Matters.

Louis, K. and Miles, M.B. (1990) *Improving the Urban High School: What Works and Why*, New York: Teachers College Press.

Lovat, T.L. and Smith, D.L. (1995) *Curriculum: Action on Reflection Revisited*, (3rd ed.), Wentworth Falls: Social Science Press.

Marginson, S. (1992) 'Educating After Finn: Shifting the Emphasis', *Independent Education*, 22, pp.4-8.

McNiff, J. (1993) *Teaching as Learning: An Action Research Approach*, London: Routledge.

McTaggart, R. (1989) 'Principles For Participatory Action Research', paper presented to the Third World Encounter on Participatory Research, Managua, Nicaragua.

Mealyea, R.J. (1989) 'Humour as a Coping Strategy in the Transition from Tradesperson to Teacher', *British Journal of Sociology of Education*, 10(3), pp.311-333.

Mezirow, J. (1991) *Transformative Dimensions of Adult Learning*, San Francisco: Jossey-Bass.

Miller, J.L. (1990) *Creating Spaces and Finding Voices: Teachers Collaborating for Empowerment*, Albany: State University of New York Press.

Ministry of Education (Schools Division) Victoria (1988) *The Technology Studies Framework: P-12*, Melbourne: Melbourne Publishing Services, Statewide School Support and Production Centre.

Powell, J.P. (1985) 'Autobiographical Learning', in Boud, D. et al (eds.), *Reflection: Turning Experience into Learning*, London: Nichols Publishing, Kogan Page.

Rappaport, J. (1986) 'Collaborating for Empowerment: Creating the Language of Mutual Help', in Boyte, H. and Reissman, F. (eds.), *The New Populism: The Politics of Empowerment*, Philadelphia: Temple University Press.

Rechter, H. (1994) 'Trespassing on Male Territory', *EQ Australia*, 4, pp.31-33.

Reid, K. et al (1989) 'Beyond the Sabre-toothed Curriculum?', in Preedy, M. *Approaches to Curriculum Management*, Milton Keynes: Open University Press.

Sanger, J. (1995) 'Making Action Research Mainstream: A Post-modern Perspective on Appraisal', *Educational Action Research*, 3(1), pp.93-104.

Shuttleworth, S. et al (1994), 'Collaborative Research for Social Change: Shared Learning between Workers and Academics', Hull: University of Hull, Centre for Continuing Development and Training.

Smyth, W.J. (1991) *Teachers as Collaborative Learners. Challenging Dominant Forms of Supervision*, Philadelphia: Open University Press.

Somekh, B. (1994) 'Inhabiting Each Other's Castles: Towards Knowledge and Mutual Growth Through Collaboration', *Educational Action Research*, 2(3), pp.357-381.

Strauss, P. (1995) 'No Easy Answers: The Dilemma And Challenges of Teacher Research', *Educational Action Research*, 3(1), pp.29-40.

Sweet, R. (1994) 'Writing to Learn', *EQ Australia*, 1, pp.44-46.

Symes, C. (1995) 'A Post-Fordist Reworking of Australian Education: The Finn, Mayer and Carmichael Reports in the Context of Labour Reprocessing', *The Vocational Aspect of Education*, 47(3), pp.247-271.

Vygotsky, L.S. (1978) *Mind in Society: The Development of Higher Psychological Processes*, in Cole, M. et al (eds.), Cambridge: Harvard University Press.

Waters-Adams, S. (1994) 'Collaboration and Action Research: A Cautionary Tale', *Educational Action Research*, 2(2), pp.195-210.

Willis, P. (1981) 'Cultural Production is Different from Cultural Reproduction is Different from Social Reproduction is Different from Reproduction', *Interchange*, 12(2-3), pp.48-67.

Winter, R. (1994) 'The Relevance for Action Research of Feminist Theories of Educational Development', *Educational Action Research*, 2(3), pp.423-426.

Zeichner, K.M. (1993) 'Connecting Genuine Teacher Development to the Struggle for Social Justice', *Journal of Education for Teaching*, 19(1), pp.5-20.

Zeichner, K.M. (1994) 'Personal Relevance and Social Reconstruction through Teacher Research', in Hollingsworth, M.S. and Sockett, H. (eds.), *Teacher Research and Educational Reform*, Chicago: Ninety-third Yearbook of NSSE.

Zeichner, K.M. and Liston, D.P. (1987) 'Teaching Student Teachers to Reflect', *Harvard Educational Review*, 57(1), pp.23-48.

Zuber-Skerritt, O. (1992) *Professional Development in Higher Education. A Theoretical Framework for Action Research*, London: Kogan Page.

8 The application of Total Quality Management to a college of further education

Jennifer A. Earnshaw

Abstract

The implementation of a Total Quality Management system has been introduced as a strategic objective by the management of many educational establishments seeking to implement the corporate transformation required to meet the needs of incorporation within the limits of funding.

Although the concepts and principles of Total Quality are in general readily applicable to an educational environment, the notion and definition of the product and identity of the customer are complex.

This chapter seeks to explore the application of an appropriate model to create, through a team approach, a structured framework for planning and implementing continuous improvement.

Introduction

The Further and Higher Education Act of 1992 established colleges as independent corporations. This resulted in a fundamental re-organisation and re-appraisal of the role, purpose and financial structure of colleges. The organisational norms are now being challenged and the process is one of organisational re-engineering rather than evolution.

Colleges are business entities and the provision of a quality product is recognised as being essential to success. The management teams of many educational establishments, guided by Department of Education directives, have accordingly examined best practice in organisational development in industry and commerce, with a view to applying a business model to education. Currently world leading companies have developed and adopted Total Quality Management as fundamental to their business policy, strategy and culture and the market domination of Japanese companies has given credibility to the success of Total Quality Management as the driving force behind corporate transformation.

Total Quality means many things to many people and this arises from the variety of directions from which it has developed. As Total Quality Management is not a single body of knowledge, there are many different interpretations and definitions of what it encompasses and the strategies which underpin the concept. The elements of Total Quality management can be defined as follows.

'**TOTAL**' means that everyone in the organisation is involved in the final product or service to the customer and that every work process or activity contributes to the success of the whole. 'Total' in this context acknowledges that the organisation operates in an environment, which, in the case of a college, is the community at large. Recognition of its role and impact on the community must, therefore, be an important strategic consideration.

'**QUALITY**' in TQM requires a common objective meaning that can be understood by all (Deming, 1992). If quality is to be managed, it must be measurable. The commonly used definitions of 'excellence' and 'best' are too subjective for measurement. A number of definitions for quality have been developed to meet the measurement criteria e.g. '**fitness for purpose**' (Juran, 1979) and '**conformance to requirements**' (Crosby, 1984). These definitions have the advantage of simplicity and provide a measurable base. However, they tend to focus on the elimination of error, which is not sufficient to maintain a competitive advantage in a dynamic marketplace. BS 4778, 1987 (USO 8402, 1986) Quality vocabulary: Part 1 International Terms, defines quality as:

> the totality of features and characteristics of a product or service that bear on its ability to satisfy states or implied needs.

Feigenbaum devised the following definition:

the total composite product and service characteristics of marketing, engineering, manufacture and maintenance through which the product and service in use will meet the expectation by the customer. (Feigenbaum, 1983)

Another definition is:

delighting the customer by continuously meeting and improving upon agreed requirements. (Macdonald, 1993)

Quality is essentially **meeting the requirements** (Oakland, 1991). It is evident, however, that in both the BS 4778 and Feigenbaum definitions, the words 'implied' and 'expectations' suggest that the concept of quality is dynamic and an organisation must be capable of meeting requirements now and in the future. Research and innovation are, therefore, essential to both stimulate and satisfy the latent expectations of customers. It must be acknowledged, however, that in education it may be difficult to identify the wants and needs of customers as the customer does not always have a clear vision of the long-term goal at the initial point of purchase. This places significant responsibility on the supplier to ensure as far as possible that the customer is provided with comprehensive information and guidance at the outset and also the opportunity to review the position at a later stage.

Deming states that quality should be aimed at the needs of the consumer, present and future, and it begins with intent, which is fixed by management. The intent is translated by functional management teams into plans, specifications and delivery of products (Deming, 1992). Thus a 'quality' organisation will have a clear mission statement and well defined strategic objectives, together with financial, marketing and operational plans embodied in an effective planning process. It is fundamental that the concept of Total Quality Management is the means by which the corporate planning process is developed and is therefore built into the organisation's ethos, and not merely bolted on at a later stage or at a lower level. Dr Joseph M. Juran, an American quality expert invited to construct the post-war regeneration of Japanese industry with Dr W. Edwards Deming, stated that quality does not happen by accident - it must be planned and is part of a quality trilogy of quality planning, quality control and quality improvement (Juran, 1974).

In education, in order to meet the present and future needs of customers, it is necessary to continually develop the curriculum, based on sound and regular market research. Hence within the marketing plan, a clear product specification must be established, from which initial resource planning can be derived. There are, however, two key TQM issues which present particular problems in this regard, i.e. who is the customer and what is the product?

On first consideration, the customer could be assumed to be the student. However, learning programmes must also fulfil the requirements of Funding Councils, examining bodies, professional institutes, the government, the community and employers, as each of these entities has a stake in the provision and outcome of the learning experience. These stakeholders have an investment in education and ultimately a right of expectation in relation to the results of the learning experience. The customer must, therefore, be considered as multifaceted. When contrasted with industry, this makes issues arising within the corporate planning process much more difficult.

It doesn't get easier! The definition of the product is also complex. As quality systems have developed within a manufacturing environment, their application to education requires interpretation and modification. Whilst it is easy to define and measure quality in physical products, this process is much more difficult in the context of education.

A valuable contribution arose from work undertaken within a jointly funded project (The Association of British Certification Bodies, The British Quality Foundation and the National Accreditation Council for Certification Bodies). Guidelines are provided which interpret the ISO 9000 International Quality Standard, extensively used in manufacturing industry, for application in further education. These guidelines define the product as follows:

> **the learning opportunity** which takes into account all processes, materials, skills and professional expertise required to develop and deliver a course or programme which will give 'value added' to a learner. Curriculum courses, programmes, services, materials and purchased products, all contribute to the overall learning opportunity ...

It is **the learning opportunity** (the product), therefore, which must **meet the requirements**, i.e. the definition of quality. It is also evident that the product is a composite of intangible and tangible elements e.g. the curriculum and the resources.

Some aspects of the multifaceted customer are explained within the guidelines by separately defining three elements of the customer as follows:

> LEARNER - the individual recipient of the education or training service e.g. student, trainee.

PURCHASER - The organisation that funds an education or training programme or funds learners to attend such programmes, e.g. FEFC, TEC, LEC, employer.

AWARDING - External validation body for particular programmes of study or training e.g. BTEC, RSA.

The guidelines are not intended to be prescriptive as the international standard itself cannot prescribe for professionalism, imagination or initiative, but can enhance these attributes by providing the means for them to flourish, underpinned by sound management practice. This is supported by eminent American quality practitioners eg. Myron Tribus, who states that 'the people work *in* a system. The job of the manager is to work *on* the system, to improve it, continuously, with their help' (Tribus undated).

The curriculum (the product) should be determined by customer need and its specification may be externally set or internally designed. Whilst curriculum design is becoming increasingly flexible to meet the needs of customers, there is a potential conflict between what the customer requires and the criteria acceptable to a validating body. A college must therefore ensure 'best fit' between customer needs and validating body requirements. As with most products, this represents a compromise, as the specific needs of every customer cannot be met by mass production in manufacturing, or group delivery of course content in an educational establishment.

The measurement of quality must relate to the degree of variation from the customer specification. In an educational context, the customer specification is established at a number of key points e.g. on validation by an accreditation body, on enrolment by the student, on meeting Funding Council criteria. If, therefore, the curriculum is correctly designed to meet customer needs and the associated resources match the specification, then the measure of quality is the consistency of delivery against specification. Hence it is necessary to measure the customer's perception of the courses delivered, the physical resources which support the curriculum, and the overall college environment.

As previously mentioned, TQM processes have their roots in manufacturing industry and care must accordingly be taken in directly translating production strategies for application in a service environment. It must be understood that in a marketing context, no physical product exists. Service organisations, such as educational establishments, are selling a 'promise'. Customer perception of the product and the organisation is therefore very important, e.g. a customer may choose an airline on the basis of in-flight service, whereas the ability of the pilot and the organisation's safety record would seem to be more valid measures. Customer perception is often based on seemingly superficial measures because it is easy to evaluate physical characteristics, e.g. catering, seating etc. whilst the assessment of the ability of the pilot and the airline's safety record cannot easily be made. In education, the physical surroundings and resources of the college present an image which is important initially in creating the right perception. However, a high quality perception can only be sustained in the long term, by delivering the promise i.e. a successful learning experience. To provide a successful learning experience, the organisation must create and maintain the requisite conditions and, to this end, educationalists can draw from the experience of successful manufacturing industries in the implementation and operation of a Total Quality model.

Excellence in education can only be achieved within the context of a successful business. It is therefore appropriate to embrace a Total Quality model which encompasses all business processes whilst recognising that the environment is dynamic and rapidly changing. The means by which TQ principles are adopted must be sufficiently flexible to cope with the diverse change process.

Comparison between a quality institution and an ordinary institution highlights the transition required in terms of quality and culture, and suggests that a quality organisation is customer, rather than internally, focussed; quality is built into the process and not 'bolted on' as a troublesome initiative. Quality is a planned long term process and is aimed at improving customer satisfaction and not seen simply as a means to cut costs (Sallis, 1993).

Traditional institutions are generally characterised by departmental barriers, lack of common mission, overbearing hierarchies and an over-reliance on rigid procedures (Porter, 1993). An appropriate Total Quality model will address these aspects.

Selection of an appropriate Total Quality model

As Total Quality Management varies tremendously in its application, there are many models. Benchmarking against other organisations is useful in gaining the necessary knowledge and experience of the concepts underpinning a Total Quality approach. However, each organisation must overlay its particular requirements to ensure that the process fits with its products, market conditions and customer needs.

The Total Quality 'gurus', whilst differing in emphasis, all tend to agree on the main drivers within a Total Quality model, e.g. customer focus, commitment from the top, involvement, teamwork, continuous improvement and measurement. Organisations generally draw from a number of different approaches and the use of a quality framework is prevalent.

The structure of quality frameworks has been influenced by an increase in quality certification, e.g. AQAP, Ford Q1, BS 5750, together with annual awards given to companies for outstanding achievement and public awards, eg. the Deming Prize, the BQA Award, the Baldrige Award and the European Quality Award. Generally awards are based on the successful implementation of a specified quality model.

Within the UK, a British Standard Guide to Total Quality Management, BS 7850, has been established, which provides advice and direction on the approach and methodology for the operation of TQM. Although this standard is not designed to be prescriptive, it lists the following investments as being central to the implementation of TQM - **investment in time and people, time to train people, time to implement new concepts, time for people to recognise the benefits and time for people to move forward into new and different company cultures**.

Perhaps the most widely recognised international model is based on the Deming Prize, which is restricted to Japanese companies, with Toshiba, Toyota and Komatsu as past winners. The model is based on the following criteria: company policy and objectives; organisation structure, including co-operation between divisions and utilisation of quality circles; education, including education in quality control; the education of sub contractors; education in process control; the use of information, including statistical information, analysis of statistics and results; standardisation; control systems, including the contribution of quality circles; quality assurance including new product development, safety procedures, measurement and inspection; quality audits; the effects of quality improvement, including the environmental impact, delivery dates, serviceability, profit, safety; and the future plans of the company, including long range plans.

As is apparent from this list, Deming's approach is statistically oriented and is criticised by some as being excessively rigid. Deming has advocated a checklist of points for management in his endeavour to transform Western management styles. His 14 points of management advocate that business should have a clear purpose which is consistently pursued to improve products and services Within Deming's 14 points 'out of crisis', there is a strong theme which places responsibility on management to train and develop employees, to break down barriers and drive out fear. (Deming, 1982)

Superficially, a number of Deming's points appear controversial. However, it is essential to read Deming's explanation. For example, Deming states that 'internal goals set in the management of a company, without a method, are a burlesque' (Deming, 1982). Thus the inference is that whilst all companies will set numerical goals, they must be associated with a clearly defined method for achievement; otherwise they are pointless.

Deming's constancy of purpose is based on a common aim and he attributes the success of the Japanese from 1950 onwards, to the fact that they adopted 'the chain reaction' principle. This emphasises the idea that improved quality eventually leads to greater productivity and an expanding business.

The Baldrige Award is based on similar criteria and was established by the US Congress in 1987 as a competitive response to the successful Japanese Deming approach. It is designed to promote the following:

(a) an awareness of quality;
(b) understanding of the requirements of quality;
(c) sharing of information on successful strategies; and
(d) the benefits derived during implementation.

The Baldrige and Deming modes both stress the non-procedural aspects of quality such as leadership, human resource management, motivation and morale, and customer satisfaction, and can be contrasted with the prescriptive approach of BS 5750 and ISO 9000, which are based entirely on procedures.

In recognition of the market dominance of the Japanese and the absence of a structured approach to TQM in Europe, the European Commission in 1988 established the European Foundation for Quality Management (EFQM). The European model was developed by the EFQM, which now has a membership of over 280 leading European businesses.

This model draws from established practices worldwide and has a sound conceptual base. It is divided into two parts - Enablers and Results, which are then subdivided into nine sections. The first part 'Enablers' is subdivided into five criteria, i.e. Leadership; Policy and Strategy; People Management; Resources and Processes. The second part 'Results' is subdivided into four criteria, i.e. People Satisfaction; Customer Satisfaction; Impact on Society; and Business Results.

The model demonstrates that Customer Satisfaction, Employee Satisfaction and Impact on Society are achieved through Leadership, driving Policy and Strategy, People Management, Resources and Processes, leading ultimately to excellence in Business Results. Each of the nine elements is a criterion that can be used to appraise the organisation's progress towards Quality Management. Processes are the means by which the organisation harnesses and releases the talents of its employees to produce results.

The score for each part of the Enablers criteria is based on the combination of two factors, ie. the degree of excellence of the **approach** and the degree of **deployment** of the approach. The assessment is, therefore, based on whether there is a methodology for achieving the stated criterion and to what extent this has been adopted within the organisation e.g. in an educational context, one criterion would be a qualitative assessment of the staff development plan and an evaluation of its deployment both departmentally and on a college-wide basis.

Similarly, the score for each part of the Results criteria is based on the combination of the degree of excellence of the **results** and the **scope** of the results. An educational example would be an assessment of how well the college has performed against target on recruitment, retention and outcome, applied in all relevant areas and facets of the organisation. Assessment of Results is graded from 'anecdotal', meaning that there is no systematic recorded evidence of results, to 'strong positive trends in all areas over at least a five year period and an excellent comparison with internal targets and competitors'. To be rated at the highest level, the college would expect to be 'best in class' in many areas of its operation.

The scope of the results would range from 'a positive result in a few relevant areas' at the lowest level, to 'results address all relevant areas and facets of the organisation' at the highest level.

The underlying principle is that in order to achieve results, the business must first establish enabling practices which drive the business forward to create a systematic process of quality improvement. If the enablers are working effectively, then the outcomes, i.e. business results should be achieved. Investors in People, for example, could be an enabler within the People Management subsection of the model, to achieve the result of People Satisfaction. It is assumed within the model that financial Business Results cannot be sustained in the long term without People Satisfaction, Customer Satisfaction and a positive Impact on Society. The heaviest weighting within the model is given to Customer Satisfaction and this must be taken as a clear signal that neglect of the views of customers in the provision of a product or service, will have negative effects on the market position of the organisation and its future business viability.

Traditional Western management practice has been to try to achieve success by emphasis primarily on the Business Results component of the model. This tends to focus attention on meeting short term targets and the negative effects of failure to achieve, rather than creating a long term culture change, empowering and motivating staff to continuously improve.

The EFQM model is designed to be used for the operation of Total Quality Management in a European organisation, where measurement of progress is achieved by self-assessment. It is also the basis on which application for the European Quality Award is made. Criteria for the Award are designed to provide a model of excellence for companies, regardless of size and type of business, and in recent years, Rank Xerox, Millikens and D2D (ICL) have been winners. The EFQM model specifically acknowledges that educational establishments can compete for the quality award, whilst Baldrige, for example, specifically excludes this category.

The application of a Total Quality model to a college environment

As the EFQM model is designed for a European context, acknowledges educational establishments within its design and is based on best practice, it would therefore seem to be currently the most appropriate model for application to a UK college environment. It is intended to be used as a self-assessment model and this process creates the essential involvement and commitment to the progression of the TQ programme.

The process of self-assessment offers a flexible approach to measurement as it allows internal appraisal of the organisation by the management and staff. Improving an organisation's effectiveness, efficiency, motivation and responsiveness can only be achieved by the active involvement of people in process improvement activities. Self-assessment involves employees in the regular and systematic review of their processes and results, thus enabling the organisation to identify its strengths and improvement opportunities.

Self-assessment can be carried out in the form of a matrix which lists the criteria, giving narrative descriptors and a scoring mechanism, from which progress can be monitored.

A matrix offers a management tool which can be used to monitor progress towards business improvement in a quick and simple way, without the use of external experts or consultants. It can provide a complete step by step framework to guide managers in the formulation of an action plan for the implementation of continuous improvement within the business unit and subsequently can help to highlight any gaps in the planning or implementation processes. The scoring mechanism can be used to monitor continuous improvement over a period of time and to monitor inter-departmental progress. However, it is important that the scoring system should not be used to create competition, as it is generally viewed that this results in reluctance to share ideas, processes and resources, and hence destroys teamwork.

Many organisations have developed their own matrix based on the EFQM criteria and by benchmarking with quality organisations who are currently using a business improvement matrix e.g. Excellence North West, support and assistance will undoubtedly be available. The EFQM criteria encourage organisations to network and Total Quality companies are most willing to share experiences.

After completion of the initial self-assessment exercise, the next stage is the formulation of an action plan to progress from the benchmark assessment to incremental improvement. This action plan is the basis for continuous improvement towards a total quality culture. Self-assessment is repeated on a regular basis to review progress and realign plans.

The Deming chain reaction describes how ultimately improvement in quality is the driving force behind business growth and also demonstrates the reason why individuals should be committed to the process. It is also possible to envisage a similar chain reaction in education, highlighting the essential elements of the planning cycle and market development which provide the funding for growth and investment. It is clear that within such a cycle, success can only be achieved by a good fit between the market needs, and the curriculum and resource provision. Thus, the wrong curriculum will either not attract students, or attract the wrong students and disappoint them at the outcome stage. Similarly, over-provision of resources will waste vital investment and under-provision will result in inadequate support to the curriculum and a poor image to the customer.

It is fundamental in this cycle that customer satisfaction is monitored on a regular basis. Thus the use of customer feedback processes, such as Student Perception of Course (SPOC) forms, Employer Perception of Course (EPOC) forms, External Verifier Reports and FEFC Inspection Reports, are key business monitors and can be used as evidence for measurement of the TQ process. In the EFQM model self assessment process, such indicators

151

would provide evidence to measure the Customer Satisfaction criterion within the 'Results' section of the model.

As delivery of the curriculum and the availability of appropriate resources are key components within the chain reaction, it is necessary to establish a process to monitor People Satisfaction. Most Total Quality organisations carry out regular Employee Opinion Surveys and use the feedback to inform their staff and resource development plans. It is important to understand the distinction between a manufacturing organisation and the delivery of a professional service. Whilst morale is undoubtedly important in both organisations, in manufacturing, the customer is unlikely to meet the producer of the product. However, in education, the product and the producer are intrinsically linked, and the morale, motivation and commitment of the lecturer, transmits immediately to the student (customer) and impacts significantly on the perception of the quality of the product.

As quality is **'meeting the requirements of the customer - now and in the future'**, the education chain reaction, if rigorously followed, ensures that Total Quality is at the centre of the planning process.

Summary

The pursuit of Total Quality can only be a long term strategic objective. It must also be recognised that most organisations setting out on the Total Quality journey do not reach their destination, but fall by the wayside - perhaps due to lack of commitment, resources, and/or lack of real desire to effect a culture change. Research suggests that there is no 'quick fix' and organisations that embarked on Total Quality Management three - five years ago, still believe that they are at the early stages of implementation, even though they may have made significant changes and improvements.

It is generally acknowledged that the impact of change to a Total Quality philosophy is greatest on management. As Total Quality is characterised by empowerment, teamwork, equality of status and open communication, it tends to challenge a traditional hierarchical structure and breaks down formal barriers between 'the management' and 'the workers'. Managers must be prepared to accept that authority to act should be vested as low down the organisation as is appropriate. Failure, within a committed workforce, should be seen as an opportunity for improvement, rather than disciplinary action.

TQ is no soft option, as an open and participative style of management creates continuous challenge from the staff in their quest to remove barriers and obstacles to progress. Many managers may find this a new and uncomfortable experience! However, the benefits of co-operation rather than conflict can release a tremendous reservoir of discretionary effort, hitherto untapped, within an organisation. The rewards are always high but perhaps even more significant in an environment where the product is totally dependent on the extent to which the lecturer is self fulfilled and his talents are fully exploited.

References

Crosby, P.B. (1984) *Quality with Tears.* New York: McGraw Hill.

Deming, W.E. (1982) Out of the Crisis, Cambridge: Mass, USA, MIT Center for Advanced Engineering Study.

Deming, W.E. (1992) *Out of the Crisis* (18th ed.). Cambridge: Mass, USA, MIT Centre for Advanced Engineering Study.

European Quality Award (1994) *Application Brochure.* Brussels: European Foundation for Quality Management.

Feigenbaum, A.V. (1983) *Total Quality Control* (3rd ed.). New York: McGraw Hill.

Juran, J.M. (1974) *Quality Control Handbook.* New York: McGraw Hill.

Macdonald, J. (1993) *TQM - Does it always work?* Letchworth: Technical Communications Publishing Ltd.

Oakland, J. (1993) *Total Quality Management.* Oxford: Butterworth-Heinemann Ltd.

Porter, L. (1993) *TQM Self-Assessment - A Discussion Paper.* Bradford: University Management Centre.

Sallis, E. (1993) *Total Quality Management in Education.* London: Kogan Page.

Tribus Myron and Yoshikazu Tsuda (undated) *Creating the Quality Company.* Massachusetts, USA: Institute of Technology, Centre for Advanced Engineering Study.

9 Mismanagement of planned educational change: lessons to be learnt from the merger of two further education colleges

Geoffrey Elliott

Abstract

This chapter sets out to examine issues arising from a merger of two further education (FE) colleges. It is argued first, that senior management of the merged colleges failed to present a vision which could win the commitment of staff in the colleges to the new institution; and second, that insufficient attention was paid by senior managers to developing a shared college culture; and third that inflexible planning led to unintended consequences and implementation failure with respect to policies and procedures. These failures are explored within a conceptual framework drawn from the management of change literature. Visioning, culture-building and flexible planning are the key elements of this framework.

Introduction

The paper is written from the point of view of an observer-participant in an art college which merged with a college of technology (the 'tech'), to form a new college of arts and technology during the summer of 1992. The merger was planned by both institutions as a response to the changing circumstances in which FE colleges found themselves in the period leading up to incorporation.

There have been operational difficulties for both former colleges following the merger, and these difficulties continue to be regarded as problematic by many staff - not least in light of the fact that senior managers regarded the merger as an opportunity for rationalisation and resource redistribution. It is argued here that the events surrounding and following the merger event can usefully be conceptualised as attempts to initiate and implement major planned change, and that therefore analytical themes drawn from the management of change literature are helpful in identifying management failure. Some lessons to be learned for mergers of educational institutions can be drawn from this chapter.

Background to the colleges

The art college was a small specialist college with some 800 full-time equivalent students. The college was established in the 1890s, and has always had a sound local reputation for its vocational art and design courses, from which most students would progress to art school or other HE institutions. There was also a small painting and decorating and leather division, which ran chiefly part-time day release courses for local industry. In 1989 a new principal was appointed, whose first major act was to set up a division of tertiary development whose role was to develop an entitlement curriculum, open access, and to broaden the curriculum offer of the college to include performing arts, media and popular music. The principal resigned after a year in post, and was replaced by the vice-principal.

The tech was built in the 1960s and as a general college of technology has always offered a range of vocational courses including caring, engineering, hair and beauty, general studies, electronics and business studies. The college was situated on a prime town centre site, and boasted around five times the student numbers of the art college. In 1989 this college also appointed a new principal who very soon gained governors' approval to move the college from a traditional departmental to a matrix structure which carried 20 or more curriculum directorates.

The possibility of a merger between the two colleges had been the subject of local political debate for the last 40 years, but had always been vigorously resisted by the staff and governors of both colleges. However, faced with the impending withdrawal of the LEA safety net, and the generally held view that only larger 'lean and fit' colleges would be able to remain solvent following incorporation, both governing bodies voted to merge the colleges in July 1992.

The timescale for the operationalisation of the merger was extremely short. Within two months of the governors' vote, the two colleges were expected to enrol students and to operate in every way as a single newly constituted college. It is argued here that it was substantially during that initial two month period that the seeds for the mismanagement of change were sown.

Visioning

The notion of visioning has a well established pedigree in business management (Peters and Waterman, 1984) and in education management (Louis and Miles, 1990). A shared vision for an educational institution will typically be generated out of the planning process, be strongly value-laden, provide a motivating force for change and improvement, and emerge gradually through shared staff involvement within the institution and linkage to existing successful initiatives (Louis and Miles, 1990). On the other hand, the picture of visioning which emerges from the business management literature is strongly tied to a charismatic leadership model. The activities of the leader are seen as crucial in determining and controlling the vision; conversely, without a 'great leader' there can (by implication) be no institutional shared vision (Peters, 1989). The subtitle of the much cited work *A Passion for Excellence* is 'the leadership difference' (Peters, 1985). The assumption here is not simply that there is a top down style of management in operation in corporate institutions, but that the activities of leaders are closely coupled to the actions of subordinates.

Weick (1988) has argued that educational organisations, far from being rational systems whose outcomes are highly predictable, are loosely coupled systems. One of the key features of such systems is that they contain ''soft' structures' which resist attempts to impose consensus and integration. He presents a forceful argument against the prospect of successful planned organisational change by drawing upon an emerging perspective in psychology:

> There is a developing position in psychology which argues that intentions are a poor guide for action, intentions often follow rather than precede

157

action, and that intentions and actions are loosely coupled. Unfortunately, organisations continue to think that planning is a good thing ...(1988)

The issue in question is one of epistemology or cognitive politics, and essentially concerns the degree of control over (in this case) a shared vision that a leader can expect to have. Questions of control bring to mind political and cultural perspectives, which can be helpful in directing our attention to the competing visions which can exist, and vie for support, when two institutions merge. Anderson (1991) has argued that adequate definitions of leadership need to take account of the extent to which the leader defines the reality of others. He makes the point that an examination of such a process of 'meaning management' necessitates focusing upon the process of cognitive politics, and that in practice 'the definition of reality promoted by principals is seldom of their own creation' (1991). This conflicts with rationalistic theories of educational management, drawn from organisation theory, which are dominating current debates on the function and future of the FE service (Elliott and Crossley, 1994).

One of the key failures of visioning in this case arose from the nature of the innovation itself: the merger had many of the characteristics of a takeover of the smaller college by the larger one. In the art college there was already in place a strong and readily identifiable vision which was expressed through a clear mission statement. Staff at all levels were clear that the vision, which related to the specialist nature and function of the art college, should be sustained following the merger. There was therefore widespread concern after it was decided not to include art college managers within the new senior management team. The exception was the vice principal, who was not appointed until shortly before the merger. There was thus little prospect of the new college vision encompassing the art college vision. In the absence of a vision shared by all staff, the art college vision took on symbolic value for the former art college staff, and became a reference point for subversive activity such as creative management information system returns.

Fullan (1991) has shown that the implementation of innovation requires restructuring which can support and sustain the implementation. Such restructuring will itself become an innovation which will form part of the dynamic of the multiple innovations which are brought about by a merger. This is perhaps the aspect given least thought by senior management (cp Caldwell and Spinks, 1992). In particular, they failed to deal adequately with the problem of where in the new college structure to place the former college of art managers. These staff would clearly be crucial in the implementation of strategies for involving college of art staff in contributing to the new college vision (cp Becher and Kogan, 1992).

Although the former art college managers had agreed that merger with the tech was the best option, given all the circumstances, they did not buy into what they regarded as the cut-throat corporatist culture of the tech. For them, the merger was instrumental - the option most likely to preserve jobs for all teaching and support staff in light of impending incorporation. There was also the view that most of the curriculum areas of the college of art were very healthy in terms of student numbers, resourcing and quality profile, and thus could survive and thrive in the new environment, potentially attracting increased resourcing within a larger and richer institution. But preserving the 'art college' identity - as a specialist college and a centre of excellence - was for them a crucial part of the deal, and a central element of their visioning.

So whilst supporting the merger, the art college managers rejected in large part the corporatist visioning of the senior managers of the new college, of which key aspects were casualisation of teaching staff, centralisation of resources and decision-making, and business model quality assurance procedures. They in turn were marginalised in that they were excluded from senior management decision-making, not consulted at all about their own new status and conditions of service or that of their staff, and subject to the vagaries of resourcing decisions based upon doubtful data emerging from a computer-based management information system.

It is clear from the management of change literature that the management strategy which resulted in the situation as outlined above falls far short of the ideal. Miles (1987) has stressed that visioning is critical to both the content and process of change. Anderson and Cox (1987) have indicated that importance of broadening the number of people committed to change, and Huberman (1992) has pointed out the inadequacy of the view that different interests are of little account when attempting to develop a shared culture. In contrast, senior managers failed to carry out any of the strategic actions identified by Louis and Miles (1990) as central to visioning: 'power sharing, rewarding staff, encouraging openness and inclusiveness in the change program efforts, expanding leadership roles, and patience, or a hands-off approach to bottom-up change.'

The present analysis follows a theme developed by Patterson et al (1986) in identifying this group of senior staff of the former college of art who used the resources at their disposal (including, crucially, their knowledge and experience of existing practices and how these could be preserved and sustained within the new college structure) to contest and alter the intended consequences of resourcing change. In acting to defend staff against what were perceived as external threats to their well-being and that of the college of art, these staff carried out a buffer role. By sustaining alternative visions which are reinforced by the failure of visioning at the higher level, such staff can undermine the dynamic of the collective vision (Louis and Miles, 1990).

Culture-building

Competing visions and conflicting cultures have been demonstrated to be important potential constraints to the successful management of change (Leithwood and Jantzi, 1990). In the implementation of a strategy for major institutional change it is vital that the differing perspectives of the participants in educational institutions are fully taken into account, in order to explore what Fullan (1991) calls 'the importance and meaning of the subjective reality of change'. Calling to mind the model elaborated by Getzels and Guba (1957), the starting point of this process is that of recognition of the ideographic dimension, that is, the existence of the diverse understandings, beliefs and expectations held by staff in each institution.

In the case of the art college, staff who went forward into the new college felt very strongly that their approaches to course organisation, teaching, and student support were undermined by senior managers. Course leaders were asked to provide a large amount of information on their students for the existing management information system. All cross-college posts were scrapped. All remission was removed from staff in relation to existing responsibilities. New procedures and guidelines were sent across to the art college senior managers, which covered areas like disciplinary procedures, staff development, insurance, and over 20 other topics for which strict rules were laid down. These acts were widely perceived as high-handed. Allusions were made to the business model which the former college of art was being expected to follow. Disparaging remarks were frequently made in staffrooms about the tech and their staff who seemingly put up with such a corporatist style of management.

The declared purpose of senior management was to regularise the new situation as quickly as possible. But the implementation of this short term objective brought about negative longer term consequences (cp Beckhard and Harris, 1987). Compliance to the plethora of new policies and procedures was achieved, but the push for art college staff to comply quickly and to the letter with the new regime led to hostility to the merger itself. Ex-art college staff were compliant to the new regime, and felt obliged to implement many of the new systems in order not to cause difficulties for themselves and their students. But compliance does not necessarily mean that the innovation will be implemented in full (Joyce and Showers, 1988), and it breeds mediocrity (Becher and Kogan, 1992). The facade phenomenon was very much in evidence in every part of the art college, and engaged in by managers, main grade teaching staff, technicians and support staff alike. A common bond was formed between these staff, who began to look back upon former practices with increased affection, and mutually to resent the imposition of a whole range of numerous forms, computer print-outs, monthly returns, registers, and other control systems. Interestingly, as contacts between former art college staff and tech staff increased it became clear that similar processes were firmly embedded in the college of technology culture. The failure to build upon any good practices in the art college, combined with senior management's failure to build a shared culture, thus resulted in the generation of a counter sub-culture among ex-art college staff, perhaps helping to weld a stronger culture in the new context of perceived adversity than would have existed before the merger.

The hostility of the college of art staff to the changes found its expression in what Firestone and Corbett (1988) call 'co-option', where the merger was used to further the ends of the art college. In one case a failure to take the pre-existing practices of the college of art into account in determining human resourcing policy led to less efficient part-time staffing allocations being made. A policy which had served its purpose in the tech was applied without question to the new situation. There was no attempt to discover whether any more efficient practices had in fact occurred at the art college. The combination of myth, division of senior management responsibility and uncritical application of numerical formula to dynamic practice was enough to undermine one of the key elements of the new culture which senior managers wished to convey: that of the efficient and effective college. This worked against the development of a sense of ownership of the culture (Miles et al, 1987). The consequences of this were that the ability of senior managers to manage essential strategic functions was called into question, the old-style tech culture was perceived to be alive and well, and a negative-efficiency factor has been built into everyday practice.

161

Flexible planning

The literature is largely silent on the need for flexible planning of major institutional innovation in the context of major national/environmental change. Inadequate information networks in the larger institution failed to sensitise senior managers to those characteristics of the smaller institution which constituted good practice. Out went the baby with the bathwater. It seems likely that the pressing demands of the environmental change brought about by incorporation left little option for senior managers but to deal arbitrarily with what existed in another unincorporated institution prior to merger.

The failure here was in not delegating authority for merging operational systems to the former art college managers, who were in a position to know where good practice existed, and how to preserve and extend it. By overloading their own agenda, senior managers, who were obliged to deal with an incessant flow of requests for information from the DfE and their consultants, Coopers and Lybrand, irreparably damaged the implementation of less pressing, but nonetheless significant, structural and operational changes. These unintended consequences of the managers' actions seem not dissimilar to those experienced by Bowe and Ball's (1992) secondary school managers, who were obliged to pay attention to external matters concerned with educational reform, and were thus perceived as 'distanced' by their staff (cp Hewton, 1982).

The speed of the merger allied to the volume of changes were undoubtedly principal factors which contributed to the mismanagement of change. James (1991) noted, in his study of the merger of a university department, that short term goals seemed to take priority over attempts to understand the complexity of the situation, and that different groups within the department were insecure in their new surroundings and 'resentful at losing their previous labels and identities' (1991). Huberman and Miles (1984) have noted that considerable time and energy is required of teachers to learn new practice and incorporate them into their repertoires.

The volume of changes required of staff consequent upon a merger is vast. The working conditions of ex-college of art staff, conditions of service, documentation, college structure, timetables and administrative procedures were all reviewed, altered, and, in many cases, altered again. Contradictory information from senior managers was not uncommon, nor was it unusual for policy and procedures to be changed two or three times in a single day.

Crisis upon crisis characterised the first couple of months of the merger, as unforeseen issues and problems emerged.

There was very little lead-in time from the merger itself to the return of the staff and students. The need to have the merged college operational from day one was vital, since over 90% of enrolments for the year took place during the first two weeks of the autumn term. Yet the haste with which roles and responsibilities were re-defined, allied to the lack of consultation with the staff concerned, was a major source of dissatisfaction and resentment for those staff. The question to be answered is whether rapid change necessarily goes along with absence of adequate consultation, respect for peoples' views, and a concern to develop a shared vision. A management of change strategy counts for nothing if it is to be thrown off course by a turbulent environment, the pace of events etc., since education has always been thus - at least during the present administration. To sustain a change strategy through rapid major multiple changes requires a flexible planning approach, which can be constantly updated, re-appraised, re-prioritised and thus work in practice as a management tool (cp Wallace, 1992).

A popular view of crisis management is that it involves abandoning planned management for problem coping (Louis and Miles, 1990). However, a flexible planning model can potentially address the predictable and unpredictable, short and medium timescales, multiple, competing, changing and often ambiguous goals (Wallace and McMahon, 1994). Such a model, however, is dependent upon a stronger degree of devolved decision-taking than is apparent in the present case. It seems likely that where control is highly centralised, and concentrated among two or three members of a senior management hierarchy, that it becomes more difficult to react fast enough to the many implications and consequences of multiple innovations. The effect of this inaction is that staff perceive senior managers as uncaring about the consequences of policy decisions in practice (cp Stenhouse, 1978).

The irony of this situation is well brought out in the management of change literature. Caldwell and Spinks (1988), focusing upon school strategic planning, argue the need to take environmental turbulence into account, yet at the same time propose a strategic planning model which utilises a three year planning cycle. In the newly merged college, the strategic plan has been a management priority. Due consultation took place with curriculum directors about their planned courses, target numbers and resourcing and marketing requirements. One week before the deadline for presentation of the plan to governors, the FEFC announced its proposals for funding learning in FE (FEFC, 1993), which led to the plan effectively being torn up, and re-written by senior managers after running funding figures through the computer. This both demonstrates the inability of rigid strategic planning to deal adequately with major external change, and also the tight grip held by senior management over the planning process itself. The staff who were involved in the earlier strategic planning consultation exercise have been left to ponder upon the degree of commitment and amount of time that they will give to any similar exercise in subsequent years.

Conclusion

In regarding the merger as a major planned change, it has been shown that failures in implementation can be understood by reference to three analytical themes of visioning, culture-building and flexible planning. It could therefore be argued that management attention to each of these themes in combination could have altered the outcome. The question is whether the themes can be used as recipe-knowledge, or whether they are more fundamentally grounded in particular management styles or cultures. Bolam (1975) is probably correct in concluding that empirical studies are probably the best way of exploring the strengths and limitations of such theoretical frameworks.

College managements are undoubtedly being placed under severe pressure by the Funding Council to adopt three year strategic planning, and by the College Employers Forum to take the toughest of lines and to pursue hard human resource management policies on personnel issues, including a move towards new (worse) contracts and conditions of service for their staff. The problem is that actions arising from these pressures have also had unintended consequences which have jeopardised the development of a shared culture for the new college.

The management of change literature confirms that working to a strategic planning model limits adaptability to rapid, frequent and unexpected changes. This model is also symptomatic of the managerialist policy of holding onto decision-taking roles, which runs counter to Fullan's (1991) prescription for successful change processes, which are 'characterised by collaboration and close interaction among those central to carrying out the changes'. This leads to an increase in the number of 'bad' decisions, which impact upon the day to day working practices of staff in an irksome and unpleasant manner. Resentment builds resistance, which serves to feed a counter-culture, which is sustained and supported by the activity of undermining initiatives which are designed to build a unified corporate culture.

It would be vital, in planning a successful merge to take full account of the organisational culture (Deal and Kennedy, 1982) and character of each constituent institution. By this I mean what Firestone and Corbett (1988) describe as '... widely shared values (which) drive behaviour and guide the settlement of disputes, thereby enabling united devotion to attaining major organisational goals'. As they also point out, 'the enactment and consequences of a change strategy are contingent on these contextual characteristics' (1988). It could therefore be predicted that where the dominant institution organises itself in such a way that it is both insensitive to such factors and unable to build and sustain a widely-shared organisational culture and vision, then there can be little reasonable expectation of successful management of change (cp Everard and Morris, 1990, 2nd ed, 231-236; Fielden, 1991, 158-166). To end on a positive point however, it would appear that a conceptual framework drawn from the management of change literature could be helpful in drawing up guidelines for the successful management of mergers.

References

Anderson, B. and Cox, P. (1987) *Configuring the education system for a shared future: Collaborative vision, action, reflection*, Andover, MA: Regional Laboratory for Educational Improvement of the Northeast and the Islands, quoted in Fullan, M. (1990) op cit. p.82.

Anderson, G. (1990) 'Cognitive Politics of principals and Teachers' in Blase, J. *The Politics of Life in Schools*, London: Sage.

Becher, T. and Kogan, M. (1992) (2nd ed) *Process and Structure in Higher Education*, London: Routledge.

Beckhard, R. and Harris, R. (1987) (2nd ed.), *Organisational Transitions: Managing Complex Change*, Reading, Mass: Addison-Wesley.

Bolam, R. (1975) 'The Management of Educational Change: towards a framework' in Houghton, V., McHugh, R. and Morgan, C. (eds.) *The Management of Organisations and Individuals, Management in Education Reader 1*, Milton Keynes: Ward Lock Educational/Open University Press.

Bowe, R. and Ball, S. (1992) *Reforming Education and Changing Schools*, London: Routledge.

Caldwell, B. and Spinks, J. (1988) *The Self Managing Schools*, London: The Falmer Press.

Caldwell, B. and Spinks, J. (1992) *Leading the Self Managing School*, London: The Falmer Press.

Deal, T. and Kennedy, A. (1982) *Corporate Cultures*, Reading, Mass: Addison-Wesley.

Department of Education and Science (1991) *Education and Training for the 21st Century*, Cm 1536, London: HMSO.

Elliott, G. and Crossley, M. (1994) Qualitative Research, Educational Management and the Incorporation of the Further Education Sector *Educational Management and Administration 22* (3), 188-197.

Everard, B. and Morris, G. (1990) (2nd ed.), *Effective School Management* London: Paul Chapman.

Fielden, J. (1991) Resource Implications of Mergers: are there any economies? *Higher Education Quarterly 45*, 254-266.

Firestone, W. and Corbett, H. (1988) 'Planned Organisational Change' in Boyan, N. (ed.) *Handbook of Research on Educational Administration*, New York: Longman.

Fullan, M. (1991) *The New Meaning of Educational Change*, London: Cassell.

Further Education Funding Council (1993) *Circular 93/16 Recurrent Funding Methodology 1994/5: Allocating Mechanism* Coventry: FEFC.

Getzels, J. and Guba, E. (1957) Social behaviour and the administrative process, *School Review, 65* Winter.

Hewton, E. (1982) *Rethinking Educational Change*, Guildford: SRHE.

Huberman, M. (1992) Critical introduction to Fullan, M. *Successful School Improvement*, Milton Keynes: Open University Press.

Huberman, M. and Miles, M. (1984) *Innovation up Close: How School Improvement Works*, London: Plenum.

James, D. (1991) Merging Educational Groups: Personal Reflections *Higher Education Quarterly, 45*, 3, 254-266.

Joyce, B. and Showers, B. (1988) *Student Achievement Through Staff Development*, New York: Longman.

Leithwood, K. and Jantzi, D. (1990) Transformational Leadership: how principals can help reform school cultures, Unpublished paper, American Educational Research Association, Boston.

Louis, K. and Miles, M. (1990) *Improving the Urban High School*, London: Cassell.

Miles, M. (1987) Practical guidelines for school administrators: How to get there, Unpublished paper presented at American Educational Research Association annual meeting, cited in Fullan, M. (1992) op cit. p.82.

Miles, M., Ekholm, M. and Vandenberghe, R. (eds) (1987) *Lasting School Improvement: Exploring the Process of Institutionalisation*, Leuven, Belgium: ACCO.

Patterson, J., Purkey, S. and Parker, J. (1986) *Productive School Systems for a Non-Rational World*, Alexandria, VA: Association for Supervision and Curriculum Development.

Peters, T. (1985) *A Passion for Excellence: the leadership difference*, London: Fontana/Collins.

Peters, T. (1989) *Thriving on Chaos*, London: Pan/Macmillan

Peters, T. and Waterman, R. (1984) *In Search of Excellence*, New York: Harper and Row.

Stenhouse, L. (1978) Case Study and Case Records: towards a contemporary history of education, *British Educational Research Journal, 4*, 2, 21-39.

Wallace, M. (1992) 'Flexible Planning: a key to the management of multiple innovations' in Bennet, N., Crawford, M. and Riches, C. *Managing Change in Education*, London: Paul Chapman/Open University Press.

Wallace, M. and McMahon, A. (1994) *Planning for Change in Turbulent Times: the case of multiracial primary schools*, London: Cassell.

Weick, K. (1988) 'Educational Organisations as Loosely Coupled System' in Westoby, A. *Culture and Power in Educational Organisations*, Milton Keynes: Open University Press.

10 Management of workplace learning

Geoff Hayton

Abstract

This chapter focuses on management of learning and training in the workplace. It reviews the trends in workplace change in Western countries and suggests a link to new approaches to skill formation at the workplace. The chapter then examines how training decisions are made in enterprises, and what triggers much of the training undertaken, based on the findings of a major study involving 42 enterprise case studies in Australia and a national survey. Issues discussed here include the conflicting approaches to training of middle management and senior management, the factors driving training in enterprises, and the role of training in enterprise strategy. The range of training practices observed in these enterprises are then described. Examples are taken from some of the case studies. The chapter includes a case study of a large home building company.

Introduction

Workplace learning has received increased attention from educators in recent years. The use of occupational competency standards in Australia, the United Kingdom, the United States and other western countries has highlighted the central role of workplace learning in the development of job competence. This has also given impetus to improving the links between education and the workplace.

If we view workplace learning in its broadest sense, some important implications emerge. The workplace is a complex working environment in which the workers are engaged for a large part of their adult lives. This provides opportunities not only for the development of job competence, but also for the development of other capacities. Thinkers as diverse as Rousseau, Mill, Owen, Marx, Gramsci and Cole have asserted that work is the central learning domain for the development of human capacity (Welton, 1991). This conception of workplace learning includes informal and incidental learning at the workplace as well as learning gained from job rotation, mentoring, coaching, on-the-job training, workshops and education programs.

Closely linked with this concept of workplace learning is the idea of worker *empowerment*. New approaches to work organisation which rely on highly-skilled workers provide greater autonomy and an active learning environment. Workers in such organisations, especially those at operative level, are given more power and choice in the work of the enterprise and greater opportunities for learning. Individuals and teams are given greater responsibility for production, service, quality and safety objectives (Hayton et al, 1993).

In Western countries in many industries, workplaces have substantially changed over recent years. Although some industries and particular enterprises show a contrary trend, there has been a widespread trend in workplaces towards some or all of the following (Gonczi, 1992):

- reducing the number of management layers;
- creating semi-autonomous teams;
- devolving responsibility for production and service objectives to operatives or teams;
- introducing new technology;
- developing a highly skilled workforce.

In such workplaces there is worker empowerment and a strong emphasis on workplace learning. With increasing competition through globalisation of national economies and other factors, workplace reform trends are expected to continue, accompanied by a growth in resources put into workplace training and education programs. A 1993 survey by the Australian Bureau of Statistics (1994) estimated that Australian employers spent 2.9% of their payroll on education and training activities. Similar surveys in 1989 and

1990 show a trend of increasing expenditure on training. In 1989 expenditure was 2.2% and in 1990 expenditure was 2.6% of payroll.

In this context of increasing expenditure on training and greater recognition of the importance of workplace learning, the federal and state governments in Australia commissioned research to acquire an improved understanding of the priorities for training within industry and of the factors which determine the level and nature of training that enterprises provide and require. The following sections describe the two major research projects that resulted, and discuss the main findings.

The research projects

Both projects were funded by the Australian National Training Authority; and undertaken by a team of researchers from the University of Technology, Sydney and Charles Sturt University. Australian Workplace Strategies joined the consortium for the 1994 project and consultants from AGB McNair were involved in the 1995 project.

The first project explored how enterprises and industry approach training decision-making, current training practices in enterprises and industry, and skill levels and training needs. These issues were examined in the context of policy issues such as the relationship between enterprise objectives and training objectives, the identification of factors underlying the demand for training, and the types of training preferred. The research was mainly based on 30 case studies in the building and construction, electronics manu-facturing and food processing industry sectors.

For the second project the brief was to:

- develop an appreciation of training practices in enterprises;
- obtain information about how enterprises approach training decision-making.
- explore the relationship between enterprise objectives and training practices;
- identify factors which appear to 'trigger' demand for training.

It was also expected that this study would result in the refinement of the model of enterprise training developed in the previous project.

The project involved a national survey of firms across all industries in Australia and a further 12 case studies in two industry sectors: the retail industry and the finance and insurance industry. The case studies were

171

designed to provide an understanding of the training practices and determinants of training in the service sector of the economy, whereas the previous study focussed on manufacturing and construction. The total of 42 case studies in the two studies included some well known national and multi-national enterprises.

The national survey provided a test of the relationships between variables in the model, including an indication of the relative strength of each determinant of training. All major industries were sampled in the survey, except government departments and community services were excluded. A net sample of 1760 worksites was obtained. Multivariate analysis of the survey data enabled an economy-wide model of enterprise training to be developed.

The main findings of these studies are presented in the following sections:

- training decision-making;
- factors driving training;
- corporate strategy and training;
- training practices;
- informal workplace learning;
- a case study.

Training decision-making

The case studies revealed a wide range of approaches to training decision-making. For medium and large organisations, decision-making is complex in many cases, with training decisions (including planning, content and expenditure) being made at two or more levels, including the individual, his or her supervisor and senior management.

Sometimes a training committee also makes decisions - in some enterprises the training committee manages the training function, while in others the committee develops a framework for training but the training function itself is managed either by line managers or through a specialist training department.

Despite the variation across enterprises and complexity in some larger organisations, aspects of training decision-making were common to most of the enterprises studied. Two levels and types of decision-making could be identified. The first level is that of the training investment decision, such as the decision to implement new structured training programs or to support a workplace initiative with an extensive training program. This level of training decision was made at relatively senior levels in most of the 42 enterprises studied (Smith et al, 1995; Noble et al, 1996). In the small to medium size organisations these decisions usually would be made at the Managing Director level, while in the large organisations these decisions usually would be made by the local senior manager, such as the Plant Manager or the Divisional Manager. For example, in the finance and insurance enterprises and the larger retailing enterprises studied, there was a strong commitment to training by the senior management. Senior managers had a critical role in these enterprises in determining the amount, direction and type of training.

The second level of training decision-making is that of training implementation. This includes identifying the needs of individuals, planning of training, timing and release patterns for participating in training programs. These training implementation decisions usually were devolved to local front line managers or middle managers.

The splitting of training decision-making between senior managers and middle or line managers has led to problems of conflicting priorities in many of the case study enterprises. While senior managers may strongly promote training and allocate resources to training in the enterprise, middle or line managers often find that training programs conflict with service or production scheduling requirements and they are reluctant to release key workers for training where it disrupts service or production schedules. In smaller enterprises this problem is obvious but many of the larger enterprises, especially those where there have been recent reductions in the size of the workforce, also face this problem. The outcome is that key staff often miss important training programs despite the strong commitment of senior managers to such programs.

A key finding also from the cases has been the critical role of the individual in determining training outcomes. This is particularly true at the managerial and professional levels, where individual initiative was the driving force behind the provision of training for these groups. In many enterprises, even those with management driven training programs aimed at large groups of employees, it was left to the individual to pursue the training that they considered necessary for their own professional development. For example, at a computer assembly factory in Victoria there was an elaborate system of management succession planning and company organised training programs. However, it was still left to the individual to *volunteer* for such training. Frequently the reason given by the individual for not attending training programs was 'pressure of work'.

In some cases, particularly in the finance and insurance industry sector, enterprises had provided a context for this individual identification of training needs. Usually this was in the form of a career development framework or a performance appraisal system. Career development frameworks tended to cover most or all employees, whereas performance appraisal systems tended to cover only management staff in the cases studied.

The national survey included a question on 'strategies to ensure adequate training' which tried to capture quantitative data on the nature of decision-making about training. Large worksites have a higher incidence of use of training decision-making compared to small worksites. The gap is greater for the more management controlled modes, with large worksites favouring formal and structured management controlled training much more than small worksites. The responses also confirm a finding from the case studies: that many worksites use more than one mode of training decision-making.

Factors driving training

Since the 1980s a number of models have been developed to attempt to account for the way in which training is carried out at the enterprise level. Of all the models reviewed, our research was informed most by the Warwick model of training in enterprises. The Warwick model has two sets of factors that affect the provision of training (Hendry and Pettigrew, 1989; Hendry, 1990):

- factors that set training in progress (triggers);
- factors that establish training within the enterprise (stabilisers).

Analysis of the information from the case studies led to the identification of several triggers of training in the enterprise, which were termed 'training drivers' in our study. The case study researchers found that in every case staff within the enterprise were able to nominate at least one factor which triggered training in the enterprise.

Although some training drivers occurred repeatedly across enterprises, there was great diversity in the training practices, even for enterprises in the same industry with a similar set of training drivers. Large enterprises reportedly spent much more on training than small enterprises, although on closer scrutiny the small enterprises tended to respond to training drivers with informal training or skill formation activities. The diversity in training across the case study enterprises was attributed to several mediating factors within the enterprise, mainly pertaining to size of organisation and training infrastructure in the organisation. The mediating factors filter or moderate the effect of the training drivers, influencing the nature and extent of training activity.

The factors discussed so far have been parameters of the enterprise - factors external to the enterprise have not been considered. Clearly some factors outside the enterprise can impact either directly on training decisions of the enterprise or indirectly on the impetus to train. Such factors were termed environmental factors in our research, emphasising that they are outside of the organisation but may permeate training decision-making within the organisation.

Thus, our research identified three types of factors which affect training by enterprises:

- training drivers;
- mediating factors;
- environmental factors.

These sets of factors have been included in a model of enterprise training, illustrated in Figure 1. A full description of this model is given in the report of the research (Hayton et al, 1996). Each of the three sets of factors will now be described.

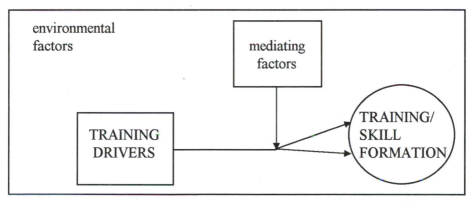

Figure 1   The model of enterprise training

Training drivers are factors within the enterprise which trigger training activity, and are perceived by those within the enterprise as the reason for training activity in one or more of its various forms. Several training drivers were clearly identified in the case studied and the national survey, and include:

- workplace change;
- new technology and product innovation;
- quality initiatives (e.g. customer service, TQM);
- industrial award coverage;
- provision of training in industrial awards;
- the inclusion of training in the enterprise business plan;
- individual performance appraisal.

Mediating factors are factors within the enterprise which intervene between the training drivers and the training activity of the enterprise. Mediating factors do not drive training directly but govern the way in which the training drivers produce a particular set of training arrangements. For example, enterprise size is a mediating variable. When comparing small and large organisations having the same set of training drivers, small enterprises tend to engage in informal types of training; large enterprises tend to engage in formal forms of training. Another mediator is the level of training decision-making. Senior managers are more likely to commit resources to long term investments in training. However, the implementation of the training rests on the actions and attitudes of lower level managers in the enterprise who may not be quite so committed to training. The actual training arrangements that are put in place will depend on the role of managers at all levels of the enterprise. The main mediating factors identified in our research included:

- size of organisation;
- industry sector;
- occupational structure;
- training infrastructure;
- level of training decision-making;
- senior management commitment to training.

Environment factors are factors in the enterprise's business environment which impact on the enterprise and tend to generate one or more training drivers. These include the level of competitive pressure experienced by the enterprise and the impact of government policy such as deregulation of product markets, legislative requirements for occupational health and safety as well as training policy. The business environment has an effect on the extent to which enterprises provide training for employees *but the impact is indirect*. That is, environmental factors do not produce training outcomes in themselves, but produce responses in enterprises that in turn drive training. Thus the deregulation of the finance industry forced the banks into a more competitive environment. Part of the response of banks to this environment has been to place a very high premium on customer service to generate increased customer loyalty. As a result, the need for improved customer service has been a major driver for training in banks. The most common response to increased competition amongst the case study enterprises was the adoption of quality assurance processes. This became a very important driver for training in many of the companies in the study. In summary, the main environmental factors identified in our research included:

- competitive pressure;
- deregulation of product markets;
- occupational health and safety regulations;
- government policies on training.

Corporate strategy and training

According to the Warwick model of enterprise training, the forces that trigger training provision are clearly linked to the strategy making process (Hendry, 1990). In this model, enterprises respond to the competitive environment through the rational process of strategy formulation. This process may lead to the identification of a skills gap as the enterprise decides to introduce new products or enter new markets. This skills gap is the source of the provision of training.

The relationship between corporate strategy and training was explored in the case studies but only indirectly in the survey through a single question on whether training and skills development constituted a section of the enterprise's business plan. The results from the case studies and the survey shed an interesting light on this supposed relationship and show that strategy, where it exists, has a much more complex relationship with training provision than the direct rationality which the Warwick model suggests. The survey shows that 74 percent of worksites have a business plan and that a further 75 percent of these claim that the business plan contains a section on skills development and training. The survey data analysis shows that the existence of a training section in the business plan is well correlated with both high diversity and volume of training.

The case studies, however, tend to highlight a more complex situation. Many of the case study enterprises did not possess a recognisable strategy except in a loose, emergent way as a series of actions taken over a period of time in response to the market conditions. This was particularly true for enterprises that had not traditionally faced a truly competitive market. For those enterprises that had traditionally existed in a more competitive environment such as the larger retail enterprises and the newer financial institutions in particular, there was much greater evidence of clear strategies for the business. In these cases, training often played a key role as an enabler of strategy. However, in none of the cases was training regarded as a strategic issue in itself. Rather training was required to help implement strategy which might contain some key human resources aspects It was unusual to find that training is referred to in strategic terms by managers. Thus, even in enterprises which had a clearly articulated strategy, training was seen as an operational issue, rather than a strategic issue, in the sense that training was usually seen as an enabler of corporate strategy rather than as a separate strategy.

These rather contradictory positions may be reconciled by viewing business planning and strategy making as separate activities. Many enterprises will have business plans that guide the direction of the business in the short to medium term. However, long term strategy-making is a quite different process. It is quite possible for enterprises to have business plans that include an element for expenditure on training. This is an operational matter, however, not a strategic process. As such, the existence of a business plan with a reference to training is quite compatible with a situation in which training plays an important operational role in the enterprise but does not figure in the strategy making process.

Training practices

Much information on training practices in Australian enterprises was obtained by the two research projects. In this section the focus will be on training infrastructure, training approaches and expenditure on training.

Training infrastructure

Across the enterprise case studies the structures for organising and managing training vary considerably; however there is a pronounced trend away from centralised training departments in all industry sectors studied. Corporate training functions still exist in some organisations, but their roles tend to focus on co-ordinating training and internal consultancy. Large enterprises stand out in having a well-developed training infrastructure, operating at two or more levels. In keeping with the internal consultancy role for training managers and others with training responsibilities, enterprises are making considerable use of external training providers.

The national survey asked about formal training infrastructure. Of the 1524 worksites which had some training over the past year, over a quarter (27 percent) of all worksites had a human resources officer, a third (33 percent) had a training manager, nearly half (46 percent) had trainers or instructors, some 15 percent had a training committee and some 40 percent had a training room. A quarter of sites had none of these facilities, but this was more common in small sites (43 percent) than medium (25 percent) or large sites (11 percent). More finance and insurance sites reported they had these facilities, and fewer food and beverage sites. The largest finance and insurance sites reported high levels of this training infrastructure. In general, there were marked differences in the training infrastructure of the small and large sites, irrespective of industry, providing support for the proposition that infrastructure is a function of increasing size of the worksite.

Training approaches

The various approaches to training by organisations mostly may be aligned with three broad types of approach: ad hoc, systematic (Hayton et al, 1988), and the 'continuous learning' approach (Senge, 1990). Our research revealed that most enterprises were somewhere between the ad hoc and systematic approach. The main indicators of a systematic approach are: the existence of training plans; formal needs analysis; evaluation of training programs; and the assessment of the costs and benefits of training. Very few enterprises had moved towards the continuous learning approach.

The approach to training varies considerably across the cases and between sectors. There are more examples of a systematic approach to training in the finance and insurance cases than in the other industry sectors. This was evident from the case studies and the national survey. Finance and insurance has more cases where training is planned rather than ad hoc, performance appraisal is linked with training and training committees are used in decision-making. The finance and insurance cases are more likely to have developed a corporate strategy that includes training, than in cases from the other industry sectors. One large financial enterprise had moved beyond the systematic approach, considering that formal needs analysis is 'out of date, expensive, rigid and not promoting the new discourse of continuous learning'.

Planning and formal needs analysis: In those enterprises that follow a systematic approach there is usually a combination of training plans and formal needs analysis linked to corporate strategy. Performance appraisal is also used by these enterprises to identify the training needs of individual employees.

The national survey revealed a moderate use of training plans or formal needs analysis. Across the whole sample, just over a third of worksites used training plans (37 percent) or systematic needs analysis (36 percent). Large worksites, consistently across all aspects, are more likely to use systematic approaches compared to medium or small worksites. However, there is little variation across industries, with only finance and insurance standing out as consistently higher in the use of systematic approaches compared to the other industry sectors.

Evaluation and assessment of costs and benefits: The case studies revealed that evaluation of training is relatively undeveloped in most enterprises across the sectors. Despite the evident commitment to training in most enterprises, there was a conspicuous lack of attention to the impact of training on productivity or profitability. The typical approach to evaluation consists of the distribution of evaluation questionnaires - euphemistically described as 'happy sheets' by one training manager - at the end of training sessions. There was little evidence of follow-up to evaluate whether training produced the expected benefits. Similarly, none of the case study enterprises attempted to measure the full costs or benefits of training.

The survey indicated that 48 percent of worksites formally evaluated any training that was delivered. There were few differences among the industry groups, with the size of the worksite making a much larger difference to whether the worksite formally evaluated training. For the four aspects of a systematic approach, a high percentage of small worksites did none of these things compared with a low percentage of large worksites, and this was a trend across the industry groups (with finance again the exception).

Training expenditure

The introduction in Australia of the Training Guarantee Act in 1989 resulted in an early focus within national training surveys upon enterprise training expenditure. Culled primarily from the three major statistical surveys published by the Australian Bureau of Statistics (ABS 1990; 1993; 1994), the statistical data presents a rather unflattering picture of enterprise training in Australia. Expenditure, although increasing, is relatively low at about 2.9 percent of payroll, with the private sector spending only 2.6 percent in 1993. The distribution of training is skewed towards male, professional employees working in the larger enterprises. Finally, employers appear to adopt a rather informal approach to training, with the emphasis on on-the-job methods and relatively low investment in training infrastructure at the enterprise level.

It is difficult to make accurate comparisons of training expenditure across the case study enterprises. Few enterprises kept complete and accurate records of training expenditure. Even in cases where complete records were kept, comparisons are problematic because the working definitions of training expenditure differ. For most of the small enterprises studied, training expenditure was not recorded. With the suspension in Australia of the Training Guarantee Act, there is no longer any compulsion to record expenditure. Moreover, enterprises adopted widely different interpretations of what constituted training expenditure. The most influential mediating factor on training expenditure was enterprise size. Training expenditure was closely correlated with the size of the enterprise. Larger enterprises tended to spend more money on training, as a percentage of payroll, than smaller enterprises.

The results from the survey in our study tend to reinforce the data from the case studies and the ABS surveys relating to training expenditure. In the survey 57 percent of worksites indicated that they spend between 1 and 5 percent of payroll on training. This figure also increases with size with 39 percent of larger enterprises indicating that they spend between 2 and 5 percent of payroll as opposed to 23 percent of smaller enterprises. The case studies, however, cast some doubt over the reliability of these survey figures.

Informal learning at the workplace

The main characteristics of informal learning or training at the workplace are that it is unplanned, unstructured and not documented. Informal internal training requires little or no training infrastructure and developmental costs are low. This type of learning was used by all enterprises studied. It was common to find informal training being used for induction, and to develop the requisite knowledge and skills to effectively serve customers. Several retailers emphasise product knowledge in this training. In some cases managers are developing a coaching role to develop the attitudes and skills of their staff.

The case study interviews indicate that few think of informal learning at the workplace as 'training', and few of the enterprises studied implemented strategies to maximise informal learning. Yet previous studies suggest that informally acquired skills are significant in the performance of middle and senior management jobs (Marsick, 1987).

Although small enterprises appear to rely more on informal learning compared to large enterprises, large enterprises seem to value informal training as much as small enterprises. They realise that informal training has the advantage of focussing on workplace issues and priorities at relatively low cost. Informal internal training per se may be insufficient to give an enterprise a competitive edge, however in conjunction with formal internal and external training it may form an important competitive strategy.

Table 1 compares the emphasis given to informal and formal training in large and small enterprises. It challenges the idea that as enterprises grow the opportunities for informal learning decrease and the requirements for formal training programs increase.

Table 1   Formal and informal external training tendencies in the cases

Firm size	Formal training	Informal training
Small	Common, except in very small enterprises. Used mainly for induction.	Used by all small enterprises.
Large	High	Increasingly common within structured framework.

Source: Hayton et al 1996

A case study

The case study enterprise is a large home builder in Australia, with corporate headquarters in Brisbane and Melbourne. This case study concentrates on the enterprise's Queensland home building operation. In 1994 annual turnover was nearly $500 million and the enterprise builds about 4,500 homes annually - about 1000 in Queensland. The direct workforce is about 2,500 nationally, with 250 direct employees and 418 contractors in Queensland.

The strategic focus of the enterprise is intensive marketing of affordable housing and refinement of a highly systematic approach to house building. The enterprise is in most segments of the domestic home construction market, but has a focus on first home buyers. The enterprise does sales (house, land and house and land packages), design, drafting, contracting, project management and manufacturing (e.g. wall frames, roof trusses); the enterprise sub-contracts building trades and, in some states, sales.

Organisation of training

There is a moderate to high level of training activity in the enterprise, both internal and external training, but with an emphasis on internal training in the enterprise's work flow procedures. The training function is a line management responsibility, with no specialist training staff in the enterprise. Most staff receive induction training and periodic internal training. Individuals who, of their own initiative, attend relevant external courses will have their fees reimbursed upon completion of the course.

Although there is a moderate level of training activity in the enterprise, the approach to training is largely non-systematic. There is no separate written training plan but training is referred to in the policy and procedures manual of the enterprise (e.g. the policy on reimbursing fees). No formal needs analyses are undertaken but some internal training is evaluated through reaction surveys and the performance of staff on the job is monitored after training.

Apprenticeship training, comprising off-the-job technical college instruction and mostly informal workplace learning, is supported by many of the enterprise's contractors. Also, in 1994 the enterprise had seven apprentices employed in Queensland. Competency standards and other elements of the national training reform agenda has had no direct impact on the enterprise. Job descriptions had recently been updated by a consultant and internal competency standards were included in these descriptions.

Determinants of training

Training has been triggered by:

- new building legislation;
- changes in procedures within the enterprise;
- new assembly or site techniques;
- monitoring of job performance - performance problems are usually addressed by retraining in standard procedures;
- new building materials;
- complaints from staff or customers;
- induction training for new staff;
- job redesign.

The first three factors have the greatest influence.

Training impediments

The cost of training is not a major impediment to training in the enterprise, but other factors were cited as impediments:

- difficulties in releasing staff to attend courses;
- the reluctance of some staff to attend internal training, when it is related to a change to the way they do their job.

The enterprise has offered training to its contractors as part of a strategy of changing work organisation and building techniques at the site. However, the contractors mostly have not readily accepted the offer of training.

References

Australian Bureau of Statistics (1990) *Employer Training Expenditure Australia*, Cat. No.6353.0.

Australian Bureau of Statistics (1993) *Employer Training Expenditure Australia*, July-September 1993, Cat. No.6353.0.

Australian Bureau of Statistics (1994) *Employer Training Expenditure Australia*, July-September 1993. Canberra: AGPS.

Gonczi, A. (ed.) (1992) *Developing a competent workforce: Adult learning strategies for vocational educators and trainers*. Adelaide: National Centre for Vocational Education Research.

Hayton, G., Garrick, J., and Guthrie, H. (1993) *Learning Construction: Skill formation in the construction industry*. Sydney: Construction Industry Development Agency.

Hayton, G., Clark, T., Guthrie, H., Fuller, D. and Oxley, S. (1988) *Training for Australian industry: a guide to research techniques for assessing industry training requirements*. Canberra: AGPS.

Hayton, G., McIntyre, J., Sweet, R., McDonald, R., Noble, C., Smith, A. and Roberts, P. (1996) *Enterprise Training in Australia: Final Report*. Melbourne: Office of Training and Further Education.

Hendry, C. (1990) *The Corporate Management of Human Resources under Conditions of Decentralisation'*. British Journal of Management, 1, 91-103.

Hendry, C. and Pettigrew, A. (1989) *'The Forces that Trigger Training'*. Personnel Management, December, 28-32.

Marsick, V.J. (ed.) (1987) *Learning in the Workplace*. London: Croom Helm.

Noble, C., Smith, A. and Gonczi, A. (1996) *Enterprise Training in Australia: Report 1 Industry Profiles and Case Studies*. Melbourne: Office of Training and Further Education.

Senge, P. (1990) *The Fifth Discipline: The art and practice of the learning organisation*. NY: Doubleday; Sydney: Random House.

Smith, A., Roberts, P., Noble, C., Hayton, G. and Thorne, E. (1995) *Enterprise Training: The Factors that Affect Demand - Final Report Volume 1*. Melbourne: Office of Training and Further Education.

Welton, M. (1991) *Toward Development Work: The workplace as a learning environment*. Geelong, Vic.: Deakin University.

11 Evaluating the development and implementation of a further education business plan

Kathy Bland

Abstract

The chapter focuses on action based research which aims to facilitate the evaluation and review of attempts to develop and implement a business plan for a business development division of a further education college.

Past developments and the current position of the Commercial Unit are examined before the framework of the business plan is explained.

The business plan represents an attempt to take forward the Commercial Unit in a way which would appear rational when external influences and constraints are considered.

Interview and questionnaire results are analysed in an attempt to evaluate the degree to which the business plan was successfully developed and implemented.

Introduction

This chapter focuses on action based research which aims to facilitate the evaluation and review of attempts to develop and implement a business plan for a business development division of a further education college. The

187

historical context is set and the current situation and business planning content and framework outlined along with the research methods employed, the results obtained and the conclusions drawn.

Historical development of the Commercial Unit

In February 1990, the Commercial Unit (offering Flexible Training Solutions) was established within the college. The Commercial Unit's aim was:

> to respond to recognised industrial needs, specific training, initially in the fluid power engineering and high technology disciplines by developing a partnership arrangement for the delivery of courses between education and industrial contributors.

The reason for setting up a separate commercial unit was to enable the college to respond to industries' needs in a flexible and efficient way without the usual constraints of timetables and academic year.

In order to 'pump-prime' the project, the college submitted an 'Industry/Education' bid to the Department of Trade and Industry (DTI) in Newcastle-upon-Tyne. Contributions from industry were received and the college contributed the staffing, which comprised one-third of a senior lecturer's time plus full-time secretarial support.

A steering group was established which was led by the Vice-Principal and included college lecturers. As well as helping with the writing of the bid, the steering group planned the identify and establishment of the commercial unit including separate stationery with a unique 'company' logo. The unit became fully established as the 'commercial arm' of the college on 1 September 1990.

The mission statement for the Commercial Unit for the period 1990 to 1991 was changed, and became:

> To deliver customised education and training to the highest quality which is innovative, competitive, flexible and accessible. Emphasis is placed on developing the potential of people.

The college was not unique in setting up its own commercial unit. The Further Education Act 1985, *Commercial Activities in Further Education,* clarified the position of colleges who were involved with profit making commercial activities and permitted the Local Education Authorities (LEAs) through their further education outlets to sell goods and services at their 'open market value'.

Current position

Since its inception, the Commercial Unit has expanded across the college to encompass all full-cost and profit making courses delivered both by the college and outside contractors. There are two distinct portfolios: standard courses which are offered at specific times throughout the year and are particularly popular in the area of Health and Safety; customer specific 'bespoke' courses which are tailored to an individual company/client's requirements. Particularly good working relationships have been established with Stockton Borough Council (SBC), Cleveland County Council (CCC), Teesside Training and Enterprise Council (TTEC), the Department of Trade and Industry (DTI) and a large majority of SMEs (small to medium sized enterprises) in the Cleveland area. High quality training packages for larger companies such as Tioxide, ICI, British Steel and Nissan have been provided.

In January 1993, the Commercial Unit was successful in gaining BS 5750 Part 1, and continued to try and enhance its image and reputation as a provider of quality training in the region by advertising the recognition achieved.

In September 1993, the Unit was divided into two distinct divisions, namely Consultancy, headed up by a Commercial Operations Manager, and Business Development, managed by the writer.

During October 1993, a business plan for the period 1 April 1993 to 31 July 1994 was drawn up. Processes for monitoring and evaluating the new Business Development Division of the Commercial Unit was facilitated by implementation of the business plan. These processes informed judgements about the progress both of the Division and its management.

The business plan itself was written by three people, each of whose contribution involved the use of a distinctly different framework and radically different content. This created some problems, not the least of which was that comparisons were made very difficult.

The Training and Commercial Director wrote the Introduction, Staffing, Strategic Objectives and Resourcing the Plan. The Commercial Operations Manager wrote the Business Plan for Consultancy, the Business Development Manager the Business Plan for Business Development and the Business Development Manager devised the Target for Income schedules for both Consultancy and Business Development. Neither the Commercial Operations Manager nor the Business Development Manager had any input into the mission statement which had been re-written sometime during late 1992 and early 1993 by senior management. The revised mission statement was that:

> Commercial operations will provide the college with the opportunity to establish its position in the North of England as a provider of quality courses. It will provide an education, training and consultancy service to meet the ever changing needs of industry, business, commerce and the service sector.

This was the first time than an 'official' business plan had been drawn up for the Commercial Unit and presented to senior management. After minor alterations in presentation, the business plan was finally accepted as a working document during November 1993.

Business plan content

The challenges that the Commercial Unit was facing when the writer commenced the new role of Business Development Manager in October 1993 were mainly to do with administrative procedures. Other areas of concern involved academic staff perceptions and how to ameliorate some of the negative aspects some people felt toward the Commercial Unit.

Although the Commercial Unit had been successful in acquiring BS 5750 Part 1, updating and revisions to the quality procedures had not occurred in any significant way.

It was felt that a business plan ought to be drawn up to formalise the Commercial Unit's intentions and provide a planning framework within which meaningful evaluations could be made.

The content of the business plan developed for the Commercial Unit was, in two important ways, heavily influenced by external factors. Firstly, this particular Business Plan Unit had to be consistent with the college mission statement and, secondly, the objectives were largely determined by college senior management. Others were added by the Business Development Manager as time went by and it became apparent that the original objectives were insufficient. On one occasion a senior manager asked that the Business Development Unit be responsible for open learning. This in turn meant that the college would have to represented at bi-monthly meetings of the North East Open Learning Network. It was also to be a requirement that the

Business Development Unit take on the development and writing of a bid to TTEC to become an accredited centre of accreditation of prior learning (APL) in Business Administration and Motor Vehicle studies as well as the managing of staff and quality audits for these curricular areas.

Other objectives which the writer was asked to include were as follows:

- To establish the college as a major local and regional centre for provision of commercial information technology courses.
- To develop and maximise the potential of a classroom for use with small *exclusive* customer groups.
- To maximise the use of the college training bus.
- To develop a vacation and weekend college consistent with the strategy presented to the Principal in March 1993.
- To monitor the progress of the business plan.

In exploring the operations of the Commercial Unit it was necessary to examine decision making processes, business planning and monitoring and review within the context of a business planning framework. This forms the focus of the next section.

The business planning framework

The framework used by the writer acknowledges the need to identify principles and to recognise the relationship that exists in a comprehensive business plan between stages of service delivery on the one hand and of policy development on the other (Newby and Prudhoe, 1993).

It is vitally important to the understanding of this framework that the terminology used here is defined.

Principles are taken here to be values or statements of belief. Their importance lies in it being necessary to keep these in mind at all times as they serve as a guide, as key values when developing and progressing the business plan.

An aim is taken to be a general statement of purpose or intent. In terms of the hierarchy of the business plan development this needs to sit at the very head of the plan as it is the most general of statements. No distinction is made here between this and other similar terms found elsewhere, such as mission statement.

An objective is used here to mean a statement of intent which is more specific than an aim. The achievement of an objective will contribute to the

191

achievement of an aim, given that they are related in this way, that is they are sequential and consistent with one another.

Having agreed aims and objective the next step in the development of a business plan would be to develop tasks or actions which relate to each objective and which contribute to the attainment of the specific objectives to which they relate. Targets are developed next. These are standards aimed for, often with a quantity or a time or completion date. There ought to be, wherever possible, at least one target for each task. This relational sequence then continues with performance indicators, selections of data or information showing whether or not targets are being met. In keeping with the pattern described thus far, there should be a performance indicator for each target.

Further terminology relates to stages in service delivery. Inputs or resources available to the productive process are the first stage in this sequence. No product can become a reality without first resources being deployed. The next stage is to do with processes, or what actually happens with and to resources as production takes place. These processes, along with the resources, should result in an output. Output is taken here to mean an amount of service or product. Finally, it is necessary to define outcomes. These are usually taken to be the view of, or satisfaction with the product expressed by users, but service outcomes, that is the impact on other services, are also used in this planning framework.

As has already been stated, the model used here attempts to bring together two sequences, firstly of aim, objective, task, target, performance indicator and lead personnel and secondly of input, process, output and outcome, at the objective stage. Thus there ought to be, in any comprehensive and complete business plan unit, objectives relating to input, process, output and outcome. Aims guide all other stages in policy development and thereby impact on the stages in service delivery. This is because inputs, process and outputs will be largely determined by the objectives, tasks and targets that it is sought to achieve. Of course, the relationship is more complex than that and, for example, a shortfall in resources or inputs could result in tasks and objectives having to be prioritised or dropped from the business plan altogether.

Research methods used

Monitoring, evaluation and review all played a part in this research. Monitoring has been described by Newby and Prudhoe (1993) as follows:

Monitoring has two main aspects. It is firstly something which is undertaken in an on-going fashion. Secondly, it focuses on hard data, perhaps quantifying output, user compliments or complaints. Such data can then be turned into useful information.

Evaluation for Newby and Prudhoe would involve the use of this and information of a qualitative nature, perhaps involving individual interviews or focus groups. Review would involve taking all of this information and examining it in relation to the business plan as a whole.

Before deciding on the methodologies which would be employed it was necessary to identify the groups whose views were to be researched. As far as the staff were concerned, it was decided that all academic staff ought to be contacted because one of the main objectives in the Business Development Business Plan was to:

Establish a business culture at the college that encourages staff to identify and develop potential commercial courses.

In terms of the senior management of the college it was decided that the views sought would be limited to those of the two Deputy Principals and the Training and Commercial Director as they were directly involved with the strategic and operational goals of the Commercial Unit.

Clearly, the views of current and past customers were of central importance to the researcher in terms of business development and market intelligence.

The relevance of this research project is clearly to help improve practice. The emphasis on this research is firstly, on monitoring the performance of the Commercial Unit and the practitioners who work in it. At a micro level, surveys, participant and interviewing studies enabled the writer to examine clients and assess the impact of the services provided. At a macro level, statistics are collected which enable income to be compared to expenditure. Secondly, following monitoring, there is a need to evaluate the new procedures and the impact of new policies. As well as the questionnaires used for monitoring, this was largely achieved via group interviews carried out at team meetings.

The term case study is commonly associated with 'qualitative' approaches to social research and, Hammersley (1993) has defined a case study:

... in terms of only one of the central features commonly associated with ethnographic and life history research: the investigation of a single case or a small number of cases.

In the context of this paper, the case study is of particular use for the writer as it allowed for the investigation of a number of 'naturally' occurring (as opposed to researcher-created) events in the course of the working period under review.

The planning of the surveys involved the writer in examining the combination of what Jupp (1993) terms as 'technical' and 'organisational' decisions and weighing up the feasibility of the study in terms of time and cost. An attempt was made to explore the various sample surveys that are commonly used in research and to balance what was practicable against what is desirable. Furthermore, a budget indicating time, cost and labour was drawn up to analyse what methods would be within the scope of this research.

Several factors ought to be closely examined before selecting a sampling method. Such factors will include cost, time, validity, relevance, representation and availability of population. By being aware of the different sample designs available, the writer was able to make a more informed decision in the planning stages as to which design would be most appropriate and most affordable. In coming to the decision about which sample design would be the most appropriate, general guidelines put forward by Moser and Kalton (1971) were followed.

They talk about the definition of the population and find it useful to:

... distinguish between the population for which the results are required, the target population, and the population actually covered, the survey population.

Though there was a wealth of secondary paperbased information, the quantitative data that was available was inappropriate for analysis for Business Development. The questionnaires were, therefore, revised and piloted. This revision affected both Business Development and Commercial Operations and, therefore, several meetings were called so that the revisions could be effected. After minor amendments the questionnaire was accepted by the Commercial Operations Unit and formalised in the BS 5750 Quality Manual.

When using highly structured data-collection methods, it is important that the researcher pilots the questionnaires to ensure that the respondents understand the questions, that the questions are asked in the 'best order' and possible answers adequately coded.

The writer followed a 'Likert' type question format which asked respondents to record their responses to a series of statements to do with service input, process, delivery and outcomes, using a standard set of six response categories ranging from 'Hardly at all' to 'Completely'. Another set of six response categories ranging from 'Poor' to 'Excellent' was also employed.

Wilson (1993) has highlighted how highly structured methods of data collection tend to be received favourably because of their 'proven methods' in the natural sciences, thus:

> ... by placing methods in the positivistic traditions of enquiry, this style of social research makes implicit claims to be regarded as a legitimate branch of the exact sciences.

Henwood and Pigeon (1993) emphasise that when carrying out interviews it is very important for the researcher to be as neutral (i.e. unbiased) as possible. Being non-directive and non-judgmental in response to questions raised by the respondents is also very important if bias is to be avoided. The interview schedule used was 'open-ended' and uncoded. This enabled exploration into the depth of understanding that each respondent had of the business planning framework. The translation of responses was done by the writer after the interviews.

Emphasis has been placed on Henwood and Pigeon's (1992) description of 'grounded theorising' and the use of this framework will help in the analysis of the interview data. Glaser and Strauss (1967) formulated this type of data analysis to help qualitative researchers make sense of usually large amounts of unstructured data. The central task in grounded theorising is the development of analytical categories. This is a creative process which relies on the researchers interpretative skills to constantly compare and contrast data and to refine and create further categories if necessary. This is sometimes referred to as the 'constant comparative method'. This process is said to continue until 'theoretical saturation' has been reached. The researcher is then able to elucidate the emerging theory. It ought to be noted that categories overlap. The writer has operationalised the categories under seven main questions.

A pilot investigation was not carried out on the interview schedule as the sample size was limited to those senior managers who were involved in the decision making processes of the Commercial Unit. Other members of the senior management team and academic staff were not directly involved in the decision-making process.

Generalisability of the results of the semi-structured interviews are unreliable as far as the college under investigation is concerned. However, Bell (1991) has stated:

> ... generalisation is unlikely, but relatability may be entirely possible. Well-prepared, small-scale studies may inform, illuminate and provide a basis for policy decisions within the institution.

Results of research on staff and customers

This section begins with a discussion of the interviews with senior college managers. Each respondent had a very different view on the usefulness of the business plan and how the framework could be used elsewhere within the college. Though all respondents agreed that the framework for the business plan was useful within the Commercial Operations Unit, only one of the respondents felt that its application could be used elsewhere in the college. All respondents felt comfortable with routine objectives being stated and implemented. Non-routine objectives, such as the Weekend and Vacation College proved a different matter and although there was no overt rejection of the proposal, it was clear that there was no universal ownership for such a scheme amongst the senior managers interviewed.

The interviews with the Principal were particularly illuminating. It was clear that the Principal was particularly keen for the Weekend and Vacation College objective to be implemented. However, problems arose which prevented such an objective being put in place. The main problem was a lack of access to the decision-making process other than through direct line managers who had the power to decide whether or not issues were presented to senior managers.

Next information acquired about levels of customer satisfaction with new business development is presented. It appears that there is a reasonably high level of customer satisfaction despite there being problems with agreeing satisfactory objectives on two of the three courses scrutinised. Other problems which emerged during the course of the eight months reviewed were dealt with on a 'one-to-one' basis with customers. Many of the problems were ameliorated quite quickly and were due to minor administrative errors.

The next part of this section examines other data collected from discussions with staff and incidental meetings.

The first objective within the business plan is to *'Establish a business culture at the college that encourages staff to identify and develop potential commercial courses'*. The plan suggests that this objective can at least start to be met by the carrying out of five tasks. These are as follows:

1   To develop and make available to senior management and their staff a proforma which will facilitate the outlining of proposed on and off site courses.
2   To agree with senior management and their staff the availability or otherwise of the resources necessary to facilitate the establishment of proposed commercial courses.
3   To cost all proposals that are put forward for commercial courses.
4   To agree with staff putting forward proposals the viability or otherwise of suggestions made.
5   To develop and distribute a procedural note indicating the steps to be gone through before, during and after the negotiation of contracts for the provision of commercial courses.

Many of the objectives contained within the Business Development Business Plan were successfully achieved. Some of the objectives, such as 'to provide information and guidance staff with course information', were largely irrelevant because of the concentration on the development of new and bespoke courses tailored to customers' needs.

Through carrying out the writing of the business plan, that is converting the general objectives set out in the college strategic plan into more specific and detailed tasks, an evaluation of how well the Commercial Operations Unit was working operationally could be made. Such an exercise proved to be invaluable in informing not only on how well strategic objectives were being implemented, but in facilitating the development and planning of future strategic plans.

Conclusion

This case study has been built around the development and implementation of the Commercial Unit Business Development Plan. The plan was produced in the hope that as rationale an approach as possible could be taken to policy development. It is such an approach that the framework tries to support. A positive outcome from this exercise has been that a similar framework has been introduced college-wide.

Some of the changes outlined in the business plan were too ambitious without a collegiate approach being taken. The weekend and vacation college for example, was too large a task for one small part of the college to undertake. The Lindblom (1979) point that organisations can, generally speaking, only change incrementally rings true here, as does Benveniste's (1977) point that doing nothing is safe and non-controversial. Whilst not drawing the conclusion that doing nothing was being advocated, a bottom up approach to objective setting was not successful. Those objectives set for the college as a whole had the necessary support for implementation, but attempts to contribute to this process of objective setting at unit level did not meet with success even though what was proposed was consistent with the rest of the business plan. The author is drawn to the conclusion that the key process of objective setting was inflexible and top down. Such an approach may be most appropriate for this organisation and this research can draw no conclusion on this point.

References

Bell, J. (1991) *Doing your Research Project, A Guide for First-time Researchers in Education and Social Science*, OU Press, Milton Keynes.

Benveniste, G. (1974) *Survival inside bureaucracy*, **In** *Decision Making, Approaches and Analysis* (ed. McGrew and Wilson) Manchester University Press, p.154-166.

Hammersley, M. (1993) *Case Study*, Principles of Social and Educational Research, Problem Formulation and Case Selection, OU Press, p.55-70.

Lindblom, C. (1979) *Still muddling, not yet through*, **In** *Decision Making, Approaches and Analysis* (ed. McGrew and Wilson) Manchester University press, p.125-138.

Moser, C.A. and Kalton, G. (1971) *Survey Methods in Social Investigation*, (2nd ed.), p.53, p.47-51.

Newby, A.K. and Prudhoe, A. (1993) *Business Planning Framework* (unpublished).

Wilson, M. (1993) *Asking Questions*, Principles of Social and Educational Research, Data Collection and Construction, OU Press p.5-30.

12 Connecting education and the workplace: some preliminary research on the Australian key competencies

Paul Hager

Abstract

In many countries there is an attempt to link together education and work-based training through the medium of vocational competencies. A number of issues are raised by this trend. There are strong traditions that make any reconciliation between education and the workplace difficult. In addition, views about how to teach by competencies effectively are also at odds, reflecting the major differences between theories of classroom learning and workplace learning. This chapter will outline these issues and illustrate them with the findings of some case studies on the role of key competencies in workplace training.

Introduction

There is an emerging worldwide interest in making better connections between education and the workplace. One example of this trend is the attempt to identify generic competencies thought to be common to performance in both education and the workplace. In Australia such generic competencies (which the Finn Report (1991) christened 'key competencies') are currently being employed in wide ranging attempts to revamp both formal education and workplace training. The Australian key competencies have their counterparts in other countries. In the United States they are known as 'workplace competencies' or 'foundation skills', in England and Scotland as 'core skills', and in New Zealand as 'essential skills'. In all cases, these competencies are thought to be generic in the sense that they underpin the acquisition of more specific competencies.

The main stimulus for this international trend is the perceived failure of schooling to develop in students all of the skills which are claimed to be essential for the high-skills workplace of the 1990s. One reading of this development is that it is part of a conservative agenda to capture education in the interests of capital. Another however, is that it is an equity initiative essential to increasing the life chances of individuals (most often those from working class backgrounds) failed by the traditional education system in an era where unskilled work is rapidly disappearing. Thus we have the interesting situation where supporters of both the political left and right are split amongst themselves, some advocating and some opposing these reforms with equal fervour.

Current Australian policy endorses eight key competencies as follows:

- collecting, analysing and organising information;
- communicating ideas and information;
- planning and organising activities;
- working with others in teams;
- using mathematical ideas and techniques;
- solving problems;
- using technology;
- using cultural understandings.

(Mayer Committee 1992a and 1992b, Queensland Department of Education 1994).

Each of these key competencies is further elaborated via a series of descriptors intended to provide further guidance for those using them to inform activities such as curriculum design, teaching, training, assessing, etc.

However, in order for these key competencies to provide significant and productive links between performance in both education and the workplace, a number of significant challenges first need to be met. One such challenge stems from the traditional tensions between education and work, based on dichotomous assumptions about general education vs vocational education;

mind vs body, education vs training, etc. These tensions are enduring and influential. One reason for this has been the belief that the proper focus of 'real' education is propositional knowledge, as exemplified in the traditional disciplines and subjects. This preoccupation has engendered the dichotomous thinking which views vocational education as mechanistic and unproblematic training in contrast to genuine education which is challenging and intellect developing (Hager, 1994). In extreme cases, the notion of 'vocational education' is itself regarded as almost a self-contradiction.

The challenge of the key competencies

So the key competencies present a formidable challenge to some entrenched educational assumptions. Given this situation, it is no surprise that a common response from traditionalist educators has been opposition to the key competencies on the grounds that they seek to subvert education to the needs of the workplace. It is argued that the outcomes of education should be far wider than vocational outcomes and must include values and orientations related to citizenship, social justice, life skills, etc. However, this overlooks the fact that the key competencies, far from being narrowly vocational, are closely related to the more general educational outcomes traditionally espoused for liberal education.

Fears that education will be subverted by the workplace seem to reflect a variety of basic assumptions including the following:

- that knowledge is superior to practice;
- that learning knowledge is more difficult than learning skills (thus more teaching is invested in the first as against the second);
- that formal education is more valuable than informal education (including workplace learning).

These assumptions reflect a view of vocational education which is both elitist and conceptually impoverished. Furthermore they ignore the potential of key competencies to liberalise vocational education as well as to further liberalise, even transform, the curriculum and pedagogy of general education. Incorporating the key competencies into vocational education and training would ensure that they become more liberal, supporting the Deweyan concept of education *through* occupations rather than specifically *for* occupations. Thus the combination of these developments in both the current vocational and general education sectors has the potential to break the destructive boundaries between general and vocational education which have characterised Western thought and practice for millennia (see Hager, 1990).

However, while these traditional assumptions about vocational education have proved to be remarkably durable throughout the entire history of formal education, some very different thinking has been emerging in recent years. Conceptualising education and the workplace in the dichotomous way discussed above inevitably divides theory from practice and creates the perennial problem of how to bring them together again when attempting to account for human action in the world. The dearth of satisfactory solutions to the theory/practice problem has generated a host of attempts in contemporary educational writings to bypass the problem. These attempts range from Schon's 'reflective practitioner' to problem-based learning. According to Yates and Chandler (1991) recent work in the cognitive psychology of knowledge shows the need to 'de-emphasise the spurious theory-and-practice connotations' that surround the declarative knowledge/ procedural knowledge and similar distinctions because 'they do not necessarily represent independent modes of functioning'.

Situated learning theory (Brown et al, 1989; Lave, 1988; Chaiklin and Lave 1993) provides another recent example of an attempt to bypass the theory/practice problem. According to Lave (1988).

'Cognition' observed in everyday practice is distributed - stretched over, not divided among - mind, body, activity and culturally organised settings (which include other actors).

Hence, Lave continues, the need to view 'cognition as a nexus of relations between the mind at work and the world in which it works'. The problem for situated learning theory is that it seems to be unable to progress beyond such holistic statements to an analysis of what they imply.

Overall, it can be said that while there is a common recognition of the need to reconceptualise the theory/practice dichotomy and its attendant limitations, no attempt thus far seems to have been completely successful. However a number of fairly clear principles about workplace learning can be drawn from this diverse work:

1   It is very different from classroom learning.
2   It is not very reliant on teachers and formal curricula.
3   Knowledge is not favoured over practice; rather the two are integrated in a seamless whole of 'know how'.

4   This 'know how' grows and develops with appropriately structured experience.
5   This 'know how' is often implicit.

Principles 3 to 5 are further illustrated by research findings on the development of expertise. According to this research, expert practitioners in a particular field have a repertoire of highly developed mental schemata which they have accumulated from experience. These schemata are drawn on by practitioners to recognise, classify and deal with the problems that confront them in their workplaces (see, e.g. Yates and Chandler, 1991). Thus novice teachers employ general principles learnt in their teacher education course to try to analyse and solve problems encountered in their first forays into classroom teaching. Expert teachers, however, rather than employing such general principles, automatically perceive new problems as reformulations of old ones and quickly fashion an appropriate response. This kind of research finding has been taken to indicate that workplace learning is richer than had been assumed previously. Rather than practitioners merely using general theories to analyse workplace problems and devise solutions, it appears that general theory may be somehow transformed by experience into mental schemata that are relatively context specific. This is reflected in the increasing realisation that graduates of academic courses are not yet equipped as competent practitioners. Hence the importance in various occupations of novices taking part in mandatory professional years, internships, probationary periods, practicums, etc.

As well as the challenge of the traditional tensions between education and work, the key competencies also generate interesting disagreements on the question of how best to teach them. Not surprisingly, these disagreements centre on views about the nature of the key competencies and about the nature of teaching. It has been very common to think of the key competencies as discrete independent skills each to be taught and assessed singly. This type of thinking has apparently been encouraged by acquaintance with the psychological literature on transfer with its emphasis on minimising and controlling variables. The logical outcome of this way of thinking is the view that the implementation of the key competencies requires that extra subjects be added to the curriculum. Once this has been judged to be impractical, the next response is to consider different ways of teaching and assessing existing subjects so as to cater for the key competencies. It has seemed to many commentators that this would involve some changes to teaching practices, as well as an increase in the amount of assessment, since the key competencies are more akin to skills than to knowledge (the major focus of current teaching and assessment practices).

These developments have served to direct attention to the questions of to what extent, and how well, do teaching and assessment of traditional subjects develop the key competencies in learners? Can these subjects be taught and assessed slightly differently so as to achieve the key competencies as well as the traditional subject outcomes? According to Lohrey (1995), based on traditional understandings of knowledge and classroom teaching, achieving this is not easy. Lohrey produces a list of principles that he claims need to be applied for successful teaching of key competencies:

- high road transfer;
- explicitness;
- self-awareness;
- integrated thinking and action;
- active and interactive learning;
- multiplicity; and
- integrated procedures.

Lohrey's principles are largely derived from the example of Alverno College in the USA which features a reportedly successful and innovative approach to teaching and assessing higher order generic competencies in professional preparation courses in teaching, business and nursing (see Hager, 1992). Teaching and assessment at Alverno are based on eight principles whose implementation requires an unusual degree of time, co-operation and commitment from staff. In the Alverno case this dedication has been forthcoming because the college is a former training institution for a religious order staffed by nuns. Lohrey's main advance on the Alverno principles is to add a linguist's perspective on the conditions needed to facilitate high road transfer. This includes a central role for metaphors and a requirement for learners to engage with the deep structure of knowledge. The magnitude of the task posed for teachers by Lohrey is clear from his assertion that '[e]xisting teaching practices and curricula in all sections of the education industry in Australia have been designed for low road transfer' (1995).

Thus, the overall picture to emerge from Lohrey's work is that there are dramatic changes needed if the key competencies are to be implemented. However, as useful and suggestive as Lohrey's work is, it is nevertheless, itself based on various assumptions about the nature of the key competencies and what is involved in learning them. While the present research projects make no claim to provide definitive answers on these questions, instances of skilled workers displaying a high level of the key competencies within the context of their workplace were common. It also seems to be very unlikely that these people went through a complex learning process as characterised by Lohrey's principles. This suggests that vocational education and workplace training may have something to offer to the debate on how to teach the key competencies.

The research projects

The two projects that will be outlined briefly were both exploratory. They were pilot projects in that, given the recency of the advent of the key competencies in Australia, there was no available research that focused on the role of key competencies in the workplace. The first research project (Gonczi et al, 1995), commissioned by the New South Wales Department of Industrial Relations, Employment, Training and Further Education, sought to ascertain the extent to which trainees/apprentices in five selected industries and courses exhibited the key competencies in their work. The research also examined, in terms of the presence or absence of the key competencies, each industry's curriculum documents, the actual training practices both formal and non-formal in the industry and also the assessment practices. The project was conducted by a team of six researchers from the University of Technology, Sydney using a variety of interview techniques as well as observations in six workplaces in each of the five industries. The five jobs studied were hairdressing apprenticeship, timber/building materials traineeship (e.g. selling customised kitchens), food and beverage traineeship, electrical installation apprenticeship and metals fabrication apprenticeship. The project was carried out in late 1994 and early 1995.

The second research project (Hager et al, 1996), commissioned by the same client, was designed to extend the findings of the first project. By working closely with selected trainers and workplaces across a range of industries, the broad aim was to develop a series of models for incorporating the key competencies into on-the-job training curriculum, into on-the-job training delivery, and into assessment and reporting practices. This second research project was conducted by a team of seven researchers from the University of Technology, Sydney. Broadly, an action research approach was adopted in which the researchers and the co-operating trainers jointly designed, carried out and modified the particular project in each workplace.

Discussion of results

There is no space to give a detailed discussion of all of the findings of these two research projects. Instead, the emphasis in what follows is on the main findings and their implications for the issues discussed in the first part of this chapter. In particular, some results from these research projects will be discussed in relation to the five broad principles about workplace learning outlined earlier:

1   It is very different from classroom learning.
2   It is not very reliant on teachers and formal curricula.
3   Knowledge is not favoured over practice; rather the two are integrated in a seamless whole of 'know how'.
4   This 'know how' grows and develops with appropriately structured experience.
5   This 'know how' is often implicit.

First, however, a few general points will be made about the overall findings and a summary will be provided of the estimated presence of the key competencies in the five occupations studied in the first project.

Despite the fact that there was little formal understanding of the key competencies amongst trainers and managers, there was a high level of commitment to the notion of generic skills. The extent of this commitment was, however, typically limited to their own workplace needs as they perceived them. In the hairdressing industry, for example, there was a strong commitment to developing communication competencies and planning competencies. In the metals traineeship there was not felt to be a major need to develop the cultural understanding of trainees or their communication competencies, but a strong need was felt to develop mathematical ideas and the ability to work in a team.

It is important that the acquisition of proficiency in the key competencies needs to be seen as a developmental process stretching over a substantial part of the life span. When trainees/apprentices start their employment with a firm, their participation is peripheral and they are seen as only partly legitimate members of that enterprise. The more that trainees/apprentices become full participants in the social and technical world of the enterprise the higher the level of the key competencies that they exhibit in their work performance. For example, fourth year apprentices in an electrical firm had higher key competency levels than the first year apprentices in the same industry. In the hairdressing industry, first year apprentices undertake a limited range of tasks such as cleaning the salon, washing clients' hair, etc. and proceed in later years to more complex tasks such as perming and colouring. Even in these later years, however, there is limited autonomous work and the qualified professional more often undertakes most of the advanced technical work. For trainees engaged in a one year program it is possible that such full participation may take a number of years to attain, depending on the complexity of the work and the enterprise.

Where the trainees are older (e.g. in the timber/building materials traineeship) they possessed greater numbers of the key competencies as well as higher levels of them. The major reason for this seems to have been the fact that the vast majority of the trainees had been members of their timber/ building firms for considerable periods before they commenced the traineeship. This suggests that adulthood and general life experiences tend to develop increasing proficiency in deployment of the key competencies.

An important finding of the first research project was that in almost all cases the trainees/apprentices do not possess all of the key competencies, and that those that they do possess, are rarely at high levels. So, if we accept the judgement of the Finn and Mayer committees that *all* of the key competencies are needed to enable young people to function effectively in a range of social, work and educational situations, then a problem does exist.

In respect of the estimated presence of the key competencies in the occupations studied in the first project, there were two main findings.

1 *Key competencies significant in all five jobs studied*

There are three key competencies which were significantly present in all five jobs at trainee level. These were 'working with others and in teams', 'using mathematical ideas and techniques', and 'using technology'. These findings reflect the fact that some teamwork is required in all of the jobs studied. Likewise, work in all five jobs requires the performance of some basic mathematical calculations. Finally, work in all five occupations studied required the use of machines of one kind or another, typically a relatively routine use.

Another key competency, 'problem solving', was rated as a somewhat significant competency for work performance in all of the five industries studied, however some hesitancy about its importance for trainees/ apprentices was evident. In the three industries centred on customer service, problem solving tended to be interpreted as dealing with a difficult or dissatisfied customer. While trainees/apprentices are expected to deal with minor customer problems, it was generally seen as the role of management to solve more difficult problems. In electrical and metals, problem solving tended to be viewed as fault finding and it was agreed that trainees/ apprentices need to do at least some of this at a basic level.

2   Key competencies significant in only some of the jobs studied

The main finding here was that several of the remaining key competencies were significantly present in the three jobs that centre on customer service but were relatively absent in the others. Thus the main examples of 'collecting, analysing and organising information' were in those jobs where it was important to find out customers' needs and present them with a range of alternatives from which to choose. In many cases, the customers' needs are only partly thought through or articulated and they are looking to the trainee for help in clarifying their options. The main jobs where this applies are hairdressing, timber/building materials and food and beverage. In the case of the electrical apprenticeships and metals traineeships, trainees did not employ this competency in their immediate work responsibilities. Similar results were found for 'communicating ideas and information' and 'planning and organising activities'.

'Cultural understanding' was not rated as a major competency for work performance in any of the five industries studied. However it was rated more highly in the three industries centred on customer service.

Thus different combinations of generic key competencies are required in different industries and occupations. Also, the customer service industries, in contrast to other industries, require a wider range of the generic key competencies. It was also noticed that in all industries studied, where enterprises engaged in training in key competencies, these enterprises tended to be regarded as successful by industry peers. While these conclusions apply to trainees, interviews with training managers indicated that further training of experienced employees would need to cover some of the generic key competencies not included in the initial training of the enterprise's trainee staff.

Three other conclusions stood out in both research projects: Firstly, the great diversity in training practices across the enterprises and industries studied. Secondly, the strong emphasis on generic key competencies, particularly 'working in teams' and 'using technology', in work based training in the enterprises. Thirdly, it was found that there is a complex web of factors that affect the nature of the training in the key competencies and the extent to which an individual trainee/apprentice develops them. While it may be possible to infer a causal relationship between the training practices and the development of key competencies in individuals, there are so many variables in each situation, that caution against drawing simplistic conclusions about this process is appropriate. Rather, the research projects suggested a number of tentative hypotheses which need further investigation.

The five interconnected variables which affect the nature of training for the key competencies across and within industries are:

- The training culture in the industry

The training culture in the industry derives from the history and traditions of training within the enterprise and/or industry. This influences both the attitudes and level of commitment to training. The training culture may also be shaped by factors such as customer service requirements, competitive pressures, quality initiatives, links between on- and off-the-job training, and industrial reform.

- The nature of the work in the industry

The nature of the work in the industry concerns the range and variety of tasks performed by trainees/apprentices and the way that these tasks are organised and performed within and across enterprises within the industry.

- The size of the firm

In relation to the size of the firm, the research projects found that, generally speaking, planned, structured and consistent training was present more frequently in large and medium-sized firms than in small firms.

- Trainers' understandings of the learning/teaching processes

The researchers noted that inadequate trainer and assessor skills often led to atomistic and mechanistic approaches to competency-based training and assessment. Such approaches were seen as likely to hinder the development of the key competencies by trainees.

- The age, experience and capacity of trainees/apprentices

To add to this complexity, each of these five variables can have a number of dimensions. Obviously these variables are not discrete categories. The researchers in these two projects were able to identify instances where all of these variables combined to produce first class training and a clear development of the key competencies in the trainees. In other instances, less happy combinations of these variables produced no real training in the key competencies and very little development of key competencies in individuals.

Finally, we turn to the findings of the two research projects in relation to the five broad principles about workplace learning outlined earlier.

1 Workplace learning is very different from classroom learning

The key competencies illustrated this principle very clearly. As noted above, the introduction of key competencies into schooling has generated debate about whether extra subjects should be added to the curriculum, or, if not, whether there should be an increase in the amount of assessment as existing subjects are taught and assessed in new ways so as to cater for the key competencies. The research on the role of key competencies in the workplace suggests a somewhat different way of looking at these issues, since in this case the key competencies are not to be thought of as 'optional extras'.

The relationship between relatively specific work skills (elements of competence) and generic skills (key competencies) is not well understood. In particular, it is not well understood that when significant work activities are considered they typically feature both specific work skills and key competencies (usually more than one) as well as aspects of the particular work context. Thus, work contexts integrate specific skills and key competencies. There were many cases of this encountered in the conduct of the two research projects. For example, the critical incident scenarios developed in hairdressing all centre on some significant workplace incident in which a competent response integrates both a range of specific skills and various key competencies.

Why is this relatively simple point so little understood? There are, no doubt, various reasons. One reason is a prevailing myth that key competencies are free floating components of work that can be described and taught in isolation. On this erroneous view, key competencies take on a life of their own and people simply have to learn them in isolation and then transfer them to new situations. In reality the key competencies are more holistic. Another reason for the lack of understanding of the key competencies is the propensity to favour specific skills descriptions when analysing work. This reliance on very narrow descriptions of specific skills makes it seem an 'objective' fact that such skills are independent of the key competencies. However, as these research projects repeatedly found, specific

210

skills are deployed in a context which typically changes somewhat from client to client, from order to order, from case to case. The requirement that skilled work take into account changing context is, on its own, usually enough to bring the key competencies into play. Thus work is seldom as narrow as task-based competency standards might suggest. Time and again in this research it was found that any significant unit of work activity can be seen as embodying simultaneously both specific skills and several of the key competencies.

Hence the conclusion that the key competencies are far from being 'optional extras' in workplace learning and training. If these activities are being carried out well then they will automatically incorporate and contextualise at least some of the key competencies. Although it is acknowledged that schooling is different in important ways from workplace learning and training, a proper understanding of the role of the key competencies in the workplace might be suggestive for thinking about their appropriate role in schooling. Could it be, for example, that all that is required in schools is some change in the emphasis of teaching and assessment practices rather than the drastic changes that some have feared?

Whether the focus of vocational learning is on-the-job in the workplace or in courses conducted in traditional vocational education institutions, these research projects supported the following recommendations:

- Use the key competencies as a vehicle for enriching training. This will encourage a more integrated, systematic and strategic approach.
- Make the key competencies more explicit in training in the same way that specific occupational knowledge and skill are made explicit. It would seem that the key competencies have not been emphasised enough in traditional vocational education and training.
- Use the key competencies to link on- and off-the-job training. In the same way as they are central to linking specific and generic within a work context, they also underpin the application of off-the-job training to particular workplace contexts.
- Emphasise the importance of the key competencies for all of the workforce in an enterprise. That is, they should be viewed as integral to successful career development and not just to the training of apprentices/ trainees.

2 Workplace learning is not very reliant on teachers and formal curricula

Once again, the key competencies provide a clear illustration of this principle. Despite the fact that trainers and managers perceive the key competencies to be important for the success of their enterprises, there is very little explicit training to develop them. The fact that the research evidence suggested that trainees/apprentices possess at least some of the key competencies indicates this may not be quite as serious a problem as it appears to be at first. If the key competencies can be developed through informal means such as job rotation schemes, work simulations eg. on foam dummies, observing experts undertaking authentic work activity, or being coached in a one-to-one situation, it is reasonable to ask is there a need for more formal training?

It appears that, as noted in the previous point, the key competencies are embedded in various combinations in ordinary work settings and that learning to operate effectively in particular settings will often lead to the development of the required levels of these competencies. At the same time, trainees appear to develop ways of understanding and knowing where their current work fits with other things learnt during their traineeship. In other words they are developing cognitive schemes at the same time as they are developing skills and attitudes. However, as mentioned above, this is a gradual process of enculturation and cognitive development. Nevertheless, the fact that some key competency development occurs as part of normal training activities, does not mean that this training could not be significantly improved by addressing the key competencies more explicitly and systematically.

3 Knowledge is not favoured over practice in workplace learning; rather the two are integrated in a seamless whole of 'know how'

As already indicated, the key competencies provide a good basis for viewing work more holistically. As a general principle, if it is found that particular units of work can be described without involving the key competencies, then the work units are probably being described too narrowly to be very useful from a training perspective.

Since clusters of the key competencies appear to underpin any significant unit of workplace performance, it follows that the key competencies are best not treated in isolation from one another in the workplace. This suggests that one way of linking education and the workplace via key competencies would be to view the development of the key competencies as becoming gradually more integrated and holistic as young people move through schooling. By the time that they are ready to move into workplaces the idea that sound performance in very many of life's situations centres on deployment of suitable combinations of key competencies could facilitate students' transition to work.

Noting the integration of the key competencies in actual workplace activities, the researchers recommended the use of the following approaches:

- Adopt an holistic and integrative training orientation. This will encourage key competency awareness. An atomistic training orientation will discourage key competency awareness.
- Emphasise that the 'situation' (or context) is crucial.
- Analyse the workplace and identify situations that have a potential for including key competencies to improve work performance. For example, answering the phone effectively may be good customer relations, but it can also involve communication and problem solving of a high order. Since the key competencies take different forms in each workplace, it is important that general descriptions be contextualised.
- Based on the second research project, methods that appear to work well include critical incident scenarios, problem-based learning, and trainer and trainee assessment tools which integrate the key competencies. Mapping activities and the development of contextualised descriptors were also useful in relating the key competencies to workplace training activities and in identifying areas in which the key competencies could be used to improve current practices.

4 Workplace learnt 'know how' grows and develops with appropriately structured experience

This principle suggests that key competencies should be thought of more broadly than just in terms of school and work. These competencies represent a basis for lifelong learning in all kinds of situations. Rather than being thought of as discrete skills that people learn to transfer, the key competencies should be seen as learnt capacities to handle an increasing variety of diverse situations. Thus transfer becomes more a growth in confidence and adaptability as learners experience ever more success in their deployment of the key competencies to a range of situations. To put it another way, perhaps it is not so much the key competencies that transfer, as growing understanding of how to deal with different contexts. In this way, non-work experiences can benefit workplace performance and vice versa.

The second research project also highlighted the need for approaches to the key competencies which maximised opportunities for integrating experiences in different learning contexts (i.e. in the workplace whether on- or off-the-job, or off-the-job in an educational institution).

5   Workplace 'know how' is often implicit

It is noted in the course of both research projects that people sometimes denied possessing key competencies though researcher observation of these same people in action in the workplace suggested otherwise. One common illustration of this was provided by the 'using cultural understandings' key competency. Many of the workplaces in the research projects featured staff and/or clients of many and diverse ethnic origins. The relative harmony and co-operation observed in the day-to-day functioning of most of these workplaces suggested that staff were proficient in this particular key competency as it related to their workplace context. Yet the researchers found that trainers repeatedly denied the relevance of the 'cultural understandings' key competency to their workplace. While this can be taken as an example of implicit 'know how', part of the problem in this case seems to be due to the way this particular key competency is described in the official literature. As currently portrayed in its descriptors, 'cultural understandings' lacks appropriate workplace connections. For example, the workplace is itself an important culture, but this is not apparent in the descriptors. The researchers in these projects repeatedly found people tending to view the descriptors for this key competency as a bureaucratically decided and imposed set of requirements which they resented. It was recommended that this key competency needs to be re-examined with the cultures of workplaces in mind.

Conclusion

The implementation of the key competencies in Australia represents a massive educational change. This chapter has argued that this major change faces at least two significant challenges. It boldly seeks to bridge the education-work dichotomy, a divide that traditional educational arrangements have institutionalised. The research evidence outlined in the chapter suggests

that a proper understanding of key competencies can meet this challenge since key competencies serve to integrate the generic and the specific within a given work context. The other challenge was uncertainty on how best to teach and assess key competencies. While not providing definitive answers, the research conducted in workplaces provided some interestingly different ways of conceptualising the problem. What is evident from the research is that the successful implementation of this major educational change is still a long way off.

References

Brown, J.S., Collins, A. and Duguid, P. (1989) 'Situated Cognition and the Culture of Learning', *Educational Researcher*, 18 (Jan-Feb), pp.32-42.

Chaiklin, S. and Lave, J. (eds.) (1993) *Understanding Practice: Perspectives on Activity and Context*, Cambridge: Cambridge University Press.

Finn Report (1991) *Young People's Participation in Post-Compulsory Education and Training*, Report of the Australian Education Council Review Committee, Canberra: Australian Government Publishing Service.

Gonczi, A., Curtain, R., Hager, P., Hallard, A. and Harrison, J. (1995) *Key Competencies in On the Job Training*, Sydney: UTS/DEET.

Hager, P. (1990) 'Vocational Education/General Education - A False Dichotomy?', *Studies in Continuing Education*, **12**(1), pp.13-23.

Hager, P. (1992) 'Teaching and Assessment of Higher Level Competencies - The Alverno Approach', in G. Scott ed. *Defining, Developing and Assessing Higher Order Competencies in the Professions*, Faculty of Education UTS Monograph Series, Sydney: UTS, pp.33-40.

Hager, P. (1994) 'Is There A Cogent Philosophical Argument Against Competency Standards?', *Australian Journal of Education*, **38**(1), pp.3-18.

Hager, P., McIntyre, J., Moy, J., Comyn, P., Stone, J. Schwenke, C. and Gonczi, A. (1996) *Workplace Keys: Piloting the Key Competencies in Workplace Training*, Sydney: UTS/DEET.

Lave, J. (1988) *Cognition in Practice: Mind, Mathematics and Culture in Everyday Life*, Cambridge: Cambridge University Press.

Lohrey, A. (1995) *Transferability in Relation to the Key Competencies*, Occasional Paper No.16, Centre for Workplace Communication and Culture, Sydney: UTS/James Cook University.

Mayer Committee (1992a) *Employment Related Key Competencies: A Proposal for Consultation*, Melbourne: Mayer Committee.

Mayer Committee (1992b) *Key Competencies*, Report of the Committee to advise the Australian Education Council and Ministers of Vocational Education, Employment and Training on employment-related Key Competencies for postcompulsory education and training, Canberra: AEC and MOVEET.

Queensland Department of Education (1994) *Cultural Understandings as the Eighth Key Competency*, Final Report to the Queensland Department of Education and the Queensland Vocational Education, Training and Employment Commission, Sydney: NLLIA Centre for Workplace Communication and Culture.

Yates, G. and Chandler, M. (1991) 'The Cognitive Psychology of Knowledge: Basic Research Findings and Educational Implications', *Australian Journal of Education*, 35(2), pp.131-53.

13 Looking back on change

John Sheehan

Abstract

This paper focuses on changes in teacher training provision for the further education sector at Huddersfield in the past 50 years. These changes are analysed at three levels. First, examples of official documents such as Acts of Parliament, circulars, papers and reports are introduced in order to provide the context in which the changes took place. Second, examples of relevant literature by practitioners in the field which appeared in the period are used as a means of charting the changes which have occurred and reflecting developments arising in practice. Third, some of the changes which occurred in the period at an institutional level at Huddersfield are identified and discussed and set in the wider context of government intentions, the evolving literature on technical teacher training, and the implications for managing these changes.

Introduction

A study of change is normally concerned with the investigation, implementation and the evaluation of here-and-now issues and problems as they arise in practice. The Monitoring Change in Education series to which this volume belongs generally focuses on contemporary matters concerning change in education. This paper is an exception because in 1997 teacher training at Huddersfield will reach the golden milestone in its development. The Editorial Board for this series therefore thought a retrospective view of change would be a contribution in marking this notable anniversary. Over and above this, an analysis of the past has the potential to chart the changes which have taken place in the period concerned. Such an approach can identify what came into fashion in the period and what has endured. It is important to learn from the past and take account of the lessons learned when formulating policies and developing practices for the future.

The approach to be used in this chapter is to deal with a decade of changes and developments at a time. For each decade examples of Acts of Parliament, circulars, papers and reports are set out in a table. Next, examples of relevant literature from the period are introduced; and, finally developments at Huddersfield are identified and the implications for management are also identified.

It is perhaps obvious that compressing 50 years of change, and attempting to take account of some governmental edicts, some of the relevant literary output and the resulting impact on the college at Huddersfield means that much will be dealt with lightly. However, the intention is to attempt to provide a flavour of what has happened at Huddersfield over the first half-century of its existence. A book would be needed to do justice to the range of issues involved and it is hoped some one will be moved to take up a pen and address the task fully.

The development of technical education

Teacher education at Huddersfield is based on a campus on Holly Bank Road which is geographically separate from the rest of the university. The campus is widely known in this country and in many other countries as 'Holly Bank' and this is the term which will be used for the remainder of this chapter.

Table 1   The 1940s

1942	Beveridge Report, Social Insurance and Allied Services	1945	Percy Report, Higher Technical Education
1943	Norwood Report, Curriculum and Examination in Secondary Schools	1946	National Insurance Act
		1946	National Health Service Act
1944	Butler Education Act	1948	Educational Foundation for Visual Aids
1944	McNair Report, Teachers and Youth Leaders		

The concept of technical teacher training in Britain was conceived in a cauldron of change. For the first half of the 1940s the energies of the nation were directed to fighting World War Two. However, before that conflict was over plans were already being laid to fight the enemies within. These were identified by Sir William Beveridge in his 1942 report as want which was to be overcome by a National Insurance Scheme; disease which was to be overcome by a National Health Service; ignorance which was to be overcome by more and better schools; squalor which was to be overcome by better houses; and idleness which was to be overcome by positive government policies to stimulate business activity.

Perusal of Table 1 shows that all societal evils identified by Beveridge were dealt with at a legislative level, except housing which received attention later. The McNair Report (1944) listed in Table 1 was concerned with teacher training and there was a need emerging to train teachers for the FE sector. The first technical teacher training college in England was set up at Bolton College in 1946; Garnett College, London was also set up in 1946; Huddersfield followed in 1947; and the college at Wolverhampton was set up in 1961. These colleges became established as the four colleges of education (technical) in England (Williams, 1962). Technical teacher training in Scotland began at Jordanhill College of Education, Glasgow, in 1966 (Niven, 1992).

Holly Bank began its existence in 1947 in a small way under the direction of Alexander MacLennan. It was accommodated in a former private house and began with 52 students and four staff. From such modest beginnings Holly Bank developed into a major provider of FE teacher training rising to a student population of approximately 2000. At first only certificate level qualifications were offered; there was, however, as we shall see later, a steady progression through the various academic levels taking in on the way diplomas, bachelor's and master's degrees and the postgraduate research degrees of MPhil and PhD. For much of its existence, Holly Bank courses were validated by the University of Leeds. A constructive and fruitful relationship with Leeds lasted for nearly 40 years. However, when degree courses were mounted in the 1970s, these were validated by the Council for National Academic Awards (CNAA). Some courses at Holly Bank were validated by Leeds and some by the CNAA for a while. The CNAA was set up in 1966 to validate and to examine courses in the polytechnic and college sector, eventually assuming responsibility for the validation of all courses, so that the involvement with Leeds eventually ceased. In the run-up to its demise in 1992 the CNAA gradually devolved responsibility for courses to institutions. Another major change occurred in 1992 when the polytechnic achieved university status, allowing the institution to validate its courses. This meant assuming responsibility for the validation and examination of the courses offered. It took approximately 45 years for Holly Bank to achieve its present degree of academic autonomy as far as the validation of courses is concerned. Policies and procedures, of course, were already in existence to maintain academic standards and to ensure quality and so on, so that the transition to the present state of autonomy was not a very radical departure from that which existed already. Nevertheless greater autonomy inevitably meant the management of change took on a new dimension.

Holly Bank has undergone a metamorphosis during its existence as far as titles are concerned It started life as a Training College for Technical Teachers. In the 1960s it became a College of Education (Technical), when there was a tendency to substitute education for training in relation to the preparation of teachers. At the merger with the polytechnic in 1974, Holly Bank became part of the Faculty of Education. A structural organisation in 1988 meant it became the School of Education within the then polytechnic. It retains this title within the University of Huddersfield.

The house where technical teacher training began in Huddersfield was only a temporary measure and was not adequate to meet the growing need for more space. Work on purpose-built accommodation began at Holly Bank in 1957 and the building as it now exists was completed in 1969.

When Holly Bank was set up in 1947 the notion of technical teacher training in Britain was, as indicated earlier, in its infancy. However, technical education has a long history; but in this paper it is only possible to pick out a few milestones in order to provide a context for technical teacher training. It may be said that it was originated by Hippocrates (460-377 BC) in a medical context for he set out the three loves as he saw them. Philantropia, a love of man; philotechnia, a love of the art of technique; philosophia, a love of wisdom (Owen, 1991). To take an enormous historical leap forward, a milestone nearer our time was the Great Exhibition at the Crystal Palace in Hyde Park in May, 1851. This was the first world fair. Developments since the Great Exhibition are to be found in Arygles (1964) who deals with progress in technical education from 1851 to 1963. A paper by Musgrave (1964) was concerned with defining the concept of technical education in the period 1860-1910. Taken together, these two sources provide a useful starting point for those wishing to understand something of the background of technical education in Britain.

Table 2   The 1950s

1956	White Paper, Technical Education	1958	Carr Report, Training for Skills
1956	Willis-Jackson Report, The Supply and Training of Teachers for Technical Colleges	1959	The Crowther Report, '16-18'
1957	Circular 323, Liberal Education		

The 1956 White Paper, Technical Education was both defensive and expansive in tone. At the defensive level concern was expressed that technical education and technology in Britain was falling behind the USA, Russia and Western Europe. On an expansive note it proposed the spending of £100 M over five years to fund the expansion of technical colleges to complement an earlier expansion of technology in the universities (MacLure, 1965).

The expansion of technical colleges inevitably meant an expansion of technical teacher training and this issue was also addressed in 1956 with the publication of the Willis-Jackson Report. This report stressed the importance of teacher training. The existing full-time, otherwise known as pre-service, courses had not recruited sufficiently well to meet the demand for teachers. The answer to the problem was seen to be the introduction of part-time courses.

Holly Bank responded in a very comprehensive and innovative way to the demand for in-service teacher training courses by establishing a network of extra-mural centres, eventually transformed into associate centres. The first of these was established at Durham in 1966, with Peter Frankland in charge. These centres grew to 30 in number and the geographical limits were Carlisle in the north and Ipswich in the south of the country. A number of models were used concerning the teaching at these centres. Sometimes a member of staff from Holly Bank was posted to a centre such as Durham. In other cases Holly Bank staff travelled to the centres to do the teaching. At other centres the staff at the host college did the teaching. The composition of the student groups at the centres was generally mixed and, for example, usually comprised engineering, office arts, construction, business studies students and so on. At the centres what was known as 'general method' was taught. This included a study of the teaching and learning strategies common to all teachers. However, Holly Bank always prided itself in having expertise in what was known locally as 'special method', engineers being taught to teach engineering by a tutor who is an engineer and so on for other groups.

The special method element of the Holly Bank teacher training courses is taught in 'blocks', now called summer schools, at Holly Bank. At one time blocks lasted two weeks, but now the summer schools last a week. Management of the blocks/summer schools presents a logistical challenge. About 600 students at a time converge on Holly Bank and, since most live in residential accommodation for the period, their basic needs for food and shelter and the like must be met before any teaching can begin. Once domestic matters are attended to the blocks are generally an enriching experience for all concerned and Holly Bank is very much alive with a wide range of activities. The diverse geographical origins of the students and the equally wide range of subjects which they represent adds to the interest and vitality of these occasions.

Mention was made earlier of a number of models being used concerning the teaching at the extra-mural centres. However, in 1991 a system of franchising was introduced. Now the teaching is done by the staff at these centres, with the students still coming to Holly Bank for the summer schools.

Circular 323 dealt with the matter of liberal education in technical colleges. Without resorting to dictionary definitions the term technical education and training is generally associated with practical activities rather than abstract thinking, although this is something of a simplification of the issues. Liberal studies, in contrast, are concerned with a liberalising and a broadening of the understanding and values of the students. In response to Circular 323, Holly Bank devised an impressive programme of what was called 'supporting studies'. These included, for example, painting, pottery, poetry, play reading, drama and so on. These supporting studies were generally highly regarded by the students. Examples of journal papers on liberal studies include Hall (1965), Neale (1966), Lawrence (1967) and Pullen (1979).

Publications in the 1950s were influential as far as technical teacher training was concerned. Programmed learning, for example, came into use as a consequence of Skinner's (1965) paper, though there were others working in the field. From 1962 onwards programmed learning was adopted as an integral part of both pre-service and in-service courses at Holly Bank and the principal exponent of the approach was Walter Corns (Corns, 1966). Programmed learning, of course, soon slipped off the educational agenda and will probably merit a footnote in history in the category of passing trends.

Behaviour objectives are a product of the 1950s. Bloom et al (1956) and Krathwohl et al (1964) were first in the field to be followed by Mager (1962) and Grondlund (1978). These publications were followed by a contribution on the topic by Holly Bank staff in the persons of Dennis Carroll, Ted Duggan and Roy Etchells (Carroll et al, 1978). There can be no doubt that objectives occupied a dominant position in technical education for a while. Then criticisms emerged concerning the prescriptive and deterministic nature of the objectives approach. Moreover, the nature of learning is such that it is not always possible to specify in advance all the learning that is likely to take place in a teaching and learning encounter. The later Tony Wesson, then a member of staff at Holly Bank, was among those to offer a critique of the objectives-based approach to education. (Wesson, 1983 a and b). Peter McKenzie, another Holly Bank colleague, went a stage further and in his paper offered an alternative to the objectives approach (McKenzie, 1985). Much of the heat has gone out of the objectives debate. Some teachers are still for them and others are definitely against them. They have not, however, slipped off the educational agenda, and now occupy a modified modest position in the scheme of things as 'learning outcomes'.

Table 3   The 1960s

Year	Event	Year	Event
1961	White Paper, Better Opportunities in Technical Education	1964	Henniker-Heaton Report, Day Release
1962	TETOC set up[1]	19641	Industrial Training Act
1963	Robbins Report, Higher Education	966	Russell Report, Training and Supply of Teachers
1963	Judges Report, Research in Technical Education	1966	Pilkington Report, Approval of FE Courses
1963	Further Education Staff (Coombe Lodge) set up	1967	Abortion Act
1964	Department of Education and Science set up	1967	Sexual Offences Act
1964	CNAA set up	1968	Linked Courses
		1968	College Government Act
		1968	Open University set up
		1969	Haslegrave Report

[1]   TETOC Technical Education and Training for Overseas Countries

The 1960s are sometimes described as the swinging 60s, though the term has been used so much that it is perhaps now no more than a cliché. However, there can be little doubt that it was an action-packed decade.

223

Harold Wilson, then Leader of the Opposition, promised in his Scarborough speech of 1963 to deliver a new Britain forged in the white heat of the technological revolution.

The term 'permissive society' has also been used to characterise the 1960s because of the enactment of the Abortion Act (1967) and the Sexual Offences Act (1967). Both of these reforms led to bitter arguments and protests. For some these reforms were timely and much needed; for others they were abhorrent pieces of legislation which would erode the moral fabric of society and lead to decadence and depravity.

Matters more specifically educational included the Robbins Report (1963) which resulted in a big expansion of the higher education sector and the creation of several new universities. The setting up of the Further Education Staff College (Coombe Lodge) in 1963 was a significant event because it provided a forum for FE staff to discuss and debate the issues of the day. Moreover, the college produced a steady stream of publications which were invaluable to FE staff. The creation of the CNAA in 1964 was to have a profound effect on the non-university sector of higher education. The validation and the examination of courses would never be the same again. Criticisms of the CNAA were that it tended to be too bureaucratic over the documentation it required relating to the courses it validated. But it could be argued that this had the effect of making curricular intentions more explicit than had been the case before. Other criticisms were that CNAA validation events were sometimes unduly confrontational. However, the practice of submitting curricular proposals for validation to a panel of well-informed peers external to the institution had much to commend it from the point of view of maintaining standards and ensuring the quality of educational provision.

The CNAA made a considerable impact on the non-university sector of higher education, but so did the 1966 White Paper, A Plan for Polytechnics and other Colleges, for it gave rise to the binary system of higher education. Universities were on one side of the binary line and the polytechnics and colleges were on the other side. These developments had implications for Holly Bank because, as we shall see later, it joined forces with the polytechnic in 1974.

Publication of the Haslegrave Report in 1969 was a significant event in technical education and led to the setting up of the Technician Education Council (TEC) in 1973 and the Business Education Council (BEC) in 1974. These bodies combined to become BTEC in 1983.

Holly Bank, as we saw earlier, expanded its activities at home and set up a large network of extra-mural centres which took in a great swathe of the country. It also extended its activities to a range of countries overseas. Members of staff act as consultants and run summer schools in many overseas countries, mainly in Africa and Asia. When TETOC was set up in 1962, Holly Bank was closely involved with it. A member of staff, Ken Brown, spent a good deal of his time on TETOC work and in representing Holly Bank visited well over 40 countries. Each year Holly Bank students are drawn from up to 10 or 12 overseas countries. Initially, these students came for courses at the Certificate level; but now Holly Bank offers a specifically-designed BEd and also a specifically designed MEd for overseas students. In addition, students from overseas are studying for research degrees at MPhil and PhD levels. A student from Brazil, for example, was recently awarded a PhD (Borges, 1994).

An indication of Holly Bank's position as a provider of education and training for overseas countries is reflected by the fact that it hosted a Commonwealth Conference on the Education and Training of Technicians in 1966. The conference was attended by 120 delegates and most of the Commonwealth countries were represented (Sparrow, 1967). A conference of Holly Bank alumni from overseas countries to mark the 50th anniversary of the institution would be a potentially interesting event.

A number of issues were reflected in the literature relating to technical education in the 1960s. At a general level the Director of Holly Bank, Alexander MacLennan, published his book on technical teaching and instruction (MacLennan, 1963). This was closely followed by the publication on a similar topic by Fred Elliott, a former Deputy Director of Holly Bank (Elliott, 1964). Both of these books contain material about the teaching and learning process which has not dated. Two issues, however, reflect the significant changes in technical education which have taken place since these books were published, namely educational technology and information technology. The range of visual aids then available, when compared with what is available now, was very limited; and the now ubiquitous microcomputer did not feature at all. Given the all-pervasive influence which computers now exert, it is difficult to imagine the conduct of education without them.

Some themes and issues which arose in the literature in the 1960s have survived the test of time. Abel (1963), for example, dealt with research in technical education and this remains a pressing issue, particularly with the coming of Research Assessment Exercises which have implications both for the prestige of the institution concerned and also for its income. The cultural background of prospective FE teachers was the subject of a paper by Dryland and Halliday (1963). A paper by Jenkinson (1965) was concerned with the technical education of Members of Parliament. It emerged that 39 MPs, mostly Labour, had experience of technical education and could, therefore, be expected to be sympathetic towards it when it came to support for it in Parliament. The effect of television broadcasts was the subject of a paper by MacFarlane Smith (1965). The Russell Report was the subject of a paper by Parry (1966). Computers, though only in an administrative capacity, were the subject of a paper by Hagger and Branson (1967). The teaching of people with learning disabilities, currently a big issue, was a matter of concern in the 1960s (Miller, 1968). Links between secondary schools and technical colleges was also an issue (Davies, 1968). MacLennan (1963) and Elliott (1964), cited earlier, made no mention of objectives in their books; but a paper by Summer (1968) was concerned with objectives in the context of craft education.

Mention was made earlier of the place of liberal studies in FE, but the introduction of non-technical studies was to continue. A paper by Musgrave (1968) discussed the place of social studies in FE. The notion of social studies in FE was still in its infancy and Musgrave (1968) adopted a defensive position to justify their inclusion in the FE curriculum. Social studies have advanced from a defensive to a dominant position in FE. Social scientists together with students from the humanities now form the biggest group on the Postgraduate Certificate in Education (PGCE) course at Holly Bank.

The 1960s was a significant decade generally and for Holly Bank in particular for a number of reasons. However, from the point of view of advancement through the academic levels the year 1969 could be said to be a watershed. In that year the first advanced qualification in the form of the Diploma in Further Education (DipFE), validated by the University of Leeds, was introduced. At first the Course Leader was Dick Hargreaves; but in 1971 Yves Bennett took over and led the DipFE course very successfully until it was replaced in 1985 by the Diploma of Professional Studies in Education (DIPSE), which was led by Jim Pollock until its demise in the early 1990s.

Table 4   The 1970s

Year	Event	Year	Event
1970	Circular 7/70 on College Government	1974	Houghton Report, Teachers Salaries
1972	Local Government Act	1974	Health and Safety at Work Act
1972	White Paper, A Framework for Expansion	1975	Bullock Report, Teaching English
1972	Manpower Services Commission set up	1975	Sex Discrimination Act
1972	James Report, Teacher Education and Training	1976	Race Relations Act
1972	Training Opportunities Scheme (TOPS)	1976	Circular 6/76, unified Vocational Preparation
1973	Employment and Training Act	1976	James Callaghan, Great Debate
1973	Russell Report, Adult Education	1977	Holland Report, Unemployed Young People
1973	Technician Education Council set up	1977	Youth Opportunities Programme (YOP)
1973	Business Education Council set up	1978	Warnock Report, Education of Handicapped

Education received attention on many fronts during the 1970s and a high point must be the speech in 1976 by the Prime Minister, James Callaghan, at Ruskin College, Oxford, which initiated the 'Great Debate'. Teacher training was the subject of two reports, the James Report (1972) and the Russell Report (1973). However, education received a different sort of attention in the late 1970s when the government decided that too many teachers were being trained and closed down approximately 30 Colleges of Education. At this time the name Crombie featured in the educational vocabulary in a big way because the terms for teachers made redundant were referred to by the single word 'Crombie'. The creation of TEC and BEC were important milestones in the education of technicians. In the Bullock Report (1975) the assertion was made that all teachers are teachers of English. Since teaching is about communicating ideas, knowledge, values, enthusiasm and so on few would argue about the centrality of language in the process.

Brief mention was made earlier of the education of people with learning difficulties. However, the publication of the Warnock Report in 1978 raised the level of awareness about the issue and placed it firmly on the educational agenda. Holly Bank responded to Warnock by making provision for a group of special needs students, to use a term current at the time, who were prepared to teach students with learning difficulties in the FE sector. The innovation started in 1986 and the tutor responsible was Leila Spencer. The group continues to develop and prosper under the guidance of David Swindells.

Unemployment, virtually unknown in the 1950s and the early 1960s, began to claim attention in the late 1970s and has been with us ever since. The publication of the Holland Report in 1977 and the setting up of the Youth Opportunities Programme in 1978 had implications for the FE sector and thus for FE teacher training.

The Sex Discrimination Act of 1975 and the Race Relations Act of 1976 have had a considerable impact on the educational process. An environment characterised by racism and sexism is not conducive to learning, particularly for those at the receiving end of such behaviour. Some racist and sexist remarks may be made unwittingly, but some may be intended. Holly Bank, an institution with a multi-ethnic population of students and staff, was actively involved in promoting a policy of equality of opportunity. At first it was at the level of raising awareness about the issue; later equality of opportunity issues were included as learning outcomes when a modular curriculum was introduced in 1991.

A perusal of the relevant literature in the 1970s reveals something of the diversity of the FE sector. Communication studies were the subject of a paper by Bratchell (1970). Now combined with media studies, this is an important area in FE. Bennett's (1970) paper related to the implications of the Haslegrave Report and the education of technicians. 'Little of the research reviewed here makes possible a calculated judgement regarding appropriate teaching aids'. This was the conclusion to a research paper on teaching aids by Power (1971). The curriculum process was the subject of a paper by Price (1972). At one time the use of objective tests had a dominant position in FE and the paper by Cross (1972) is an example of their use in government examinations. A paper by Randall (1976) provided an insight into the nature of a TOPS course. Flander's Intervention Analysis Categories (FIAC) was devised by Ned Flanders (Flanders, 1970),. FIAC had its attractions in that it appeared to be a precise way of observing and recording teaching behaviour. However, for some it was too atomistic an approach for analysing teaching and it fell out of favour. The paper by Leighton (1977) is an example of an interest in FIAC.

It is not surprising that the reference to the Great Debate appeared in the literature in the period and the paper by Brennan (1977) is an example. At the level of teaching and learning strategies, team teaching had its advocates and the paper by Joyner (1977) is an example of an interest in the subject. In an era not dominated by concerns about staff/student ratios (SSRs) team teaching had its attractions. A team of teachers coming together to offer their perspectives on some issue or problem had much to commend it and had the potential of offering students a very rich educational experience. However, when the stress was placed on raising the SSRs, now somewhere about 18:1 and rising inexorably to 20:1, then team teaching becomes rapidly ruled out because of these considerations. In its heyday Dennis Carroll and Alan Taylor, among others, were leading exponents of the team teaching approach.

One of the most fundamental managerial changes at an institutional level at Holly Bank came in 1974 when it was incorporated into the then Polytechnic of Huddersfield. As would be expected, there were mixed reactions to this change of status. The change involved Holly Bank losing its autonomous status and its own governing body and becoming part of the Faculty of Education of the polytechnic. The other elements in the new faculty were the Department of Education, which was concerned with preparing teachers for the schools sector, and the then Department of Behavioural Sciences. The merger inevitably meant for some, or at least threatened, a loss of identity. Other factors such as loyalty to Holly Bank and a preference for the status quo rather than change also featured in the transition to the new status. However, there was of course, another side to the coin. The economy of scale arguments were dominant at the time and it was questionable whether Holly Bank could have survived as an independent institution. Monotechnics, as Holly Bank was before incorporation, cannot offer the same range of resources and the same variety of educational experience to students as polytechnics, hence another reason for joining forces. Incorporation, mergers, amalgamations, take-overs or whatever are rarely painless and the merger with the polytechnic was no exception in that respect. However, despite the vicissitudes experienced on the way, the merger has reached its 21st anniversary and has thus reached the age of majority.

In 1974 Holly Bank extended its range of provision when it added a course for nurse tutors to the range of courses it offered. The tutors responsible for this course were John Sheehan and Maureen Jones. It began as a full-time course, but starting in 1977 the part-time course was offered at a number of the extra-mural centres. The provision for nurse tutors expanded considerably and the expansion was of two sorts. While the full-time course took in about 30 students each year, the intake to the part-time mode at one time almost trebled this number and it was not unusual to have 80 nurse tutors attending the summer blocks/summer schools. As well as a numerical increase, the nurse tutors progressed through the academic level of courses on offer. In 1976 a BEd (Hons) was offered, led by Peter McBride, and a significant number of nurse tutors studied for this qualification. Later on, in 1982, a highly innovative BEd based on distance learning coupled with block attendance at Huddersfield was offered by Holly Bank. This course was led initially by the late John Furness, later by Keith Squire, and currently the leadership is shared by Philip Mitchell and Ralph Tuck. It attracted significant numbers of nurses from all over the country, with smaller numbers coming from Scotland and the Isle of Man.

Nurse tutors are definitely an upwardly mobile group as far as level of academic qualifications is concerned. When a part-time MEd was offered in 1982, led initially by the late Tony Wesson and now led by Grant Roberts, nurse tutors were a significant, and sometimes a numerically dominant group, within the course. In the early 1980s when research degrees, first MPhils and later PhDs, were offered nurse tutors came forward in significant numbers to join the ranks of postgraduate research students. Of the 40 or so students currently studying for postgraduate research degrees, nearly half of them are drawn from the ranks of nurse tutors.

Table 5   The 1980s

1980	MacFarlane Report, Education for 16-19	1985	Swann Report, Education of Children from Ethnic Minorities
1981	Education Act		
1981	White Paper, New Training Initiative	1986	National Council for Vocational Qualifications
1982	Information Technology Year	1988	Training and Enterprise Councils set up
1983	BTEC establishment		
1983	Youth Training Scheme	1988	Employment Act
		1988	Education Reform Act

The publication of the MacFarlane Report in 1980, the Education Act of 1981 and the White Paper, the New Training Initiative, were doubtless important events, but the declaration of 1982 as Information Technology Year had perhaps the most noticeable effect at the sharp end of the teaching and learning process. From now on Information Technology (IT) was to assume a dominant position on the education agenda. Holly Bank responded to the IT challenge in two ways. IT was added to the curriculum for the Certificate in Education (Cert Ed) and Postgraduate Certificate in Education

(PGCE). Students and staff were made aware of the essentials and potential of computer technology for the teaching and learning process. The second way Holly Bank responded was that it provided the base for the IT in NAFE (Information Technology in Non-Advanced Further Education) project. Starting in 1985, the project ran for three years and was funded by the Department of Education and Science. The project was staffed by Rob Owen and George Allan initially and others joined later. The project was linked by 40 colleges of FE within 11 Local Education Authorities and it served the dual purpose of raising awareness relating to IT and also acting as a resource centre.

The setting up of the National Council for Vocational Qualifications (NCVQ) in 1986 was significant for the FE sector and for Holly Bank since it prepares teachers for that sector. A major effect was the need to respond to the notion of national standards for a whole range of vocational qualifications based on competence. At first only NVQs were involved, but later GNVQs were introduced as an alternative to the traditional A levels. Apart from raising the awareness about these developments, the main implication for Holly Bank arising out of the introduction of NVQs and GNVQs was that of the assessment of learning. Teachers assessing students for these qualifications are required to have Training and Development Lead Body (TDLB) qualifications. For Holly Bank this meant incorporating TDLB D32 and D33 qualifications within the Cert Ed and the PGCE courses. A significant number of students have gained these qualifications.

In 1988 the Training and Enterprise Councils (TECS) were set up with a mandate to take over the planning and oversight of vocational education and training. The setting up of the TECs marked a significant shift of responsibility in relation to vocational education from central and local government to the private sector. Two-thirds of the members of TECs must be from private sector employers (Hall, 1990). Since TECs and the FE sector have common interests, there is a strong case for co-operation. Fortunately, a good relationship has been established between Holly Bank and the local TEC.

A variety of themes emerge from the literature of the 1980s. Around that time the Keller Plan as a teaching and learning strategy was in vogue and the paper in Sheehan (1981) is an evaluation of a workshop on the topic for nurses. A paper by Benett (1980) was concerned with attitudes towards curriculum evaluation; and Brannen et al (1980) also deal with the issue of curriculum evaluation. Guggenheim and Lazenby (1980), both members of staff, wrote about computer managed learning in TEC courses.

231

Mike Guggenheim and the late Peter Lazenby put computing on the map within the college. The paper by Hobart and Harris (1982) focused on Performance-Based Teacher Education (PBTE). At Holly Bank Eric Tuxworth was active in this area of work. Although things have inevitably moved on, the model for initial teacher training at Holly Bank now is competence-based. The paper by Barr (1982) concerning the changing role of FE colleges is of interest for two reasons. First, Frank Barr was the Deputy Director of Holly Bank in 1974 at the time of the merger and went on to become a member of the Rectorate of the polytechnic. Second, his paper was based on an address to the British Association for the Advancement of Science and therefore it is of interest to have FE matters discussed in such a forum.

Open learning is, while variously defined, in essence a flexible approach to education which gives students more control over their learning than would be the case in traditional approaches to education. References to open learning in the literature in the 1980s include Coffey (1976), Bagley and Challis (1981) and Birch and Cuthbert (1981). Holly Bank became involved in open learning in 1985 when it became the centre for the West Yorkshire Open Learning Federation (WYOLF) scheme. WYOLF was a partnership of training organisations and institutions of further and higher education (WYOLF, 1987). Philip Mitchell was the Holly Bank tutor responsible for WYOLF when it was set up and he published a paper on the topic (Mitchell, 1986). Later Loraine Powell and then John Baptiste were responsible for the project.

A publication by the CNAA (1986) on Credit Accumulation and Transfer Schemes (CATS) was to have a profound effect on curriculum development at Holly Bank and throughout the further and higher education sectors. The change in the delivery of education which CATS represented could be said to be revolutionary in a Kuhnian sense (Kuhn, 1970) in that a new paradigm was introduced. The modular design of the curriculum used in CATS is radically different from the curricular models previously in use. A feature of the CATS approach is to give credit towards awards for previous learning which may be of two sorts. APL (Accreditation of Prior Learning) is concerned with relevant prior learning which is already certificated, either within the institution of elsewhere. APEL (Accreditation of Prior Experiential Learning) is concerned with giving credit for learning experience which was not formally assessed at the time it was gained. One of the implications, among many, of setting up CATS was the need to establish procedures for the award of APL and APEL. Holly Bank was the first school in the polytechnic/university to introduce CATS in the early 1990s. Other schools in the institution adopted CATS as also has most of the higher education sector.

While developments at Holly Bank such as IT in NAFE, WYOLF and CATS were undoubtedly important, other developments which took place in the early 1980s were pioneering in nature, as far as Holly Bank was concerned, and had the effect of opening up new territories for exploration. These were the introduction of the part-time MEd, which meant working at a higher academic level for the first time; the supervision of postgraduate research degrees (MPhil/PhD) by, for example Yves Benett, Grant Roberts and John Sheehan; the conduct of funded research by colleagues such as Yves Benett and Jim Pollock. From modest beginnings these initiatives bore fruit in a significant way. The MEd developed to an extent that more students have graduated from this programme than any other taught masters programme in the university. In the early days there was only a handful of MPhil/PhD students; now there are approximately 40 such students and the number is rising. Income from funded research to date has exceeded £1.5 M. Research activity at Holly Bank received recognition in the Research Assessment Exercise in 1992, when it was awarded a rating of two. A five point scale is used for this assessment, with five at the best end of the scale. While a rating of two may seem a modest achievement, it needs to be borne in mind that Holly Bank was a relative newcomer as far as research is concerned and was in competition with universities with long traditions and a wealth of experience in the field of research.

Table 6   The 1990s

1991	White Paper, Education and Training	1992	Further and Higher Education Act
1992	White Paper, Choice and University	1993	Education Act

Education continues to be an important item on the political agenda. Holly Bank originated in the wake of the Butler Education Act of 1994 and the McNair Report of 1944. As we have seen from the tables relating to the decades since the 1940s there has been a steady stream of Acts, circulars, papers and reports in the intervening years, and the trend seems set to continue. The Queen's Speech of 1992, for example, promised measures to raise standards in education; to promote vocational training for young people and adults; to improve teacher training; and to extend choice in education (Hansard, 1992).

The literature emerging in the 1990s, even when a tiny sample is considered, reflects the emergence of new issues and problems. A paper by Tudor (1991) was concerned with the issue of APEL. This is an example of an aspect of CATS entering the educational debate. Quality issues, always important, have become a major issue of the 1990s and the paper by Sutcliffe and Pollock (1992) was concerned with the matter. The Ancient Greeks it seems, introduced the notion of mentoring to the world, since most writers on the topic seem to refer to its Hellenic origins, but it appears to have had a renaissance somewhere in the 1980s. A paper by Lunt et al (1992) dealt with the issue of mentoring in the context of a youth training scheme. A paper by Boulogne et al (1994) dealing with links with St Lucia provides evidence of Holly Bank's continuing involvement with overseas countries. Mention has already been made of the part-time MEd and the extent to which it developed. A paper (Anon, 1994) citing the abstracts of MEd dissertations completed in 1991 lists 18 for Holly Bank. This paper, as well as providing an insight into the range of topics chosen for these dissertations, gives an indication of the number of students who completed the course successfully in that year. The final paper to be considered in this section is one by Gregory (1995) and deals with the implications of introducing the Doctor of Education degree (EdD) in British universities. It poses the question, which has echoes of a certain advertisement for beer, whether the EdD can reach parts the PhD cannot. At a general level the PhD has had a clear field in Britain as far as earned doctoral degrees are concerned. The introduction of the EdD is therefore an innovative and, some would say, an imaginative venture. At a specific level, plans are proceeding well for the introduction of an EdD at Holly Bank. Growth and development thus continues apace.

Holly Bank, in common with other institutions of its kind, has been subject to many changes over the years. Perhaps one of the most radical happened as a result of the Further and Higher Education Act of 1992. The effect of this Act was to change the status of the institution from that of a polytechnic to that of a university, with the prestige and autonomy which is subsumed within that status. The founding fathers - I believe they were all men - of Holly Bank were undoubtedly people with foresight and imagination and their embryo institution grew to have a national and an international reputation and progressed through the various levels of hierarchies relating to educational institutions to reach the zenith which is university status. It is unlikely that the founders thought or dreamt that such progression would be possible, and that their successors would assume the role of university dons. It seems to be so that a case study of an institution which uses a longitudinal approach can identify changes which occur over time and provide a useful perspective on the institution, though inevitably a retrospective one.

Conclusion

The intention of this paper was to convey something of the flavour of the Holly Bank experience in the fifty years of its existence; a more rigorous analysis of the associated issues and problems was not possible within the confines of the space available. At a general level Holly Bank may be characterised as a friendly and welcoming place with a tradition for treating people well. Many other factors, of course, have contributed to the development of Holly Bank, but diversification must be regarded as a very important factor. Holly Bank spread its activities, as we have seen, widely both at home and overseas. Diversity is a characteristic of the EE sector and this diversity of expertise was mirrored by the staff at Holly Bank, though this is becoming increasingly difficult to sustain. During it development Holly Bank has diversified concerning the level of courses offered; now the whole spectrum is covered, including carrying out funded research.

It is likely, given the developmental pattern of the last fifty years, that many changes and thus challenges for management of the institution will have to be faced in the future. Among these is the status of the mandatory award for initial teacher training in the FE sector. If the rumbles about the matter become a reality, this would present a major challenge for the management of the institution. Maintaining a good research grading in the face of intense competition also presents a challenge and has income implications. Other challenges will undoubtedly present themselves. The franchising arrangements, for example, represent a very important change and will need to be developed and nurtured. This means an extended range of relationships for Holly Bank which will continue to contribute to the diverse nature of the institution. It also means, from the point of view of management, that there will be a need to continue to ensure a free flow of information, so vital for the effective functioning of any organisation, but particularly important in a franchise relationship. The complexity of the franchising arrangements for the associate centres has implications for fundamental issues such as the assessment of learning, academic standards and quality. It may be that in future there will be more emphasis on validating and monitoring courses at associate centres, than on the actual delivery of courses at Holly Bank. Changes in the future may be much more radical than suggested here, since prediction is an uncertain business. What can be predicted, however, is that there will be changes, and thus challenges for management, because change is synonymous with growth and development; a non-changing state is therefore not an option (Sheehan, 1990).

Acknowledgement

It is a pleasure to acknowledge the help I received from many colleagues, too numerous to mention individually, at Holly Bank in the course of writing this paper; it is much appreciated. I would like to say, however, that I absolve them from blame for any errors or omissions which may be evident: the responsibility for these is entirely mine.

References

Abel, R.A. (1963) Research in technical education in the National Foundation for Education Research. *The Vocational Aspect of Education*. 15, p.151-153.

ANON (1994) Abstracts of masters dissertations completed in 1991. *The Vocational Aspect of Education*. 46, pp.195-201.

Argyles, M. (1964) *South Kensington to Robbins: An account of English Technical Education since 1851*. London: Longmans.

Bagley, B. and Challis, B. (1981) *Inside Open Learning*. Bristol: Further Education Staff College.

Barr, F. (1982) Challenge and Response: the changing role of Further Education Colleges. *The Vocational Aspect of Education*. 34, pp.89-98.

Benett, Y. (1970) The education of mechanical engineering technicians and the Haslegrave Report. *The Vocational Aspect of Education*. 22, pp.53-56.

Benett, Y. (1980) Teachers' attitudes to curriculum innovation: making explicit a psychological perspective. *The Vocational Aspect of Education*. 32, pp.71-76.

Birch, W. and Cuthbert, R.E. (1981) *Costing open learning in Further Education*. London: Council for Educational Technology.

Bloom, B.S., Englehart, M.D., Faust, E.J., Hill, W.H. and Krathwohl, D.R. (1956) Taxonomy of educational objectives, Handbook 1, Cognitive domain. London: Longmans Green.

Borges, M.N. (1994) The design and implementation of a knowledge-based system for curriculum development in engineering, PhD thesis, The University of Huddersfield.

Boulogne, T., Benett, Y. and McKenzie, P. (1994) Education and business links with St Lucia. *The Vocational Aspect of Education.* 46, pp.81-88.

Brannen, R., Holloway, D. and Peeke, G. (1980) Curriculum evaluation in Further Education: the Diploma for the Training and Further Education of Mentally Handicapped Adults, *The Vocational Aspect of Education.* 32, pp.27-32.

Bratchell, D.F. (1970) Communication studies and vocation, *The Vocational Aspect of Education.* 22, pp.63-66.

Brennan, E.J.T. (1977) The Great Debate; some personal reflections, *The Vocational Aspect of Education.* 24, pp.99-101.

Carroll, D., Duggan, J.E. and Etchells, R. (1978), *Learning by Objectives.* London: Hutchinson.

Coffey, J. (1976) *Development of an open learning system in Further Education: a report*, working paper 16. London: Council for Educational Technology.

Corns, W. (1966) Teaching the fundamentals of programmed learning with a programmed text in a college of education, *The Vocational Aspect of Education.* 18, pp.35-40.

Council for National Academic Awards (1986) *The Credit Accumulation and Transfer Scheme.* London: CNAA.

Cross, M. (1972) The use of objective test in government examinations, *The Vocational Aspect of Education.* 24, pp.133-139.

Davies, J.L. (1968) Collaboration between secondary schools and technical colleges in the education of the 15-18 age group: the linked course, *The Vocational Aspect of Education.* 20, pp.211-216.

Dryland, A.R. and Halliday, L.R. (1963) The cultural background of prospective teachers in Further Education, *The Vocational Aspect of Education.* 25, pp.200-205.

Elliott, F. (1964) *A technical teachers certificate course.* London: Cassell.

Flanders, N.A. (1970) *Analysing teaching behaviour.* London: Addison-Welsey.

Gregory, M. (1995) Implications of the introduction of the Doctor of Education Degree in British Universities: can the EdD reach parts the PhD cannot? *The Vocational Aspect of Education*. 47, pp.177-188.

Gronlund, N.E. (1978) *Stating objectives for classroom instruction*, (2nd ed.), New York: Macmillan.

Guggenheim, M.J. and Lazenby, P. (1980) Micro-computer management of learning for TEC courses, *The Vocational Aspect of Education*. 32, pp.13-17.

Hagger, C.A. and Bramson, M.J. (1967) The computer as an aid to resource allocation in a college of technology, *The Vocational Aspect of Education*. 19, pp.3-16.

Hall, M. (1965) Accommodation for liberal studies: an outline, *The Vocational Aspect of Education*. 27, pp.121-129.

Hall, V. (1990) *Maintained Further Education in the United Kingdom*. Bristol: The Further Education Staff College.

Hansard (1992-93) House of Commons Official Report, sixth series, volume 207: London: Her Majesty's Stationery Office.

Hobart, R.B. and Harris, R.McL (1982) P.T.B.E. or not to be, that is the question, *The Vocational Aspect of Education*. 34, pp.37-43.

Jenkinson, A.J. (1965) The technical education of Members of Parliament, *The Vocational Aspect of Education*. 27, pp.171-177.

Joyner, T.F. (1977) Team teaching in physics at a college of Further Education, *The Vocational Aspect of Education*. 24, pp.23-30.

Krathwohl, D.R., Bloom, B.S. and Masia, B.B (1964) *Taxonomy of educational objectives*, handbook two, affective domain. London: Longmans.

Kuhn, T.S. (1970) *The structure of scientific revolutions*. (2nd ed.), Chicago: University of Chicago.

Lawrence, G. (1967) Circular 323 and after, *The Vocational Aspect of Education*. 19, pp.185-190.

Leighton, B. (1977) Influences on classroom teaching behaviour: a research design for language teachers in adult education, *The Vocational Aspect of Education*. 19, pp.49-57.

Lunt, N., Benett, Y., McKenzie, P. and Powell, L. (1992) Understanding mentoring, *The Vocational Aspect of Education*. 44, pp.135-141.

MacFarlane Smith, I. (1965) an experimental study of the effect of television broadcasts on the G courses in engineering science. *The Vocational Aspect of Education*. 17, pp.89-104.

MacLennan, A. (1963) *Technical teaching and instruction.* London: Oldbourne.

MacLure, J.S. (1969) *Education documents: England and Wales, 1816-1968.* London: Methuen.

Mager, R.F. (1962) *Preparing instructional objectives.* California: Fearon.

McKenzie, P. (1985), Behavioural objectives and an alternative, *Nurse Education Today.* 5, pp.151-158.

Miller, B.K. (1968) Teaching office arts to the deaf, *The Vocational Aspect of Education.* 20, pp.195-199.

Mitchell, P. (1986) The provision of an open learning scheme - the context and some problems, *The Vocational Aspect of Education.* 38, pp.75-79.

Musgrave, P.W. (1964) The definition of technical education: 1860-1910, *The Vocational Aspect of Education.* 16, pp.105-111.

Musgrave, P.W. (1968) The place of social studies in Further Education, *The Vocational Aspect of Education.* 20, pp.167-177.

Neale, R.S. (1966) On liberal studies, *The Vocational Aspect of Education.* 18, pp.206-224.

Niven, S.M. (1992) *The first 25 years: an account of the development by the Scottish School of Further Education of post-initial courses of professional training for the further education service in Scotland.* Glasgow, Scottish School of Further Education: Jordan Hill College.

Owen, D. (1991) The third Lord Cohen Lecture: the wider responsibilities of the physician, *Royal Society of Health Journal.* 101, pp.85-88.

Parry, J.P. (1966) The Russell Report: the supply and training of teachers for Further Education, *The Vocational Aspect of Education.* 18, pp.157-163.

Power, T.V. (1971) Folklore of teaching aids: a review of some research papers, *The Vocational Aspect of Education.* 23, pp.109-113.

Price, T.K. (1972) The curriculum process - with special reference to business studies, *The Vocational Aspect of Education.* 24, pp.119-122.

Pullen, P.C. (1979) The part-time liberal studies lecturer in Further Education, *The Vocational Aspect of Education.* 31, pp.55-60.

Randall, E. (1976) The TOPS preparatory course: a pilot scheme, *The Vocational Aspect of Education.* 28, pp.7-10.

Sheehan, J. (1981) An evaluation of a workshop for teachers of nursing by comparing the members' expectations with their opinions of the outcome, Journal of Advanced Nursing. 6, pp.483-489.

Sheehan, J. (1990) Investigating change in a nursing context, *Journal of Advanced Nursing.* 15, pp.819-824.

Skinner, B.F. (1954) *The science of learning and the art of teaching.* Harvard Educational Review. 24, pp.86-97.

Sparrow, W.G. (1967) The training of technicians: a Commonwealth conference, *The Vocational Aspect of Education.* 19, pp.86-93.

Sumner, R. (1968) The objectives of craft education, *The Vocational Aspect of Education.* 20, pp.137-149.

Sutcliffe, W. and Pollock, J. (1992) Can the total quality management approach used in industry be transferred to institutions of higher education? *The Vocational Aspect of Education.* 44, pp.11-27.

Tudor, A. (1991) The accreditation of prior experiential learning (APEL) in Great Britain - some implementation issues in vocational education, *The Vocational Aspect of Education.* 43, pp.191-204.

Wesson, A. (1983a) Behaviourally defined objectives: a critique, Part One, *The Vocational Aspect of Education.* 35, pp.51-58.

Wesson, A. (1983b) Behaviourally defined objectives: a critique, Part Two, *The Vocational Aspect of Education.* 35, pp.75-79.

West Yorkshire Open Learning Federation (1987) *Guide to Courses,* Huddersfield: The Polytechnic of Huddersfield.

Williams, J.H. (1962) The Wolverhampton Training College for Technical Teachers, *The Vocational Aspect of Education.* 14, pp.3-7.

COMPETENCE & ACCOUNTABILITY IN EDUCATION

Edited by
Peter McKenzie, Philip Mitchell and Paul Oliver

MONITORING CHANGE IN EDUCATION

In a world of apparently diminishing resources, there have been consistent calls for more effectiveness and efficiency in education, and there can be no question that those involved in education will face calls for increased accountability.

Meanwhile the competence 'movement' has stressed the idea that education and training should be primarily concerned with achieving measurable outcomes, particularly those which have credence in the workplace. Opponents suggest that this is often to the detriment of the knowledge and understanding normally regarded as crucial to competent performance, yet it is likely that this kind of measurement will increasingly become an index of accountability.

The papers presented in this volume examine these concepts in a variety of contexts, ranging from school-based teacher training to the assessment of NVQs, and from recent government legislation to the Smithers Report. A variety of views are expressed, which should be of interest to all those concerned with current trends in education.

1995   168 pages   1 85742 279 1   £25.00

Price subject to change without notification

ENVIRONMENTAL ISSUES IN EDUCATION

Edited by
Gill Harris and Cynthia Blackwell

MONITORING CHANGE IN EDUCATION

Effective environmental education is an essential requirement for a sustainable future, yet it is acknowledged that public understanding of major environmental issues remains poor. This book provides an overview of recent research on the degree of understanding of environmental matters and surveys resources available to support the delivery of environmental education and the development of environmental policies.

The findings of research on attitudes to the environment and on understanding of environmental issues among children and young people in the UK and across Europe are presented, together with a survey of practising teachers' awareness of environmental matters.

The book also examines the link between environmental education and green consumerism, and looks at the contribution which both formal education - in schools, further and higher education - and informal education via the media can make to the development of environmental awareness.

Finally, the book attempts to establish indicators for the evaluation of environmental education programmes, to secure the development of positive attitudes and a genuine, life long responsibility for the environment.

1996   224 pages   1 85742 331 3   £27.50

Price subject to change without notification

PARENTS, EDUCATION & THE STATE

Edited by
Cedric Cullingford

MONITORING CHANGE IN EDUCATION

The role of parents in the education system is crucial and increasingly recognised as being so, not only by teachers, but by parents themselves and politicians. Parents are seen to have an influential part to play in support of schools and are also asked to take a more controlling role.

This book examines the reality of parents' place in the education system: How important is their contribution? What do they think of it? What do teachers and children think of this? What kind of impact do parents have on the academic and social futures of their children? And what do their parents really think about the political changes?

This book brings together original research and distinguished contributors, to deal with important issues. It analyses what is going on based on empirical evidence from parents, children and teachers, and draws out the political implications.

1996   196 pages   1 85742 338 0   £30.00

Price subject to change without notification

arena

Psychology and Education
for
Special Needs

Recent developments and future directions

Edited by Ingrid Lunt, Brahm Norwich
with Ved Varma

The education service is in the process of basic changes in curriculum, organisation and funding. This inevitably affects special needs education which, while adapting and undertaking significant changes, is retaining the progress made since the implementation of the 1981 Education Act. This edited book provides an overview of and commentary on the broad areas of policy and organisational aspects, and curriculum and teaching matters concerning special needs education. Within these pages the reader will find pointers for future developments in the field.

The book is in three sections and shows that special needs education relates to all aspects and levels in the education system:

• Provision for special needs, which includes chapters on early identification, provision for clumsy children, specific learning difficulties and those with communication difficulties.

• Teaching, assessment and support approaches, which includes chapters on school-based developments to meet the needs of children experiencing difficulty in learning, individual strategies for investigation and intervention, and reflection on the role of educational psychologists.

• Policy, organisation and training, which includes chapters on implementing the 1981 Education Act, school clusters, international perspectives, lobbying and teacher education for special needs.

1995   264 pages   1 85742 306 2   £35.00
Price subject to change without notification

arena

The Dictionary of
Educational Terms

David Blake & Vincent Hanley

Contact ratio, Key Stages, hidden curriculum, opting out – but what does it all mean? If you have ever felt bewildered by the constantly changing language in the school world this is the book for you!

This convenient and easy-to-use book of reference to education in England and Wales brings together information on the National Curriculum, the world of schools, the legal framework of education, key educational ideas and much more. The extensive cross-referencing and comprehensive list of abbreviations and acronyms make it an ideal tool for teachers, governors and parents alike. **The Dictionary of Educational Terms** is an invaluable guide to a complicated field – can you afford to be without it?

David Blake and *Vincent Hanley* are Principal Lecturers in Education at the West Sussex Institute of Higher Education.

1995   203 pages
Hbk   1 85742 256 2   **£30.00**
Pbk   1 85742 257 0   **£14.95**
Prices subject to change without notification